Hands-On Activities With Scripture Values

TEACHER GUIDEBOOK

ISBN #1-58938-150-5

Published by The Concerned Group, Inc.
700 East Granite • PO Box 1000 • Siloam Springs, AR 72761

Authors **Dave & Rozann Seela**
Publisher **Russ L. Potter, II**
Senior Editor **Bill Morelan**
Project Coordinator **Rocki Vanatta**
Creative Director **Daniel Potter**
Proofreader **Renee Decker**
Step Illustrations **Steven Butler**
Character Illustrations **Josh Ray**
Colorists **Josh & Aimee Ray**

Printed on recycled paper in the United States

For more information about **A Reason For®** curricula, write to the address above, call, or visit our website.

www.areasonfor.com
800.447.4332

TABLE OF CONTENTS

Overview

How To Use This Guidebook

Weekly Lessons

Assessment

*"A sound grounding in science strengthens many of the skills that people use every day, like solving problems creatively, thinking critically, working cooperatively in teams, using technology effectively, and valuing life-long learning."**

**National Science Education Standards*, 1999 Washington, D.C.: National Academy Press. (p. ix)

A NEW PARADIGM

A Reason For® Science was designed for children, the handiwork of an infinite God — young minds created with an unlimited capacity to think, to learn, and to discover!

Because of this emphasis on children and how they learn, ***A Reason For® Science*** is based on a different paradigm from the traditional textbook approach. Why? In an effort to address standards and accountability, many of today's science textbooks seem to get learning backwards. They focus primarily on building a knowledge base, assuming students will later attach meaning to memorized facts. The problem is that few elementary students master information presented this way because they simply never become engaged with the material.

By contrast, ***A Reason For® Science*** is based on the premise that learning science is an *active* process. It's "something children do, not something done to them."[2]

According to the **National Science Education Standards**, ". . . active science learning means shifting emphasis away from teachers presenting information and covering science topics. The perceived need to include all the topics and information . . . is in direct conflict with the central goal of having students learn scientific knowledge with understanding."[3]

To paraphrase William Butler Yeats, "Teaching is not filling a pail. It's lighting a fire!"

INQUIRY-BASED LEARNING

A Reason For® Science is designed to teach basic Life, Earth, and Physical Science concepts through fun, hands-on activities. Its focus is to make learning both fun and meaningful.

But hands-on activities by themselves are not enough. To truly master a concept, students must have "minds-on" experiences as well! This means actively engaging the material through a variety of activities such as group discussion, problem solving, and journaling. It also requires thought-provoking questions that help develop higher-level cognitive skills. The weekly format of ***A Reason For® Science*** is designed to reflect this inquiry-based model.

According to the **National Science Education Standards**, "Inquiry is central to science learning. When engaging in inquiry, students describe objects and events, ask questions, construct explanations, test those explanations against current scientific knowledge, and communicate their ideas to others . . . In this way, students actively develop their understanding of science by combining scientific knowledge with reasoning and thinking skills."[4]

Since different students achieve understanding in different ways and to different degrees, the flexible format of ***A Reason For® Science*** also encourages multiple learning styles and allows for individual differences. Activities challenge students to develop their own unique skills, and encourage them to come up with creative solutions.

NATIONAL STANDARDS

National standards referred to in ***A Reason For® Science*** come from the **National Science Education Standards**[1]. More specifically, they reflect the "K-4 Science Content Standards" (p.121 - 142) and "5-8 Science Content Standards" (p. 143 - 172).

The Teacher Guidebook includes a list of content standards that relate to each individual lesson. References are based on the NSES alphabetic format, plus a numeric code to indicate the bulleted sub-topic. For example, **C1** in a fourth grade lesson would indicate Content Standard **C** and sub-topic **1**. (A detailed description of this content standard can be found on pages 127 - 229 of the **Standards**.)

As noted above, lower grade and upper grade standards are found in different sections of the book. A **C1** reference for a third grade lesson, for example, would be found on page 127 (characteristics of organisms). By contrast, a **C1** reference for a seventh grade lesson would be found on page 155 ("structure and function in living systems").

METHODOLOGY

Master teachers know that a science curriculum is much more than information in a textbook. It has to do with the way content is organized and presented in the classroom. It is driven by underlying principles, and by attitudes and beliefs about how learning occurs. It is expressed in the practices and procedures used in its implementation.

In other words, textbooks don't teach science — *teachers* do!

That's why it's important for you to understand how this curriculum is designed to be used, and how you can enhance the learning process in your classroom.

Concepts, Not Content

The needs of children in elementary school are very different from high school students, especially when it comes to science education. The presentation of the Periodic Table provides a good example. High school students may find it useful to memorize each element, its atomic weight, and its position on a chart. By contrast, elementary school students must first understand the concept of such a table. What is it? How is it used? Why is it arranged this way? Has it always looked like this? How (and why) has it changed over time? Such an approach leads to a foundational understanding of a concept, rather than a body of memorized "facts" that may change over time.*

As Nobel prize winner, Dr. Richard Feynman, once said, "You can know the name of a bird in all the languages of the world, but when you're finished, you'll know absolutely nothing whatever about the bird . . . (that's) the difference between knowing the name of something and knowing something!"

* *For example, less than 30 years ago many students were still being taught the "fact" that matter only has three states (solid, l Alfven won the Nobel prize for identifying a fourth state of matter (plasma). There are many such examples in education — includ able charts themselves, which are being replaced in many colleges by a new 3D computer model that offers new insights into relationships bet*

Multi-Sensory Learning

In addition to focusing on concepts instead of just content, ***A Reason For® Science*** uses a multi-sensory approach to learning that supports multiple learning styles.

Visual events include watching teacher demonstrations, studying diagrams and illustrations, and reading summaries. **Auditory** events include participating in group discussions with team members, listening to teacher directions and explanations, and hearing the unique sounds associated with the activities. **Kinesthetic** events include tactile interaction with activity materials, hands-on experimentation, and taking notes, writing answers, and drawing diagrams in individual Student Worktexts.

Omitting any of these components can significantly weaken the learning process, especially for children with specific learning disabilities.

Student-Driven, Teacher-Directed

As long-time educators, the authors of this series recognize that many elementary teachers don't consider themselves "science people." Therefore, this series avoids unnecessary technical jargon, and deals with complex interactions in simple, easy-to-understand language that's reinforced with concrete, hands-on activities.

The Teacher Guidebook is designed to give you the confidence that you need to teach science effectively. In addition to the usual answer keys and explanations, it includes several sections just for teachers.

"Additional Comments" offers tips and techniques for making each lesson run smoothly. "Teacher to Teacher" provides expanded science explanations to increase your understanding. "Extended Teaching" presents a variety of extension ideas for those who wish to go further.

During the first year, we strongly recommend that you try every activity a day or two in advance. Although most activities are relatively simple, this added practice will give you a better feel for any potential problems that might arise.

Most of all, remember that one of the primary goals of this series is to make science FUN for the participants. And that includes you, too!

COMPONENTS

The following are some of the key components in this series:

Letter to Parents

Positive communication between home and school is essential for optimum success with any curriculum. The "Letter to the Parents" (page 3, Student Worktext) provides a great way to introduce ***A Reason For® Science*** to parents. It covers the lesson format, safety issues, connections with national standards, and the integration of Scripture. Along with the opening sections of this Guidebook, the parent letter provides information you need to answer common questions about the series.

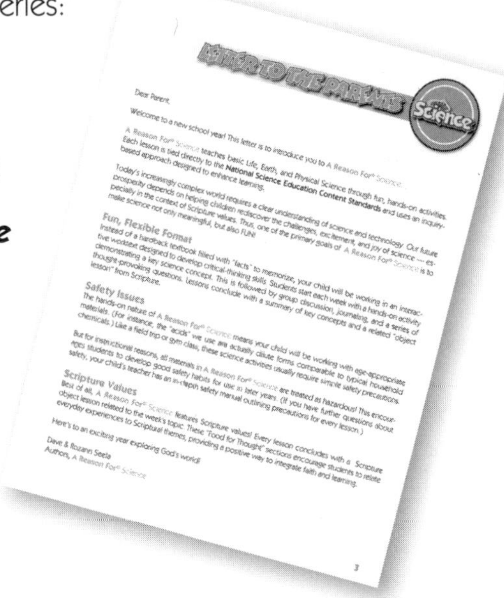

LETTER TO THE PARENTS

Dear Parent,

Welcome to a new school year! This letter is to introduce you to *A Reason For® Science*.

A Reason For® Science teaches basic Life, Earth, and Physical Science through fun, hands-on activities. Each lesson is tied directly to the **National Science Education Content Standards** and uses an inquiry-based approach designed to enhance learning.

Today's increasingly complex world requires a clear understanding of science and technology. Our future prosperity depends on helping children rediscover the challenges, excitement, and joy of science — especially in the context of Scripture values. Thus, one of the primary goals of *A Reason For® Science* is to make science not only meaningful, but also FUN!

Fun, Flexible Format

Instead of a hardback textbook filled with "facts" to memorize, your child will be working in an interactive worktext designed to develop critical-thinking skills. Students start each week with a hands-on activity demonstrating a key science concept. This is followed by group discussion, journaling, and a series of thought-provoking questions. Lessons conclude with a summary of key concepts and a related "object lesson" from Scripture.

Safety Issues

The hands-on nature of *A Reason For® Science* means your child will be working with age-appropriate materials. (For instance, the "acids" we use are actually dilute forms comparable to typical household chemicals.) Like a field trip or gym class, these science activities usually require simple safety precautions.

But for instructional reasons, all materials in *A Reason For® Science* are treated as hazardous! This encourages students to develop good safety habits for use in later years. (If you have further questions about safety, your child's teacher has an in-depth safety manual outlining precautions for every lesson.)

Scripture Values

Best of all, *A Reason For® Science* features Scripture values! Every lesson concludes with a Scripture object lesson related to the week's topic. These "Food for Thought" sections encourage students to relate everyday experiences to Scriptural themes, providing a positive way to integrate faith and learning.

Here's to an exciting year exploring God's world!

Dave & Rozann Seela
Authors, *A Reason For® Science*

3

Student Research Teams

A Reason For® Science was created to model the way scientific study works in the adult world. Students are divided into "research teams" to work through activities cooperatively. Ideally, each research team should be composed of three to five students. (Fewer students per team makes monitoring more difficult; more students per team minimizes participation opportunities.) The best groupings combine students with different "gifts" (skills or abilities), complimentary personalities, etc. — the same kinds of combinations that make effective teams in the corporate or industrial world.

In addition, ***A Reason For® Science*** encourages collaboration between the different teams, again modeling the interactions found in the scientific community.

Individual Student Worktexts

Although students collaborate on activities and thought questions, the Student Worktexts provide opportunities for individual reaction and response. The importance of allowing students to write their own response to questions, keep their own notes, and journal about their individual experiences cannot be underestimated. (While collaboration is essential in the scientific community, no true scientist would neglect to keep his/her own personal notes and records!)

Individual Student Worktexts also provide teachers with an objective way to monitor student participation and learning throughout the school year.

Materials Kits

Quality materials are an integral part of any "hands-on" curriculum. ***A Reason For® Science*** offers complete, easy-to-use materials kits for every grade level. With some minor exceptions*, kits contain all the materials and supplies needed by one research team for an entire school year. Materials for each team come packaged in an attractive, durable storage container. You can choose to restock consumable portions of the kit from local materials, or purchase the convenient refill pack.

Personal Science Glossary

A glossary is a common component in many science textbooks, yet students rarely use traditional glossaries except when assigned to "look up" a word by the teacher. Since words and terms used in elementary science are not highly technical, this activity is better served by referring students to a standard dictionary.

A more effective approach to helping students learn science words at this level is to encourage them to develop and maintain a **personal science glossary**. This can be a plain spiral-bound notebook with one page (front and back) dedicated to each letter of the alphabet. Throughout the school year, students continually add new words and definitions — not only from their own reading and research, but from the findings of their team members as well. (For your convenience, a black-line master for a glossary cover is included in Appendix A.)

** To help minimize expenses, kits do not include common classroom supplies (pencils, paper, etc.) and a few large items (soft drink bottles, tin cans, etc.) that are easily obtained by the teacher. Kit and non-kit materials needed for each lesson are clearly marked in this Teacher Guidebook.*

SAFETY ISSUES

When using hands-on science activities, teachers must be constantly aware of the potential for safety problems. Even the simplest activities, using the most basic materials, can be dangerous when used incorrectly. **Proper monitoring and supervision is required at all times!**

Although the publisher and authors have made every reasonable effort to ensure that all science activities in ***A Reason For® Science*** are safe when conducted as instructed, neither the publisher nor the authors assume any responsibility for damage or injury resulting from implementation.

It is the responsibility of the school to review available science safety resources and to develop science safety training for their teachers and students, as well as posting safety rules in every classroom.

An excellent source of science safety information is the Council of State Science Supervisors at: http://csss.enc.org/safety. The CSSS website offers a FREE, downloadable safety guide, "Science and Safety, Making the Connection." This booklet was created with support from the American Chemical Society, the Eisenhower National Clearinghouse for Mathematics and Science Education, the National Aeronautics and Space Administration, and the National Institutes of Health.

To support appropriate safety instruction, every ***A Reason For® Science*** Student Worktext includes a special section on safety. In addition to the safety precautions above, it is strongly recommended that every teacher verify all students clearly understand this information *before* beginning any science activities.

ASSESSMENT METHODS

Authentic assessment is an important part of any quality curriculum. ***A Reason For® Science*** offers a duel approach to assessment. First, participation, understanding, and higher-level thinking skills and can be assessed by periodically collecting and reading students' responses to the essay-style questions in the Student Worktext.

Second, this Teacher Guidebook provides black-line masters for a "weekly quiz" (see page 163). These quizzes offer a more traditional assessment based on fact acquisition. Questions are similar to the type that students might face on any standardized test.

In addition, you can use both these methods to create a customized quarterly or yearly assessment tool. Simply select a combination of true/false and multiple choice questions from the quizzes and essay-style questions from the Student Worktext.

SCRIPTURE CONNECTION

Integrating faith and learning is an essential part of a quality religious education. A unique component of ***A Reason For® Science*** is the incorporation of Scripture Object Lessons into every unit. As students discover basic science principles, they are encouraged to explore various spiritual connections through specific Scripture verses.

Since some school systems may prefer one Scripture translation to another, Scriptures are referenced by chapter and verse only, rather than direct quotations in the text.

CREATIONISM

Many people (including many notable scientists) believe that God created the universe and all the processes both physical and biological that resulted in our solar system and life on Earth.

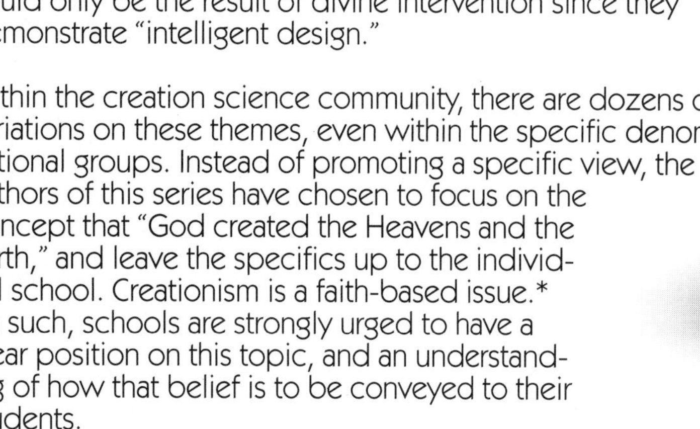

However, advocates of "creation science" hold a variety of viewpoints. Some believe that Earth is relatively young, perhaps only 6,000 years old. Others believe that Earth may have existed for millions of years, but that various organisms (especially humans) could only be the result of divine intervention since they demonstrate "intelligent design."

Within the creation science community, there are dozens of variations on these themes, even within the specific denominational groups. Instead of promoting a specific view, the authors of this series have chosen to focus on the concept that "God created the Heavens and the Earth," and leave the specifics up to the individual school. Creationism is a faith-based issue.* As such, schools are strongly urged to have a clear position on this topic, and an understanding of how that belief is to be conveyed to their students.

** For that matter, so is the theory of evolution.*

[1] *National Science Education Standards*, 1999 Washington, D.C.: National Academy Press. (p. ix)
[2] *Ibid.* (p. 2)
[3] *Ibid.* (p. 20)
[4] *Ibid.* (p. 2)

This Teacher Guidebook . . .

is based on a simple, easy-to-understand format. Lessons throughout the series follow the same pattern, so once you're familiar with the format for one lesson, you can find information quickly for any other lesson. The samples on the following pages explain the purpose of each section.

Category
All lessons are divided into one of three primary categories — Life Science, Earth Science, or Physical Science. Physical Science is further divided into two parts — Forces or Energy/Matter.

Focus
"Focus" states the topic of the lesson.

Objective
"Objective" describes the purpose of the lesson.

National Standards
"National Standards" refers to content standards found in the **National Science Education Standards**. (For details on standards, see page 6.)

Materials Needed:
"Materials Needed" is a comprehensive list of materials used in the lesson. **Bold-faced** words indicate items provided in the Materials Kit.

Safety Concerns:
"Safety Concerns" provides details about potential safety hazards. (For more on Safety, see page 9.)

Category
Life Science

Focus
Germination

Objective
To explore growth in plants

National Standards [1]
A1, A2, B1, B2, B3, C1, C2, C3, E3, F2, F3, F4, G1

Materials Needed [2]
petri dishes (3)
pipette
seeds (assorted)
water
paper towels
tape
scissors

Safety Concerns
4. Sharp Objects
Remind students to be careful using scissors.

[1] See page xx for a description of standards source and code.

[2] Bold-face type indicates items included in Materials Kit.

LESSON 1

Additional Comments
Seeds provided for this activity are common American grain crops: oats, corn, wheat, and soybeans. If students wish to repeat this activity, have them try seeds like alfalfa, radish, sunflower, or pumpkin. Be sure to clean petri dishes thoroughly after each use to sterilize.

Overview
Read the overview aloud to your students. The goal is to create an atmosphere of curiosity and inquiry.

Here's a great way to introduce this activity: Seat two students at the front of the class. Ask them both to point straight down. Praise their accuracy. Now blindfold them. Repeat your request to point down. Praise their ability again, remove their blindfolds, and have them return to their seats. Ask the class, "Do you think animals might have this same ability?" Follow this by asking, "What about fish?" Then ask, "What about living things with no brains, like plants? Do they have this ability, too?" Many students respond "no" to this last question, setting the stage to explore the answer.

LIFE 15

Additional Comments: "Additional Comments" offers tips and techniques for making each lesson run more smoothly.

Overview: The "Overview" provides lesson summaries, thoughts on introducing the lesson, ideas for dealing with materials, and other valuable lesson-specific tips.

What To Do

"What to Do" expands on the Steps found in the Student Workbook. It outlines potential problems, offers alternatative procedures, and explains ways to enhance the lesson.

WHAT TO DO

Monitor student research teams as they complete each step.

Step 2

Grouping instructions are purposely ambiguous to allow several options. Depending on class size and materials available, 1) have each research team create their own set of three, 2) have each team create only one dish, then combine dishes to create groupings, 3) create a unique combination to meet your specific classroom needs. Regardless of the total number of dishes, at least one dish must lie flat, one must be on edge with seeds up, and one must be on edge with seeds down. These three environments are necessary for the primary comparisons.

Step 4

Emphasize the instruction, *"Don't change their position in any way!"* If dishes are moved, the results will be invalid.

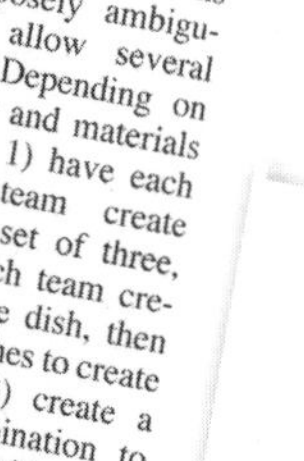

Teacher to Teacher

Another name for the energy stored in seeds is endosperm. Humans and animals use plant endosperm as a food source, too. For instance, flour is ground-up wheat endosperm!

Be sure students realize the two phases of a plant's life cycle that are involved: sprouting and growing. The sprouting process only requires warmth and water. A seed soaks up moisture, swells, splits, and a new plant emerges. But light is needed for the next stage. Light stimulates the new plant into producing the chemical chlorophyll (the green in plants). Without chlorophyll, plants have no way to make food once they've used up the energy in the endosperm. The process of using chlorophyll to direct more food is called photosynthesis.

16 LIFE

Teacher To Teacher

"Teacher to Teacher" offers expanded science explanations designed to increase teacher understanding.

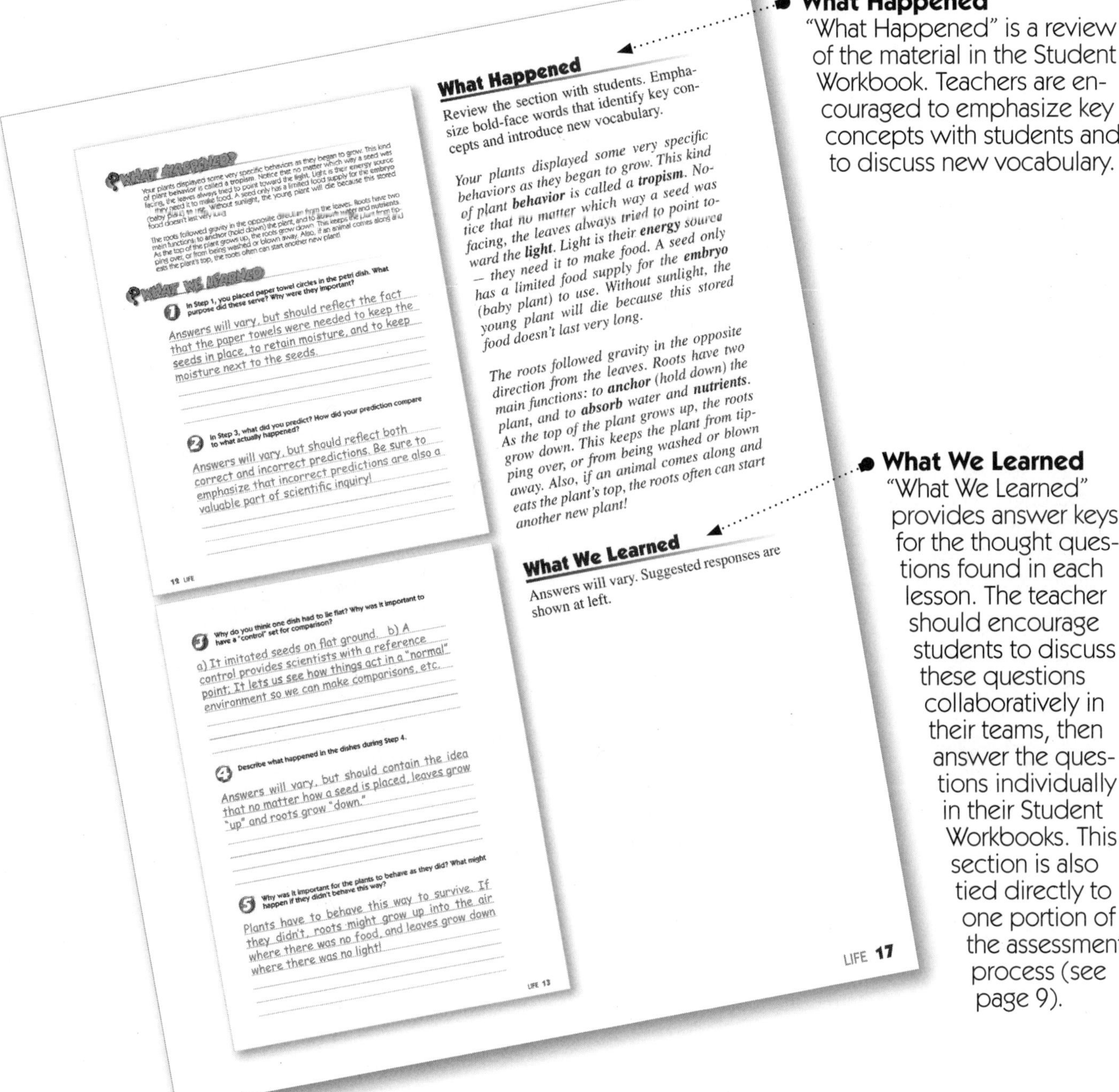

What Happened

In Step 1, you placed paper towel circles in the petri dish. What purpose did these serve? Why were they important?

Answers will vary, but should reflect the fact that the paper towels were needed to keep the seeds in place, to retain moisture, and to keep moisture next to the seeds.

In Step 3, what did you predict? How did your prediction compare to what actually happened?

Answers will vary, but should reflect both correct and incorrect predictions. Be sure to emphasize that incorrect predictions are also a valuable part of scientific inquiry!

12 LIFE

Why do you think one dish had to lie flat? Why was it important to have a "control" set for comparison?

a) It imitated seeds on flat ground. b) A control provides scientists with a reference point; It lets us see how things act in a "normal" environment so we can make comparisons, etc.

Describe what happened in the dishes during Step 4.

Answers will vary, but should contain the idea that no matter how a seed is placed, leaves grow "up" and roots grow "down."

Why was it important for the plants to behave as they did? What might happen if they didn't behave this way?

Plants have to behave this way to survive. If they didn't, roots might grow up into the air where there was no food, and leaves grow down where there was no light!

LIFE 13

What Happened

Review the section with students. Emphasize bold-face words that identify key concepts and introduce new vocabulary.

Your plants displayed some very specific behaviors as they began to grow. This kind of plant ***behavior*** *is called a* ***tropism****. Notice that no matter which way a seed was facing, the leaves always tried to point toward the* ***light****. Light is their* ***energy*** *source – they need it to make food. A seed only has a limited food supply for the* ***embryo*** *(baby plant) to use. Without sunlight, the young plant will die because this stored food doesn't last very long.*

The roots followed gravity in the opposite direction from the leaves. Roots have two main functions: to ***anchor*** *(hold down) the plant, and to* ***absorb*** *water and* ***nutrients****. As the top of the plant grows up, the roots grow down. This keeps the plant from tipping over, or from being washed or blown away. Also, if an animal comes along and eats the plant's top, the roots often can start another new plant!*

What We Learned

Answers will vary. Suggested responses are shown at left.

LIFE 17

What Happened

"What Happened" is a review of the material in the Student Workbook. Teachers are encouraged to emphasize key concepts with students and to discuss new vocabulary.

What We Learned

"What We Learned" provides answer keys for the thought questions found in each lesson. The teacher should encourage students to discuss these questions collaboratively in their teams, then answer the questions individually in their Student Workbooks. This section is also tied directly to one portion of the assessment process (see page 9).

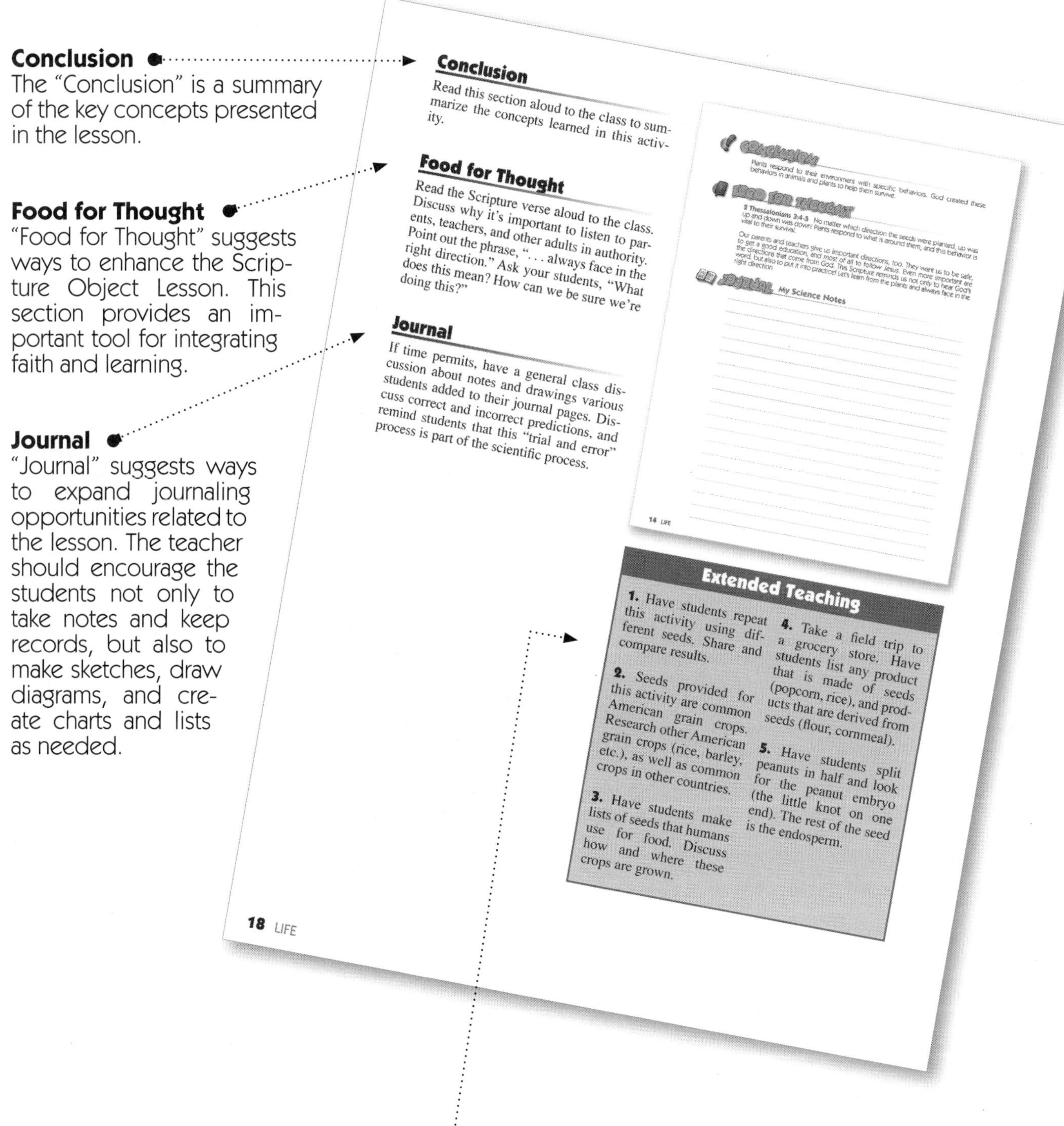

Conclusion
The "Conclusion" is a summary of the key concepts presented in the lesson.

Food for Thought
"Food for Thought" suggests ways to enhance the Scripture Object Lesson. This section provides an important tool for integrating faith and learning.

Journal
"Journal" suggests ways to expand journaling opportunities related to the lesson. The teacher should encourage the students not only to take notes and keep records, but also to make sketches, draw diagrams, and create charts and lists as needed.

Extended Teaching
"Extended Teaching" presents a variety of extension ideas for those who wish to go further.

Lessons
a reason for
2

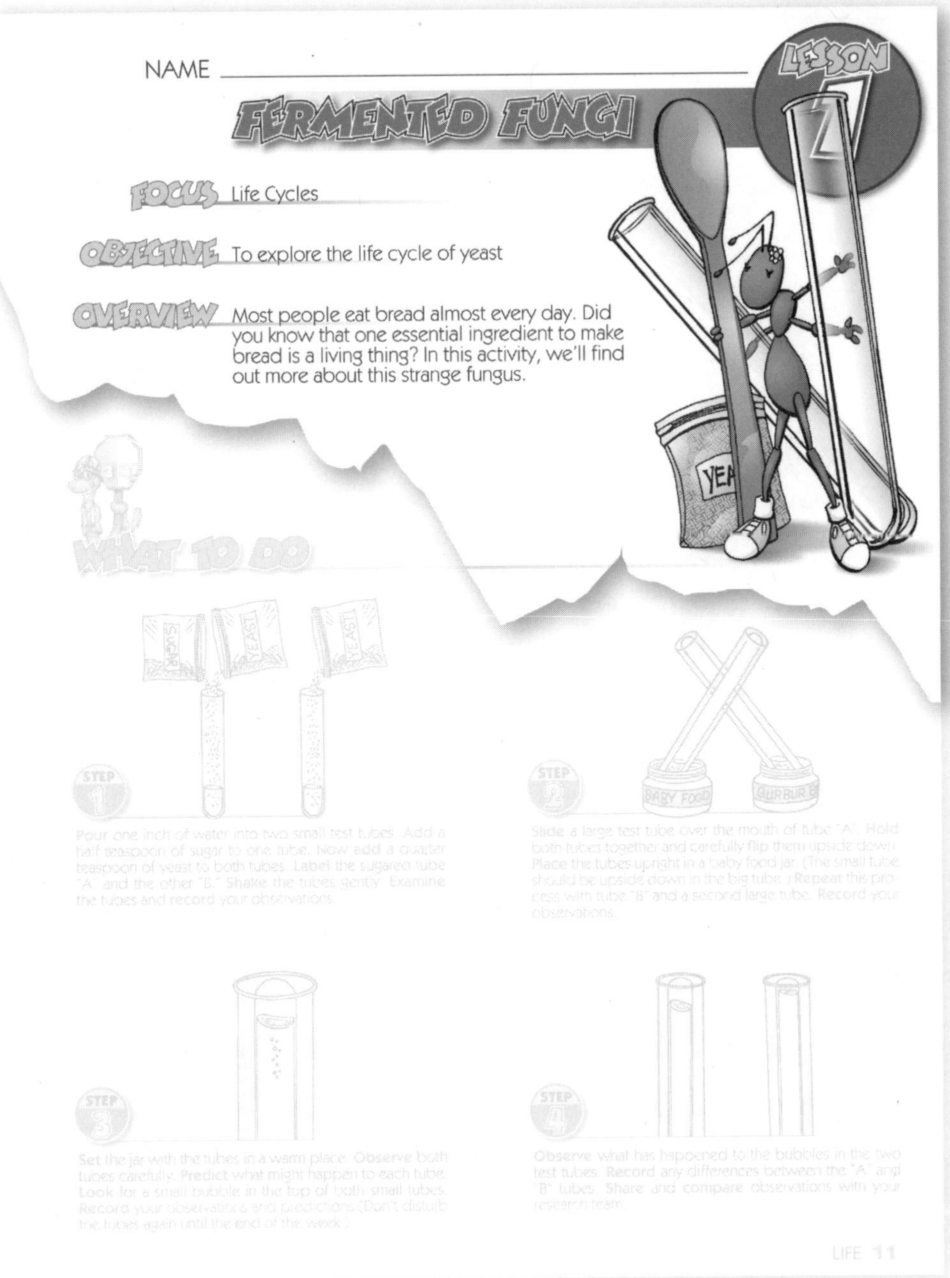
NAME

LESSON 1

FERMENTED FUNGI

FOCUS Life Cycles

OBJECTIVE To explore the life cycle of yeast

OVERVIEW Most people eat bread almost every day. Did you know that one essential ingredient to make bread is a living thing? In this activity, we'll find out more about this strange fungus.

WHAT TO DO

STEP 1 Pour one inch of water into two small test tubes. Add a half teaspoon of sugar to one tube. Now add a quarter teaspoon of yeast to both tubes. Label the sugared tube "A" and the other "B." Shake the tubes gently. Examine the tubes and record your observations.

STEP 2 Slide a large test tube over the mouth of tube "A". Hold both tubes together and carefully flip them upside down. Place the tubes upright in a baby food jar. (The small tube should be upside down in the big tube.) Repeat this process with tube "B" and a second large tube. Record your observations.

STEP 3 Set the jar with the tubes in a warm place. Observe both tubes carefully. Predict what might happen to each tube. Look for a small bubble in the top of both small tubes. Record your observations and predictions. (Don't disturb the tubes again until the end of the week.)

STEP 4 Observe what has happened to the bubbles in the two test tubes. Record any differences between the "A" and "B" tubes. Share and compare observations with your research team.

LIFE 11

Category

Life Science

Focus

Life Cycles

Objective

To explore the life cycle of yeast

National Standards [1]

A1, A2, B1, B2, B3, C1, C3, D1, E3, F1, F4, G1

Materials Needed [2]

small test tubes - 2
large test tubes - 2
sugar
yeast
baby food jars - 2
spoon
water

Safety Concerns

3. Hygiene
Remind students to wash their hands after handling this activity.

4. Slipping
There is a potential for spills with this activity. Remind students to exercise caution.

4. Breakage
Remind students to exercise caution when handling test tubes and jars.

[1] *See page 6 for a description of standards source and code.*

[2] *Bold-face type indicates items included in Materials Kit.*

Additional Comments

Depending on room temperature, the time needed for this activity will vary from overnight to the rest of the week. When fermentation appears to have stopped, dump all the liquids down the drain and wash up immediately. Any clear container can replace the baby food jar. Be sure to remove labels.

Overview

Read the overview aloud to your students. The goal is to create an atmosphere of curiosity and inquiry. Focus on discovering whether this dry, hard yeast is a living thing.

WHAT TO DO

Monitor student research teams as they complete each step.

Step 1

Picture only illustrates what materials should be added to each tube. To avoid messes, have students carefully use a spoon to add material to test tube.

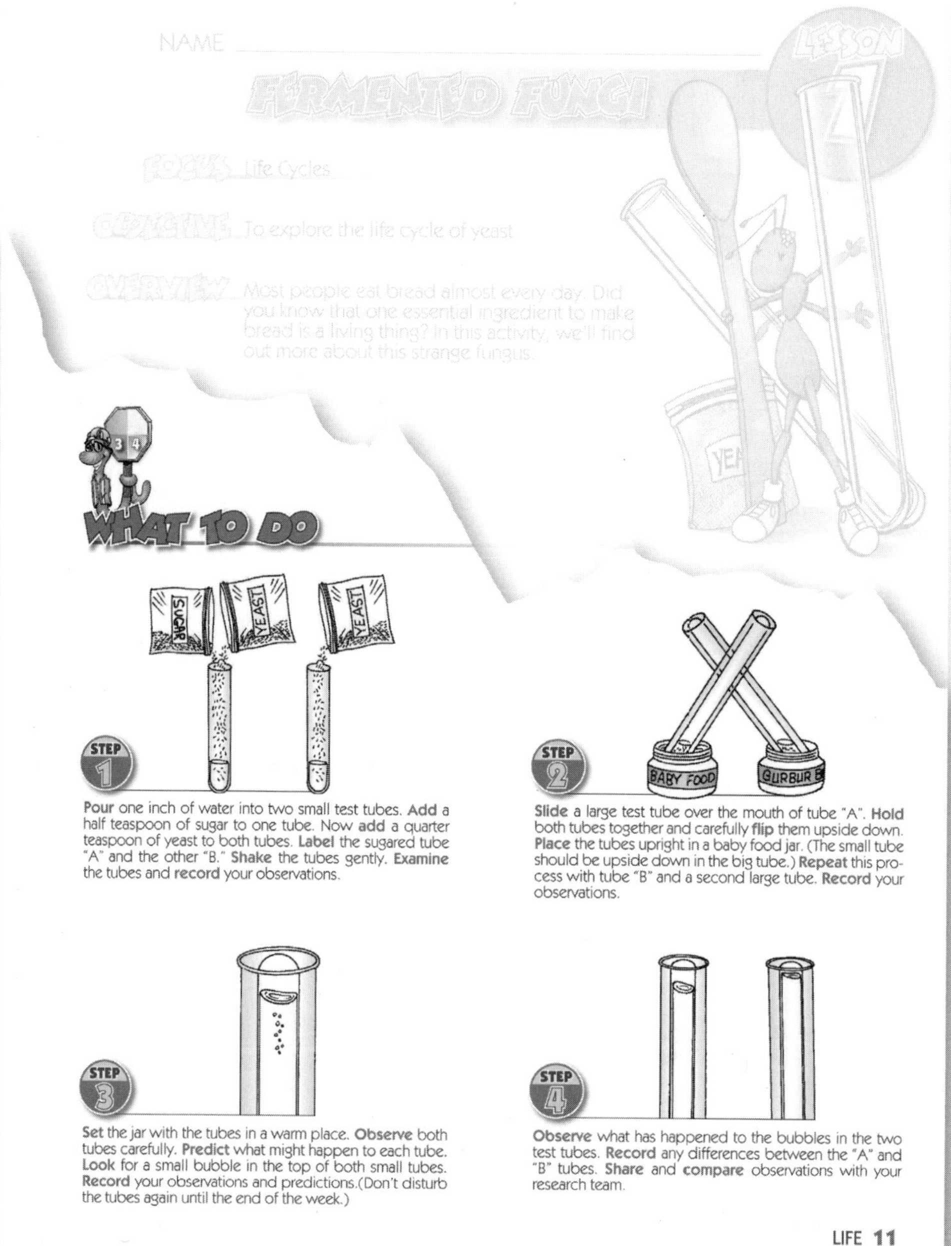

Teacher to Teacher

All living things are divided into five basic kingdoms. They are *Animalia* (animals), *Plantae* (plants), *Mycetae* (fungi like yeast), *Protista* (protozoa and algae) and *Prokaryotae* (bacteria). *Mycetae* are primarily decomposers — the original recyclers! These are very versatile creatures. For instance, the fermentation process that *Mycetae* use (anaerobic respiration) works just fine, even without any oxygen from the atmosphere.

WHAT HAPPENED?

The yeast we used in this activity belongs to the group of living things that scientists call fungi. Some fungi can be very helpful, like the yeast we use to make bread. Other fungi, like toadstools and some mushrooms, are very poisonous!

When yeast is combined with sugar, it creates a chemical reaction called fermentation. Fermentation gives off carbon dioxide gas (the same gas you breathe out). Notice that the tube with the sugar created a much bigger bubble of carbon dioxide. As far as the yeast is concerned, sugar is food and carbon dioxide is just a by-product. Sugar and water allow the yeast to continue its life cycle — the process of birth, growth, reproduction, and death. Of course, the life cycle of yeast is much, much faster than that of humans!

WHAT WE LEARNED

How were the test tubes and their contents different in Step 1? How were they similar?

a) different: only one had sugar added

b) similar: same test tubes, same amount of solution, same temperature, etc.

2 What was the purpose of Step 2? Do you think yeast needs air to grow? Why or why not?

a) to seal the tubes so no air could get in

b) no

c) because the changes in one tube showed growth

3 What did you predict in Step 3? How did your prediction reflect what actually happened in Step 4?

a) answers will vary

b) answers will vary, but should show logical relationships

4 How were the test tubes different in Step 4? What change did you observe?

a) tube A had sugar in the solution

b) air bubble grew much larger in Tube A

5 Based on your observations about yeast's life cycle, what does it produce to help make bread? How does this help?

a) bubbles, gas, etc.

b) it helps bread rise, making it light and fluffy

What Happened

Review the section with students. Emphasize bold-face words that identify key concepts and introduce new vocabulary.

*The **yeast** we used in this activity belongs to the group of living things that scientists call **fungi**. Some fungi can be very helpful, like the yeast we use to make bread. Other fungi, like toadstools and some mushrooms, are very poisonous!*

*When yeast is combined with sugar, it creates a **chemical reaction** called **fermentation**. Fermentation gives off **carbon dioxide** gas (the same **gas** you breathe out). Notice that the tube with the sugar created a much bigger bubble of carbon dioxide. As far as the yeast is concerned, sugar is food and carbon dioxide is just a by-product. Sugar and water allow the yeast to continue its **life cycle** — the process of **birth**, **growth**, **reproduction**, and **death**. Of course, the life cycle of yeast is much, much faster than that of humans!*

What We Learned

Answers will vary. Suggested responses are shown at left.

Conclusion

Read this section aloud to the class to summarize the concepts learned in this activity.

Food for Thought

Read the Scripture aloud to the class. Talk about the concept of "spiritual food." Discuss steps we can take to lead a healthier spiritual life.

Journal

If time permits, have a general class discussion about students' journal entries. Share and compare observations. Be sure to emphasize that "trial and error" is a valuable part of scientific inquiry!

Conclusion

There are many kinds of fungi — some useful, others harmful. Like all living things, fungi have a life cycle of birth, growth, reproduction, and death. We can use yeast's life cycle to help make bread.

Food for Thought

Matthew 4:4 Yeast uses the sugar in bread dough as food to help it go through part of its life cycle. This produces carbon dioxide, which is what makes bread fluffy and delicious! To stay healthy, it's important for us to eat good food, too.

Scripture reminds us that physical food isn't the only thing we need. Spiritual food is even more important! Reading God's Word and attending church help feed our souls. Just as good food makes our bodies healthy, so the good news of Jesus makes our souls stronger. Take time every day to fill your body with both kinds of food!

Journal My Science Notes

14 LIFE

Extended Teaching

1. Invite a parent or grandparent who makes bread to visit your classroom. Have them demonstrate the proper procedure for making bread by hand. Challenge teams to create posters showing this process.

2. Make two loaves of bread in class. Purposely leave the yeast out of one recipe to show the difference in the final product. Have students write a paragraph or two describing the results.

3. Tell students about the five kingdoms all living things are divided into. Using the Internet or an encyclopedia, have them find several examples for each kingdom. Create a bulletin board showing these divisions.

4. Have students research important chemical products of fermentation. What living things cause these fermentations? Have each team describe a specific kind of fermentation process and its uses to the class.

5. Have students research the history of bread making. Make a list of different breads made around the world. If possible, bring various ethnic breads to class for students to sample.

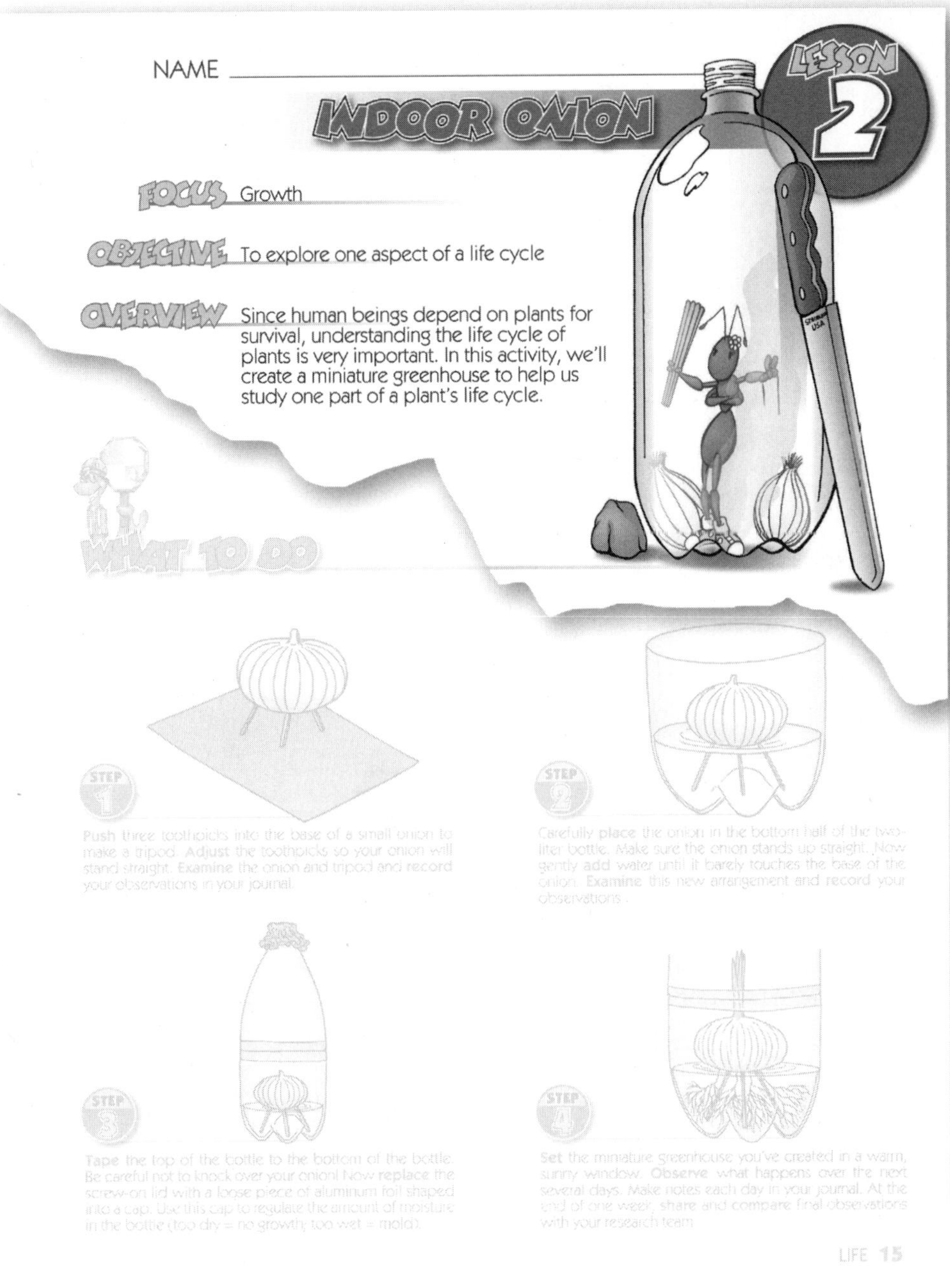

NAME ______________________

INDOOR ONION

LESSON 2

FOCUS Growth

OBJECTIVE To explore one aspect of a life cycle

OVERVIEW Since human beings depend on plants for survival, understanding the life cycle of plants is very important. In this activity, we'll create a miniature greenhouse to help us study one part of a plant's life cycle.

WHAT TO DO

STEP 1
Push three toothpicks into the base of a small onion to make a tripod. Adjust the toothpicks so your onion will stand straight. Examine the onion and tripod and record your observations in your journal.

STEP 2
Carefully place the onion in the bottom half of the two-liter bottle. Make sure the onion stands up straight. Now gently add water until it barely touches the base of the onion. Examine this new arrangement and record your observations.

STEP 3
Tape the top of the bottle to the bottom of the bottle. Be careful not to knock over your onion! Now replace the screw-on lid with a loose piece of aluminum foil shaped into a cap. Use this cap to regulate the amount of moisture in the bottle (too dry = no growth; too wet = mold).

STEP 4
Set the miniature greenhouse you've created in a warm, sunny window. Observe what happens over the next several days. Make notes each day in your journal. At the end of one week, share and compare final observations with your research team.

LIFE 15

Category

Life Science

Focus

Growth

Objective

To explore one aspect of a life cycle

National Standards

A1, A2, B1, B2, B3, C1, C3, D1, E3, F1, F4, G1

Materials Needed

toothpicks - 3
small onion
soft drink bottle - 2 liter
water
tape
aluminum foil
knife

Safety Concerns

4. Sharp Objects
Remind students to be careful when using the knife.

4. Slipping
There is a potential for spills. Remind students to exercise caution with water.

Additional Comments

Depending on your group, you may choose to cut the bottles in half yourself before class. This will avoid students using knives. These miniature greenhouses do best in a bright, sunny spot. The onion sets garden stores sell in the spring work equally well for this activity.

Overview

Read the overview aloud to your students. The goal is to create an atmosphere of curiosity and inquiry. Remind students that what they see taking place in the bottom of the bottle usually happens underground.

WHAT TO DO

Monitor student research teams as they complete each step.

Step 4

Since bottles will probably be clustered in the same sunny location, be sure to have students label them to avoid confusion. Empty and clean bottles after activity is finished. Save them for the next lesson.

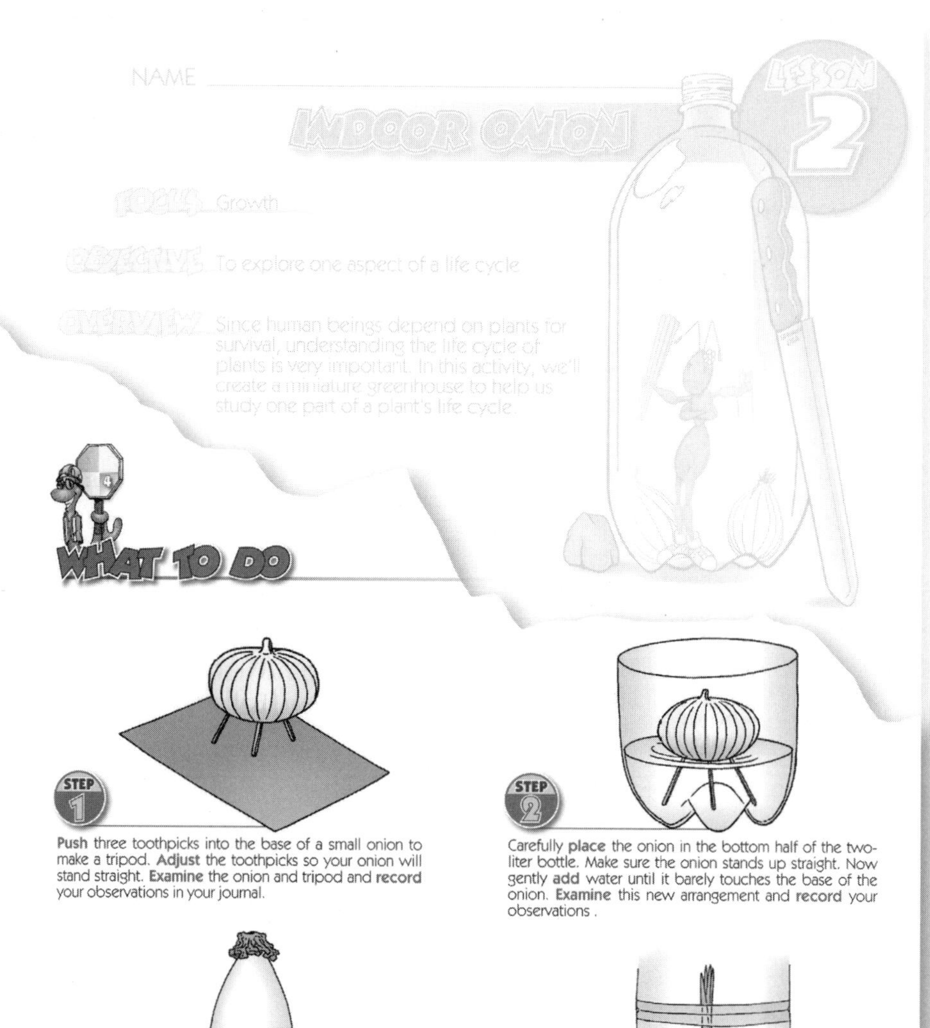

NAME

LESSON 2

INDOOR ONION

FOCUS Growth

OBJECTIVE To explore one aspect of a life cycle

OVERVIEW Since human beings depend on plants for survival, understanding the life cycle of plants is very important. In this activity, we'll create a miniature greenhouse to help us study one part of a plant's life cycle.

WHAT TO DO

STEP 1

Push three toothpicks into the base of a small onion to make a tripod. **Adjust** the toothpicks so your onion will stand straight. **Examine** the onion and tripod and **record** your observations in your journal.

STEP 2

Carefully **place** the onion in the bottom half of the two-liter bottle. Make sure the onion stands up straight. Now gently **add** water until it barely touches the base of the onion. **Examine** this new arrangement and **record** your observations .

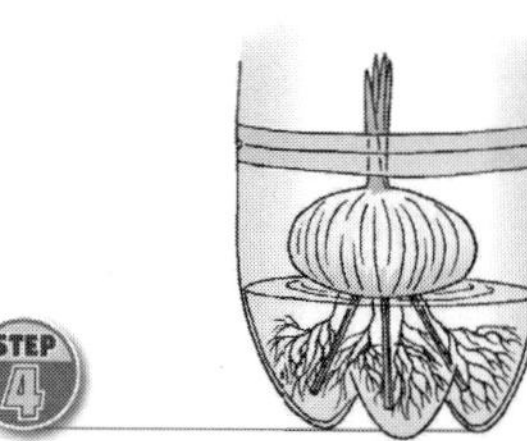

STEP 3

Tape the top of the bottle to the bottom of the bottle. Be careful not to knock over your onion! Now **replace** the screw-on lid with a loose piece of aluminum foil shaped into a cap. Use this cap to regulate the amount of moisture in the bottle (too dry = no growth; too wet = mold).

STEP 4

Set the miniature greenhouse you've created in a warm, sunny window. **Observe** what happens over the next several days. Make notes each day in your journal. At the end of one week, **share** and **compare** final observations with your research team.

LIFE 15

Teacher to Teacher

Photosynthesis is a complicated chemical process. It not only creates food for the plant, but also the food and oxygen needed by animal life. During photosynthesis, energy from the sun helps convert carbon dioxide and water into glucose and oxygen. The reverse of photosynthesis is respiration — "burning" food to release energy. Plants can both create food and use it. Animals can only use it.

All living things have a life cycle. They begin, they grow, they reproduce, and they die. The bodies of all living things contain nutrients (chemicals needed for life). After they die, the nutrients can be recycled by other living things. In this activity, we saw part of the cycle as the onion started to grow.

A clear bottle was needed for your miniature greenhouse so the maximum amount of light energy could get through. Plants need this light for a complicated chemical process called photosynthesis. Photosynthesis helps create food for plants (and the creatures that eat them). Your greenhouse not only let in light, but also regulated (controlled) air flow, kept water from evaporating, and held in heat — all things that plants need to thrive!

WHAT WE LEARNED?

1 **Why were the toothpicks important in Step 1? Why not lay the onion on the bottom of the bottle?**

Answers will vary, but should include the idea that onions won't grow if completely immersed in water.

2 **Why did you need to add water in step 2? Why was the level of the water important?**

a) plants need water to grow

b) too low, the plant couldn't use it; too high, the plant would be immersed

 **Why didn't you seal the bottle completely in step 3? What might have happened if you did?**

a) so heat, water, air could be regulated

b) might have gotten too hot, too dry, etc., for plant to grow

 **What happened to your onion in Step 4? What would happen to the onion if you left it there for several weeks? Why?**

a) it grew, it put out shoots, it put down roots, etc.

b) would keep growing, but eventually would die because no nutrients were available from the soil

 **How does a greenhouse help plant growth? Why do most have glass roofs? What form of energy entered your mini-greenhouse?**

a) helps regulate heat, water, air, etc.; controlled conditions

b) to let the sun in

c) solar (sun) energy

What Happened

Review the section with students. Emphasize bold-face words that identify key concepts and introduce new vocabulary.

All living things have a ***life cycle****. They* ***begin****, they* ***grow****, they* ***reproduce****, and they* ***die****. The bodies of all living things contain* ***nutrients*** *(chemicals needed for life). After they die, the nutrients can be* ***recycled*** *by other living things. In this activity, we saw part of the cycle as the onion started to grow.*

A clear bottle was needed for your miniature greenhouse so the maximum amount of ***light energy*** *could get through. Plants need this light for a complicated chemical process called* ***photosynthesis****. Photosynthesis helps create food for plants (and the creatures that eat them). Your greenhouse not only let in light, but also regulated (controlled) air flow, kept water from* ***evaporating****, and held in* ***heat*** *— all things that plants need to thrive!*

What We Learned

Answers will vary. Suggested responses are shown at left.

Conclusion

Read this section aloud to the class to summarize the concepts learned in this activity.

Food for Thought

Read the Scripture aloud to the class. Talk about the importance of putting down strong "spiritual roots." Discuss ways that students can do this.

Journal

If time permits, have a general class discussion about students' journal entries. Share and compare observations. Be sure to emphasize that "trial and error" is a valuable part of scientific inquiry!

Like all living things, plants have a life cycle. Plants grow best in the right environment. Plants need certain things to grow properly, includiing light, air, water, and warmth.

FOOD FOR THOUGHT

Matthew 15:3-9 Roots were one of the things you saw growing in your miniature greenhouse. Roots absorb nutrients from the soil, pull in water, and work as anchors. Wind, water, and animals can't easily uproot plants that have strong roots.

This Scripture tells us that people who don't believe in God have shallow roots or no roots at all. Plants with good roots are like people who belong to God. They have grown strong through the power of God's love, and are able to withstand the storms of life. Remember to sink your roots deep into God's Word!

JOURNAL **My Science Notes**

18 LIFE

Extended Teaching

1. Challenge students to make detailed, colored drawings of their onion as it grows. They should create one drawing each day. Have them compile drawings to create an "Onion Growth" book.

2. Using the Internet or an encyclopedia, have students research how greenhouses trap heat. Challenge teams to create posters that depict their findings.

3. Take a field trip to a commercial greenhouse. Ask the owner to explain its operation. Have students take notes, then write a paper about the experience.

4. Invite a gardener to visit your classroom. Have him/her share some of his/her "secrets" for growing great flowers and vegetables. Discuss ways to keep plants healthy.

5. Start a school garden. Peppers, squash, and tomatoes are all fairly simple to grow. Have students keep careful records (planting date, watering, weeding, fertilizing, etc.).

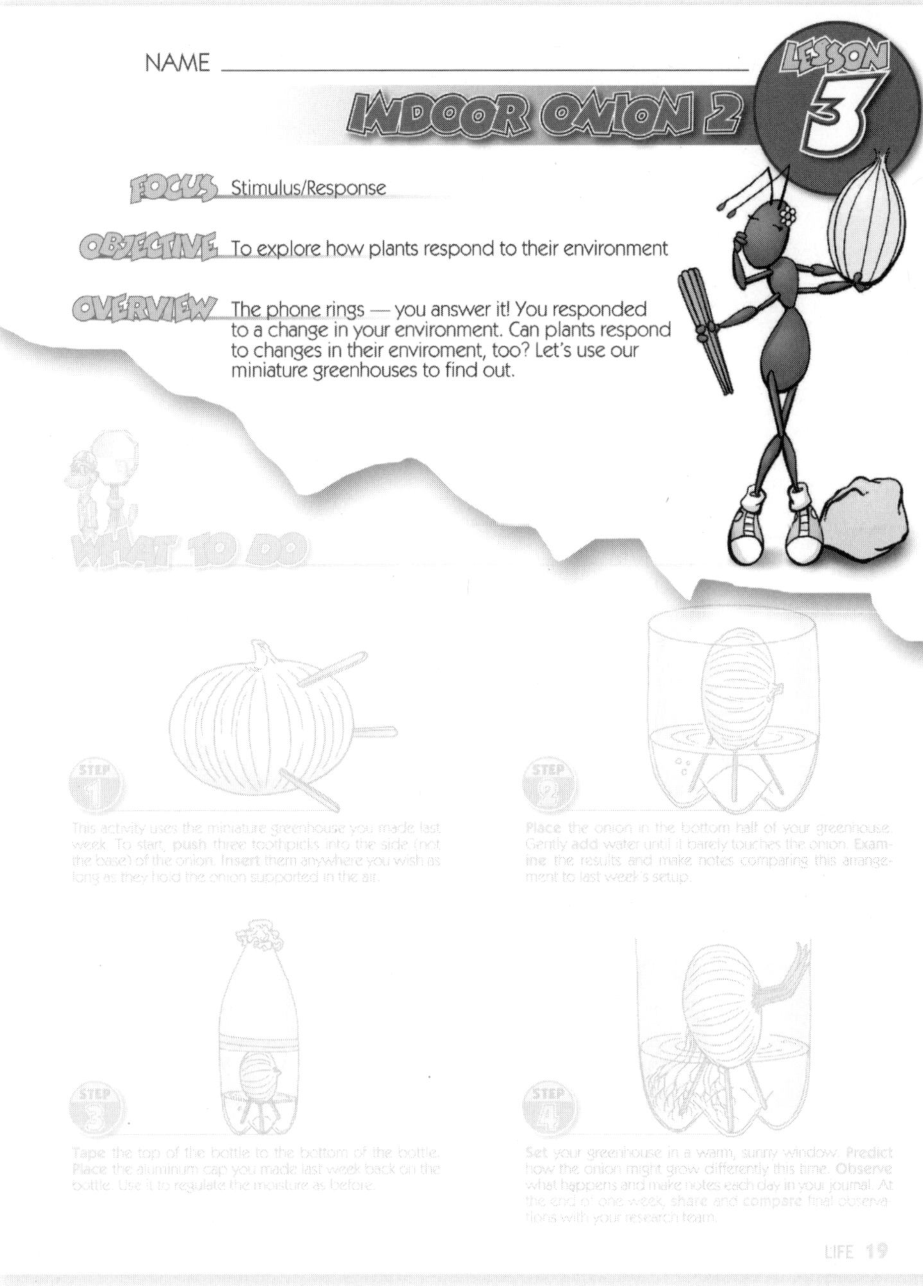
NAME ____________________

INDOOR ONION 2

LESSON 3

FOCUS Stimulus/Response

OBJECTIVE To explore how plants respond to their environment

OVERVIEW The phone rings — you answer it! You responded to a change in your environment. Can plants respond to changes in their enviroment, too? Let's use our miniature greenhouses to find out.

WHAT TO DO

STEP 1

This activity uses the miniature greenhouse you made last week. To start, **push** three toothpicks into the side (not the base) of the onion. **Insert** them anywhere you wish as long as they hold the onion supported in the air.

STEP 2

Place the onion in the bottom half of your greenhouse. Gently **add** water until it barely touches the onion. **Examine** the results and make notes comparing this arrangement to last week's setup.

STEP 3

Tape the top of the bottle to the bottom of the bottle. **Place** the aluminum cap you made last week back on the bottle. Use it to regulate the moisture as before.

STEP 4

Set your greenhouse in a warm, sunny window. **Predict** how the onion might grow differently this time. **Observe** what happens and make notes each day in your journal. At the end of one week, **share** and **compare** final observations with your research team.

LIFE 19

Category
Life Science

Focus
Stimulus/Response

Objective
To explore how plants respond to their environment

National Standards
A1, A2, B1, B2, B3, C1, C3, D1, E3, F1, F4, G1

Materials Needed
toothpicks - 3
small onion
bottle *(from Lesson 2)*
water
tape
aluminum foil

Safety Concerns
4. Sharp Objects
If additional bottles are made, remind students to be careful using the knife.

4. Slipping
There is a potential for spills. Remind students to exercise caution with water.

Additional Comments
Encourage students to be creative. The more angles they use in setting up their onions, the greater number of growth patterns you'll have for comparison! When this activity is complete, students should discover that shoots always grow up and roots always grow down.

Overview
Read the overview aloud to your students. The goal is to create an atmosphere of curiosity and inquiry. Focus on the concept of stimulus/response.

WHAT TO DO

Monitor student research teams as they complete each step.

Step 4

As in the last lesson, have students label bottles to avoid confusion.

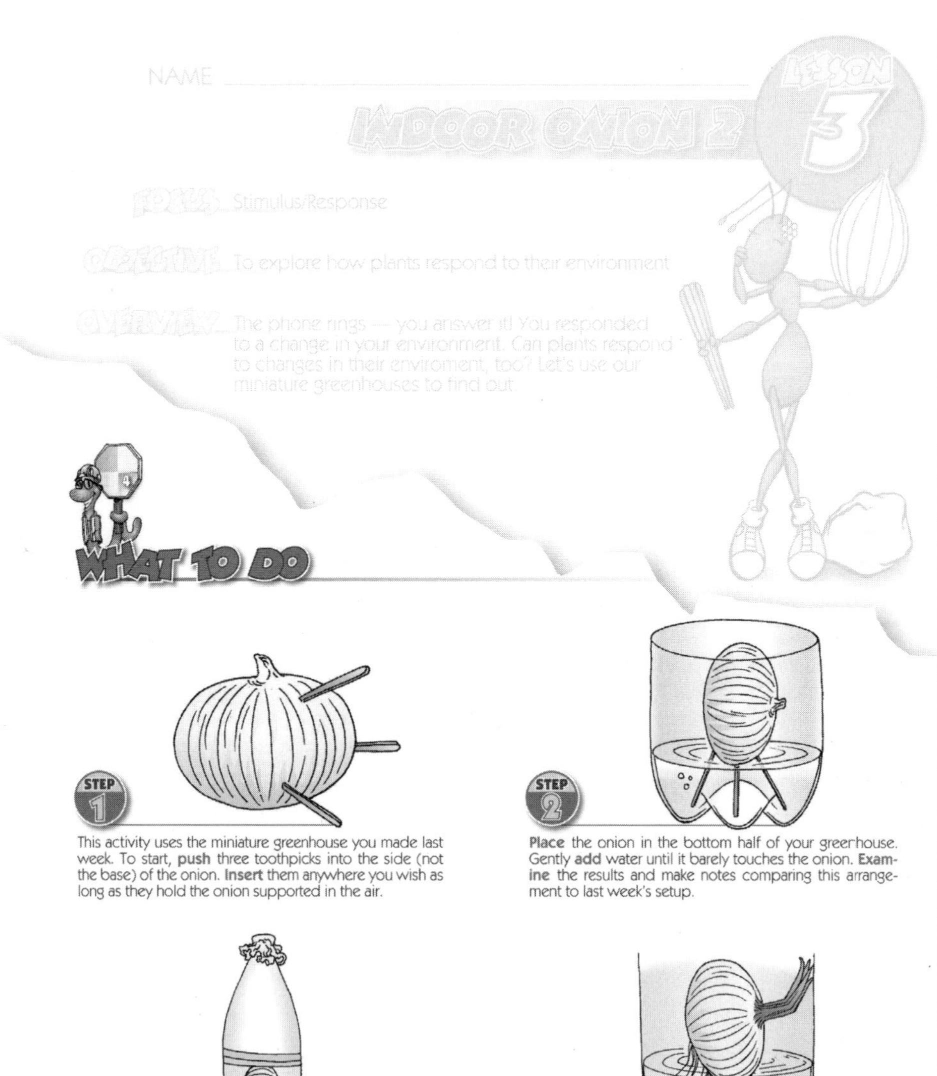

NAME

LESSON 3

INDOOR ONION 2

FOCUS Stimulus/Response

OBJECTIVE To explore how plants respond to their environment

OVERVIEW The phone rings — you answer it! You responded to a change in your environment. Can plants respond to changes in their environment, too? Let's use our miniature greenhouses to find out.

WHAT TO DO

STEP 1

This activity uses the miniature greenhouse you made last week. To start, **push** three toothpicks into the side (not the base) of the onion. **Insert** them anywhere you wish as long as they hold the onion supported in the air.

STEP 2

Place the onion in the bottom half of your greenhouse. Gently **add** water until it barely touches the onion. **Examine** the results and make notes comparing this arrangement to last week's setup.

STEP 3

Tape the top of the bottle to the bottom of the bottle. **Place** the aluminum cap you made last week back on the bottle. Use it to regulate the moisture as before.

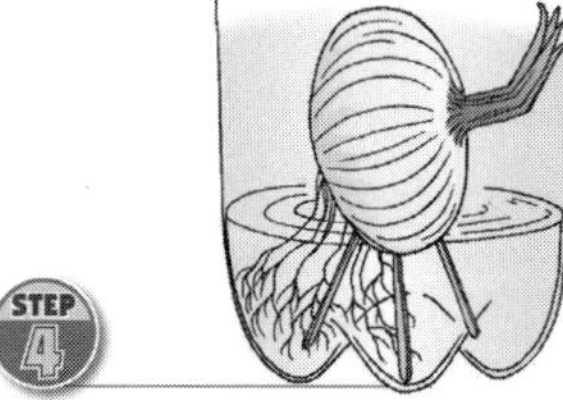

STEP 4

Set your greenhouse in a warm, sunny window. **Predict** how the onion might grow differently this time. **Observe** what happens and make notes each day in your journal. At the end of one week, **share** and **compare** final observations with your research team.

LIFE 19

Teacher to Teacher

Tropisms are simple plant behaviors. This activity demonstrated geotropism — a plant's response to gravity. Geotropism helps plants orient their roots downward to reach the nourishment of the earth. The activity also demonstrated phototropism — a plant's response to light energy. Phototropism helps plants orient their shoots and leaves upward toward the sun so that photosynthesis can take place. Both of these tropisms are necessary for a plant's survival.

What Happened?

Just as you react to a ringing phone in your house, plants and animals react to a stimulus (something that happens) in their environment. Scientists call this reaction a response.

In this activity, the stimulus was gravity. Even though you tried to confuse it, your plant responded to gravity in a predictable way. No matter how a plant is positioned, roots always grow down and leaves always grow up. As gravity pulls, the roots of a plant will grow toward the pull and the leaves will grow away from it.

At the beginning of this lesson, we asked, "Can plants respond to changes in their environment?" The results of this activity helped show that they can and do!

What We Learned

1. **Compare Step 1 of this lesson to Step 1 of Lesson 2. How was your onion placement different?**

   answers will vary

2. **Why was it important to keep environmental conditions the same for both of these lessons?**

   Answers will vary, but should include the idea that you should only change one variable in an experiment.

3. **What did you predict in Step 3? How did your prediction reflect what actually happened in Step 4?**

   Answers will vary, but should reflect logical comparisons.

4. **What happened to your onion in Step 4? How was this similar or different from results of Lesson 2?**

   a) the roots grew down, the shoot grew up

   b) answers will vary, but should reflect the fact that the onion's position didn't matter

5. **Why must plants and animals be able to respond to a stimulus in their environment? What might happen if they didn't?**

   a) response to a stimulus helps them survive

   b) they might die

What Happened

Review the section with students. Emphasize bold-face words that identify key concepts and introduce new vocabulary.

*Just as you **react** to a ringing phone in your house, plants and animals react to a **stimulus** (something that happens) in their **environment**. Scientists call this reaction a **response**.*

*In this activity, the stimulus was **gravity**. Even though you tried to confuse it, your plant responded to gravity in a predictable way. No matter how a plant is positioned, roots always grow down and leaves always grow up. As gravity **pulls**, the roots of a plant will grow toward the pull and the leaves will grow away from it.*

At the beginning of this lesson, we asked, "Can plants respond to changes in their environment?" The results of this activity helped show that they can and do!

What We Learned

Answers will vary. Suggested responses are shown at left.

Conclusion

Read this section aloud to the class to summarize the concepts learned in this activity.

Food for Thought

Read the Scripture aloud to the class. Talk about the analogy used in this verse. Discuss ways students can "sink roots" into God's love.

Journal

If time permits, have a general class discussion about students' journal entries. Share and compare observations. Be sure to emphasize that "trial and error" is a valuable part of scientific inquiry!

CONCLUSION

Plants have the ability to respond to a stimulus in their environment. In response to the stimulus of gravity, roots always grow down, and leaves always grow up. This response helps plants survive.

FOOD FOR THOUGHT

Isaiah 11:1-3 No matter what angle you placed the onion, the stalk grew up and the roots grew down. This automatic response of plants helps keep them alive. Imagine how impossible it would be for an onion to grow with its roots in the air!

Scripture compares the coming Messiah (Jesus) to a plant. The "roots" are a reminder of Jesus' family heritage. The "fruit" or "shoot" growing from the stump foretells Jesus' death and resurrection. Jesus' life was grounded in obedience to God. What about your life? Don't leave your roots sticking into thin air! Take time to plant the love of Jesus firmly in your heart.

JOURNAL My Science Notes

22 LIFE

Extended Teaching

1. Using the Internet or an encyclopedia, have students research other plant tropisms. Ask each team to give a report on what they found, and how these tropisms help plants survive.

2. Invite a biologist or professional gardener to visit your classroom. Talk about how nutrients are brought into plants through the roots. Discuss other plant behaviors.

3. Have students fill the bottom of the bottle with potting soil, then plant seeds along its outside edge so they can watch them grow. Challenge them to make comparisons with Lesson 3.

4. Using the NASA website, have students research what happens to plants when exposed to the minimal gravity of space. Have teams create posters depicting their findings.

5. Have students research other plant tropisms. Some interesting subjects are "touch sensitive" plants (like *Mimosa*) and "insectivorous plants" (like Venus Flytrap). Have them share their findings with the class.

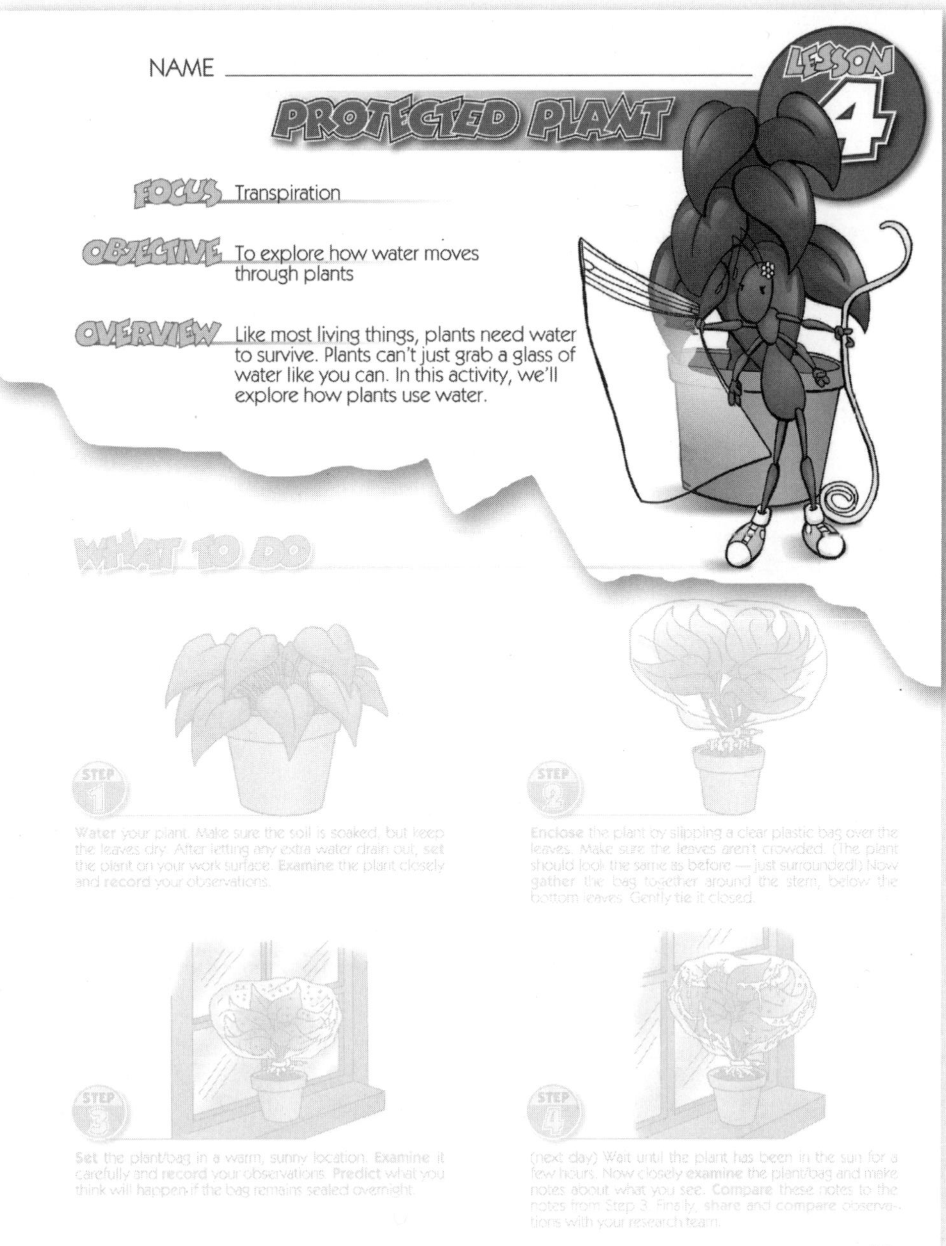

NAME ____________________

LESSON 4

PROTECTED PLANT

FOCUS Transpiration

OBJECTIVE To explore how water moves through plants

OVERVIEW Like most living things, plants need water to survive. Plants can't just grab a glass of water like you can. In this activity, we'll explore how plants use water.

WHAT TO DO

STEP 1 Water your plant. Make sure the soil is soaked, but keep the leaves dry. After letting any extra water drain out, set the plant on your work surface. Examine the plant closely and record your observations.

STEP 2 Enclose the plant by slipping a clear plastic bag over the leaves. Make sure the leaves aren't crowded. (The plant should look the same as before — just surrounded!) Now gather the bag together around the stem, below the bottom leaves. Gently tie it closed.

STEP 3 Set the plant/bag in a warm, sunny location. Examine it carefully and record your observations. Predict what you think will happen if the bag remains sealed overnight.

STEP 4 (next day) Wait until the plant has been in the sun for a few hours. Now closely examine the plant/bag and make notes about what you see. Compare these notes to the notes from Step 3. Finally, share and compare observations with your research team.

LIFE 23

Category

Life Science

Focus

Transpiration

Objective

To explore how water moves through plants

National Standards

A1, A2, B1, B2, B3, C1, C3, D1, E3, F1, F4, G1

Materials Needed

potted plant
clear plastic bag
water
string

Safety Concerns

none

Additional Comments

Inexpensive plants from a garden center work just fine. Be sure to choose plants with large leaves and a single stem. Plastic bags must be large enough to completely surround the plant without crowding. The brighter and sunnier the location, the faster transpiration will take place.

Overview

Read the overview aloud to your students. The goal is to create an atmosphere of curiosity and inquiry.

WHAT TO DO

Monitor student research teams as they complete each step.

NAME

LESSON 4

PROTECTED PLANT

FOCUS Transpiration

OBJECTIVE To explore how water moves through plants

OVERVIEW Like most living things, plants need water to survive. Plants can't just grab a glass of water like you can. In this activity, we'll explore how plants use water.

WHAT TO DO

STEP 1

Water your plant. Make sure the soil is soaked, but keep the leaves dry. After letting any extra water drain out, **set** the plant on your work surface. **Examine** the plant closely and **record** your observations.

STEP 2

Enclose the plant by slipping a clear plastic bag over the leaves. Make sure the leaves aren't crowded. (The plant should look the same as before — just surrounded!) Now **gather** the bag together around the stem, below the bottom leaves. Gently **tie** it closed.

STEP 3

Set the plant/bag in a warm, sunny location. **Examine** it carefully and **record** your observations. **Predict** what you think will happen if the bag remains sealed overnight.

STEP 4

(next day) Wait until the plant has been in the sun for a few hours. Now closely **examine** the plant/bag and make notes about what you see. **Compare** these notes to the notes from Step 3. Finally, **share** and **compare** observations with your research team.

LIFE 23

Teacher to Teacher

Water is vital for plant survival. Acting much like blood in a human body, water transports nutrients to all the plant's cells. It also provides support (called "turgor pressure") to keep the plant from drooping. Eventually the water is released into the air through transpiration. A full-grown tree can release many gallons of water through transpiration every day!

How did some of the water from the plant's roots get into the sealed bag? The answer is found in the structure of the plant's leaves. The underside of each leaf contains tiny cells that open and close like little gates. These cells are called guard cells and the openings are called stomata.

If the sun is bright and the plant has plenty of water, the guard cells swell and the stomata opens. This allows carbon dioxide to enter (for use with photosynthesis) and excess oxygen and water (in the form of water vapor) to be released. Scientists call this transpiration. But if the sun is dim or the plant is short on water, the guard cells shrink, closing the stomata. This allows the plant to conserve water until conditions improve.

1. Why was plenty of water essential as part of Step 1? Why was it important to keep the leaves dry?

   a) need enough for transpiration.

   b) to prove wetness came from transpiration, not left over from watering

2. What was the purpose of the bag in step 2? Why not put the entire plant in the bag?

   a) to create a controlled environment

   b) water might have come from the soil, not just the plant

24 LIFE

3. What did you predict in Step 3? How did your prediction reflect what actually happened in Step 4?

   Answers will vary, but should reflect logical comparisons.

4. Where did the water vapor come from in Step 4? What outside energy source helped in the process?

   a) from watering the soil

   b) energy from the sun

5. Based on your observations, what might happen to a plant without sufficient water on a hot, sunny day?

   It would wilt, it would droop, it might die, etc.

LIFE 25

What Happened

Review the section with students. Emphasize bold-face words that identify key concepts and introduce new vocabulary.

*How did some of the water from the plant's roots get into the sealed bag? The answer is found in the **structure** of the plant's leaves. The underside of each leaf contains tiny cells that open and close like little gates. These cells are called **guard cells** and the openings are called **stomata**.*

*If the sun is bright and the plant has plenty of water, the guard cells swell and the stomata opens. This allows **carbon dioxide** to enter (for use with **photosynthesis**) and excess oxygen and water (in the form of water **vapor** to be released. Scientists call this **transpiration**. But if the sun is dim or the plant is short on water, the guard cells shrink, closing the stomata. This allows the plant to conserve water until conditions improve.*

What We Learned

Answers will vary. Suggested responses are shown at left.

Conclusion

Read this section aloud to the class to summarize the concepts learned in this activity.

Food for Thought

Read the Scripture aloud to the class. Talk about the enduring promises found in God's word. Discuss ways students can learn to trust God more.

Journal

If time permits, have a general class discussion about students' journal entries. Share and compare observations. Be sure to emphasize that "trial and error" is a valuable part of scientific inquiry!

Conclusion

Like most living things, plants need water to survive. Water is absorbed by a plant's roots and released from its leaves through stomata. Plants also take in carbon dioxide and give off oxygen.

Food for Thought

Isaiah 40:6-8 In this activity, we saw how water can move through a plant. Plants cannot survive without this precious resource. If a drought comes and the plant runs out of water, it dies!

Scripture reminds us that everything eventually dies — the plants, the animals, and even all humans. Nothing in this world is permanent except for God's Word! Isaiah reminds us that the Word of God will stand forever. No matter what happens, we can know that God's Word is always true. Those who learn to trust in God's Word will live forever!

Journal My Science Notes

26 LIFE

Extended Teaching

1. Have students research droughts. Discuss how droughts negatively impact an area. Have each team choose some aspect of a drought and report their findings to the class.

2. Invite a representative from your local water facility to visit your classroom. Discuss how water is purified and some of the challenges facing water facilities.

3. Using the Internet, have students research new, more efficient forms of irrigation being tested in agriculture. Have each team produce a poster showing at least one form of irrigation.

4. Challenge students to discover how desert plants survive such harsh climates. How does this relate to stomata, leaves, roots, etc.? Have them write a paper detailing at least one example.

5. Have students research the "Oklahoma Dust Bowl" era. Challenge each team to make a poster showing how this affected the U.S. economy, families, and the migration of people.

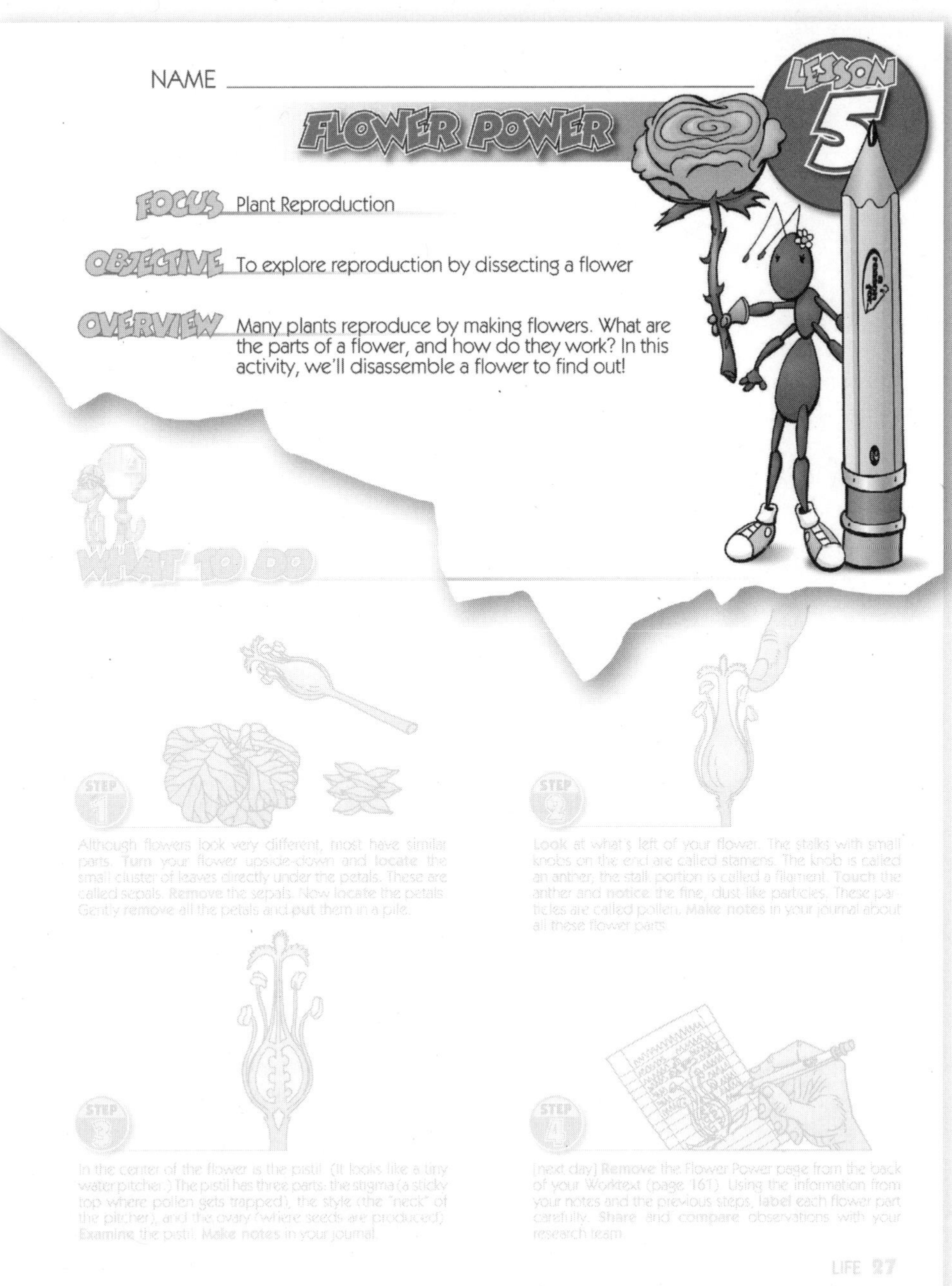
NAME ______________________

LESSON 5

FLOWER POWER

FOCUS Plant Reproduction

OBJECTIVE To explore reproduction by dissecting a flower

OVERVIEW Many plants reproduce by making flowers. What are the parts of a flower, and how do they work? In this activity, we'll disassemble a flower to find out!

WHAT TO DO

STEP 1

Although flowers look very different, most have similar parts. Turn your flower upside-down and locate the small cluster of leaves directly under the petals. These are called sepals. Remove the sepals. Now locate the petals. Gently remove all the petals and put them in a pile.

STEP 2

Look at what's left of your flower. The stalks with small knobs on the end are called stamens. The knob is called an anther; the stalk portion is called a filament. Touch the anther and notice the fine, dust-like particles. These particles are called pollen. Make notes in your journal about all these flower parts.

STEP 3

In the center of the flower is the pistil. (It looks like a tiny water pitcher.) The pistil has three parts: the stigma (a sticky top where pollen gets trapped), the style (the "neck" of the pitcher), and the ovary (where seeds are produced). Examine the pistil. Make notes in your journal.

STEP 4

[next day] Remove the Flower Power page from the back of your Worktext (page 161). Using the information from your notes and the previous steps, label each flower part carefully. Share and compare observations with your research team.

LIFE 27

Category

Life Science

Focus

Plant Reproduction

Objective

To explore reproduction by dissecting a flower

National Standards

A1, A2, B1, B2, B3, C1, C3, D1, E3, F1, F4, G1

Materials Needed

Flower Power worksheet *(student worktext, p. 163)*
flower

Safety Concerns

3. Skin Contact
Some students may have allergies to flowers. Check in advance and adjust accordingly.

Additional Comments

Local florists may be willing to donate older, fading flowers. Roses are excellent, but other flowers work well, too. Be sure to remove thorns from stems before using! If you wish, allow students to use a microscope to examine pollen more closely. Leftover petals can be used to make classroom potpourri!

Overview

Read the overview aloud to your students. The goal is to create an atmosphere of curiosity and inquiry. Make sure there is ample time for every student to identify every part.

WHAT TO DO

Monitor student research teams as they complete each step.

Step 2

Following this step, you will need to slice each team's stalk in half with a sharp knife. This will help them see the interior more clearly in Step 3.

NAME

LESSON 5

FLOWER POWER

FOCUS Plant Reproduction

OBJECTIVE To explore reproduction by dissecting a flower

OVERVIEW Many plants reproduce by making flowers. What are the parts of a flower, and how do they work? In this activity, we'll disassemble a flower to find out!

WHAT TO DO

STEP 1

Although flowers look very different, most have similar parts. **Turn** your flower upside-down and **locate** the small cluster of leaves directly under the petals. These are called sepals. **Remove** the sepals. Now **locate** the petals. Gently **remove** all the petals and **put** them in a pile.

STEP 2

Look at what's left of your flower. The stalks with small knobs on the end are called stamens. The knob is called an anther; the stalk portion is called a filament. **Touch** the anther and **notice** the fine, dust-like particles. These particles are called pollen. **Make notes** in your journal about all these flower parts.

STEP 3

In the center of the flower is the pistil. (It looks like a tiny water pitcher.) The pistil has three parts: the stigma (a sticky top where pollen gets trapped), the style (the "neck" of the pitcher), and the ovary (where seeds are produced). **Examine** the pistil. **Make notes** in your journal.

STEP 4

[next day] **Remove** the Flower Power page from the back of your Worktext (page 161). Using the information from your notes and the previous steps, **label** each flower part carefully. **Share** and **compare** observations with your research team.

LIFE **27**

Teacher to Teacher

Flowers that have both male and female reproductive organs are called "perfect flowers." Flowers that have only male or only female organs are called "imperfect flowers." Flowers that have petals, sepals, a pistil, and stamens are called "complete flowers." Flowers that are missing one or more of these parts are called "incomplete flowers."

A flower is actually the core of a plant's reproductive system. No two flowers are exactly alike, but most have similar parts. Flowers contain male and female cells, pollen, and eggs, which combine in the process called fertilization.

In some varieties, one plant has "male" flowers (with pollen) and another plant has "female" flowers (no pollen). In others, male and female flowers can be found on the same plant. Common methods of pollination include air currents (wind) and insects (like bees).

The disassembly process you used is called dissection. When you dissect something, you carefully and systematically take it apart. Scientists (including doctors and veterinarians) often use dissection to help them understand how living things work.

1. Describe the sepals and petals you removed in Step 1.

Accept any reasonable descriptions.

2. Describe the stamens, anther, and filament you removed in Step 2.

Accept any reasonable descriptions.

3. Name and describe the three parts of the pistil.

Atigma, style, ovary; accept any reasonable descriptions.

4. What is the primary purpose of flowers?
Name three plants that reproduce using flowers.

a) reproduction

b) answers will vary, but must be flowering plant

5. Name two methods of pollination.
How does a flower's bright color help with its pollenation?

a) air currents, insects

b) it attracts insects that transfer pollen from plant to plant

What Happened

Review the section with students. Emphasize bold-face words that identify key concepts and introduce new vocabulary.

*A **flower** is actually the core of a plant's **reproductive system**. No two flowers are exactly alike, but most have similar parts. Flowers contain male and female cells, **pollen**, and **eggs**, which combine in the process called **fertilization**.*

*In some varieties, one plant has "male" flowers (with pollen) and another plant has "female" flowers (no pollen). In others, male and female flowers can be found on the same plant. Common methods of **pollination** include **air currents** (wind) and **insects** (like bees).*

*The disassembly process you used is called **dissection**. When you dissect something, you carefully and systematically take it apart. Scientists (including doctors and veterinarians) often use dissection to help them understand how living things work.*

What We Learned

Answers will vary. Suggested responses are shown at left.

Conclusion

Read this section aloud to the class to summarize the concepts learned in this activity.

Food for Thought

Read the Scripture aloud to the class. Talk about the complexity of our world and its environment. Relate this to the complexity of our lives and our need to trust God.

Journal

If time permits, have a general class discussion about students' journal entries. Share and compare observations. Be sure to emphasize that "trial and error" is a valuable part of scientific inquiry!

Conclusion

All living things must reproduce to survive. Plants use flowers in the reproduction process. Some species have both male and female flowers on one plant. Other species require flowers from two plants to reproduce.

Food for Thought

Job 38:4-35 When you dissected the flower, you discovered the complexity of its marvelous design. This is just a tiny sample of God's handiwork!

Humans create grand designs, too. But as brilliant and complex as those designs might be, they never last forever. Some great designs (like the Titanic) even lead to tragedy. But as Job realized, what God creates lasts forever. Imagine how complex it must have been to create an entire planet with its interlocking environmental systems. Now imagine creating an entire universe! Don't put your faith in the things that humans create. Put your trust in God!

Journal My Science Notes

Extended Teaching

1. Take a field trip to a local market. Have each team find and list 10 products that involved some form of pollination in their development. (Hint: honey, fruit, anything grain based, etc.). Back at school, have them share and compare lists.

2. Have students make a bulletin board of different flowers. Use discarded garden magazine pictures, pressed flowers, and student drawings.

3. Challenge students to research spices (which are made from various plant parts). Have each team choose a spice and report their findings to the class.

4. Have students research bees. Challenge each team to make a chart showing the importance of bees in the pollination process.

5. Using the Internet, have students research cross-pollination. What are some of the resulting products? How does this relate to new crop varieties?

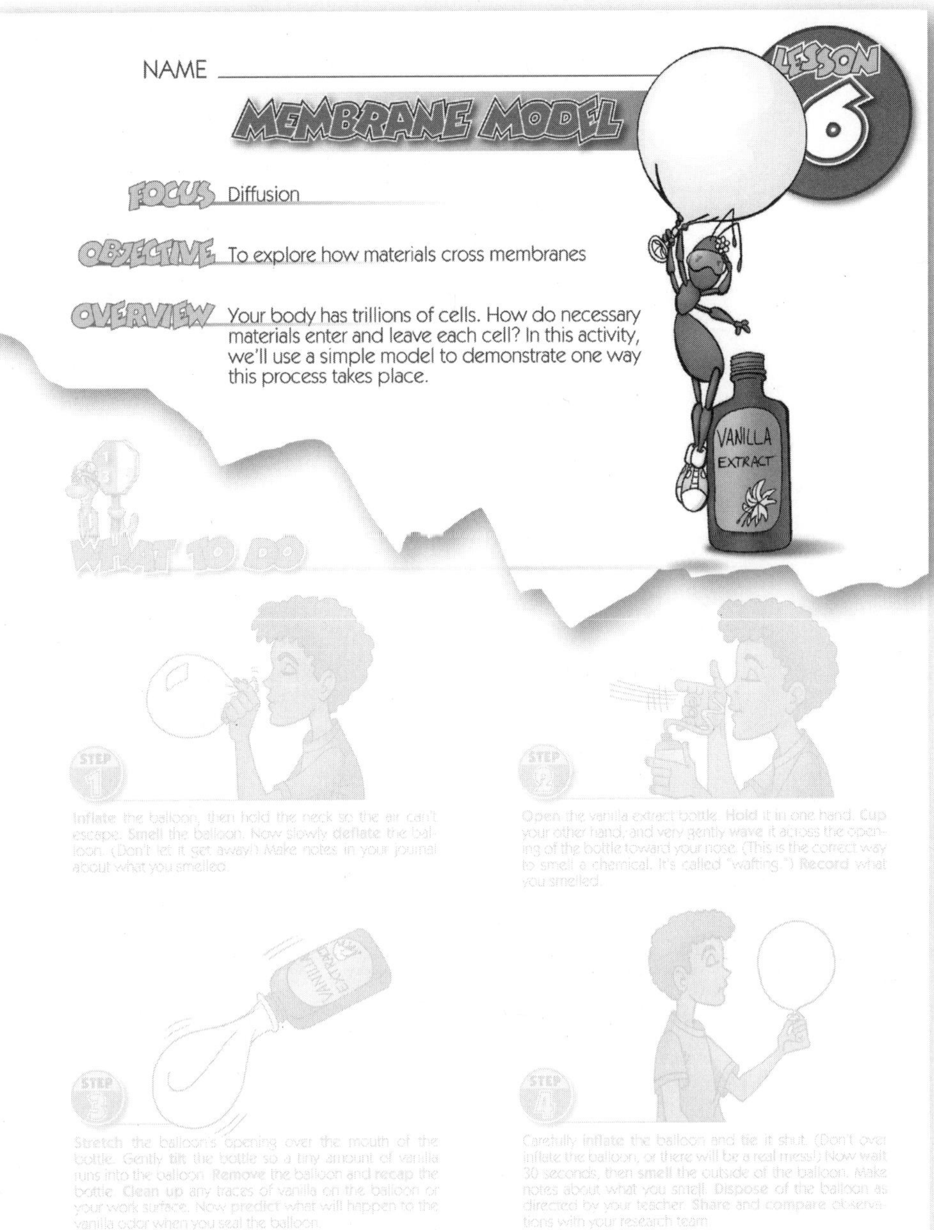

NAME ______________________

LESSON 6

MEMBRANE MODEL

FOCUS Diffusion

OBJECTIVE To explore how materials cross membranes

OVERVIEW Your body has trillions of cells. How do necessary materials enter and leave each cell? In this activity, we'll use a simple model to demonstrate one way this process takes place.

WHAT TO DO

STEP 1
Inflate the balloon, then hold the neck so the air can't escape. Smell the balloon. Now slowly deflate the balloon. (Don't let it get away!) Make notes in your journal about what you smelled.

STEP 2
Open the vanilla extract bottle. Hold it in one hand. Cup your other hand, and very gently wave it across the opening of the bottle toward your nose. (This is the correct way to smell a chemical. It's called "wafting.") Record what you smelled.

STEP 3
Stretch the balloon's opening over the mouth of the bottle. Gently tilt the bottle so a tiny amount of vanilla runs into the balloon. Remove the balloon and recap the bottle. Clean up any traces of vanilla on the balloon or your work surface. Now predict what will happen to the vanilla odor when you seal the balloon.

STEP 4
Carefully inflate the balloon and tie it shut. (Don't over inflate the balloon, or there will be a real mess!) Now wait 30 seconds, then smell the outside of the balloon. Make notes about what you smell. Dispose of the balloon as directed by your teacher. Share and compare observations with your research team.

LIFE 31

Category

Life Science

Focus

Diffusion

Objective

To explore how materials cross membranes

National Standards

A1, A2, B1, B2, B3, C1, C3, D1, E3, F1, F4, G1

Materials Needed

balloon, medium size
vanilla extract

Safety Concerns

3. Skin Contact
Remind students to carefully wash their hands after this activity.

4. Goggles
Goggles are a good precaution against flying vanilla from exploding balloon

Additional Comments

Don't let students over-inflate balloons. Caution them to use only a very tiny amount of vanilla — a few drops is plenty! Depending on your group, you may to wish to use only one "teacher-controlled" balloon to reduce the possibility for a vanilla-flavored explosion.

Overview

Read the overview aloud to your students. The goal is to create an atmosphere of curiosity and inquiry.

WHAT TO DO

Monitor student research teams as they complete each step.

Step 3

Caution students to use only a tiny amount of vanilla. A few drops are enough for this activity to work.

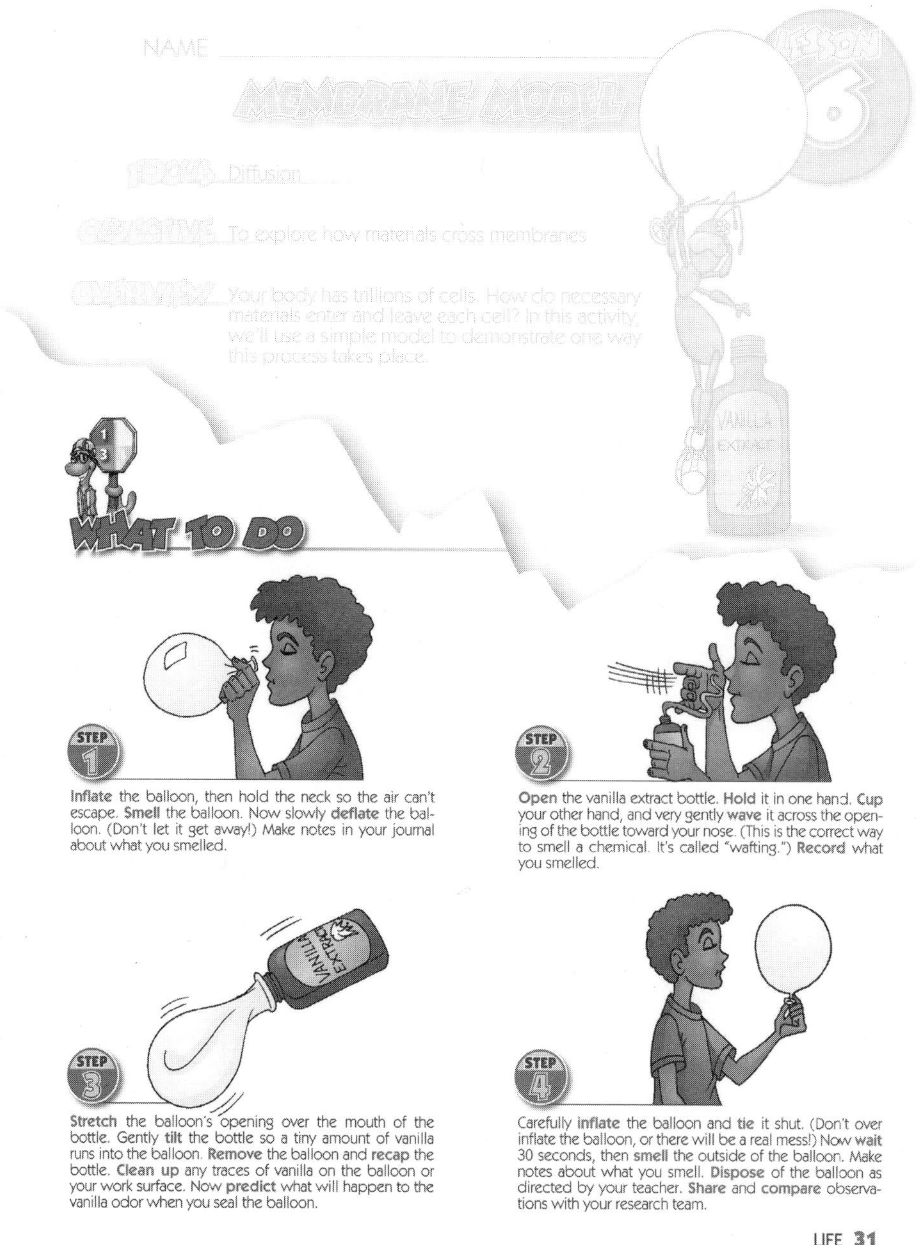

NAME

LESSON 6

MEMBRANE MODEL

TOPIC Diffusion

OBJECTIVE To explore how materials cross membranes

OVERVIEW Your body has trillions of cells. How do necessary materials enter and leave each cell? In this activity, we'll use a simple model to demonstrate one way this process takes place.

WHAT TO DO

STEP 1 **Inflate** the balloon, then hold the neck so the air can't escape. **Smell** the balloon. Now slowly **deflate** the balloon. (Don't let it get away!) Make notes in your journal about what you smelled.

STEP 2 **Open** the vanilla extract bottle. **Hold** it in one hand. **Cup** your other hand, and very gently **wave** it across the opening of the bottle toward your nose. (This is the correct way to smell a chemical. It's called "wafting.") **Record** what you smelled.

STEP 3 **Stretch** the balloon's opening over the mouth of the bottle. Gently **tilt** the bottle so a tiny amount of vanilla runs into the balloon. **Remove** the balloon and **recap** the bottle. **Clean up** any traces of vanilla on the balloon or your work surface. Now **predict** what will happen to the vanilla odor when you seal the balloon.

STEP 4 Carefully **inflate** the balloon and **tie** it shut. (Don't over inflate the balloon, or there will be a real mess!) Now **wait** 30 seconds, then **smell** the outside of the balloon. Make notes about what you smell. **Dispose** of the balloon as directed by your teacher. **Share** and **compare** observations with your research team.

LIFE 31

Teacher to Teacher

Diffusion is when molecules spread out from an area of *greater* concentration to an area of *lesser* concentration. The concentration of molecules inside the balloon was very high. As they bumped and shoved each other around, a few (including some vanilla molecules) were pushed out through the balloon's walls into the air. Even without a leak, a balloon will go flat over time — another example of diffusion at work.

WHAT HAPPENED?

Material enters and exits the cell through the cell membrane. One common process is called diffusion. Imagine a cloud of smoke. First it's thick and dark, then it begins to spead thinner and thinner, then eventually it disappears. The smoke molecules diffuse because air molecules are always moving — and as they move around, they shove the smoke molecules farther and farther apart!

The balloon in this activity was filled with vanilla extract molecules. As they moved around in the balloon, some vanilla molecules got pushed out through the molecules of the balloon. (That's why you smelled them!)

Diffusion always spreads things out. The vanilla extract molecules went from where there were many (inside the balloon) to where there were few (outside the balloon).

WHAT WE LEARNED

1. Describe what the balloon smelled like in Step 1.

No smell, or just the "rubbery" smell of the balloon.

2. What process did you use to smell the bottle's contents in Step 2? Describe what you smelled.

a) wafting

b) the smell of vanilla

3. What did you predict in Step 3? How did your prediction reflect what actually happened in Step 4?

Answers will vary, but should reflect logical comparisons.

4. Describe what the balloon smelled like in Step 4. Compare this with what it smelled like in Step 1.

a) it smelled like vanilla

b) answers will vary, but should reflect a lack of smell

5. Explain how this activity modeled the transfer of materials through a cell membrane. Why is it important for materials to be able to go in and out of a cell?

a) the vanilla molecules passed through the balloon's wall

b) to let in nutrients and let out waste

What Happened

Review the section with students. Emphasize bold-face words that identify key concepts and introduce new vocabulary.

*Material enters and exits the **cell** through the **cell membrane**. One common process is called **diffusion**. Imagine a cloud of smoke. First it's thick and dark, then it begins to spread thinner and thinner, then eventually it disappears. The smoke **molecules** diffuse because air molecules are always moving — and as they move around, they shove the smoke molecules farther and farther apart!*

*The balloon in this activity was filled with vanilla extract molecules. As they moved around in the balloon, some vanilla molecules got **pushed** out through the molecules of the balloon. (That's why you smelled them!)*

Diffusion always spreads things out. The vanilla extract molecules went from where there were many (inside the balloon) to where there were few (outside the balloon).

What We Learned

Answers will vary. Suggested responses are shown at left.

Conclusion

Read this section aloud to the class to summarize the concepts learned in this activity.

Food for Thought

Read the Scripture aloud to the class. Talk about the analogy used in this verse. Discuss ways we can be a "beautiful fragrance" to those around us.

Journal

If time permits, have a general class discussion about students' journal entries. Share and compare observations. Be sure to emphasize that "trial and error" is a valuable part of scientific inquiry!

Conclusion

Diffusion is one way materials move in and out of living cells. Diffusion allows the transfer of materials through the cell membrane. Diffusion can move materials from high concentration areas to low.

Food for Thought

2 Corinthians 2:16 Didn't that vanilla smell good? Psychologists tell us that smells are powerful memory triggers! Perhaps this vanilla brought back a special memory, like someone in your family cooking a holiday meal.

In this Scripture, Paul tells us that Christians who spread the good news of Jesus are like a beautiful fragrance filling a room. Like the vanilla, such great smells tend to spread out and fill a large area. This is exactly what happened to the story of Jesus. It spead from the tiny town of Bethleham until it filled the entire world!

Journal My Science Notes

34 LIFE

Extended Teaching

1. Have students drop food coloring in a clear container of water to see diffusion in action. Let them experiment with hot and cold water, and record any difference in the rate of diffusion.

2. Invite a nurse to visit your classroom. Find out why they advise people to drink lots of liquids when they're ill. Have him/her explain what's going on in terms of dehydration.

3. Have students find a picture of a cell membrane in a Biology book or on the Internet. Research what it's made of and how it works. Challenge teams to create posters based on their findings.

4. Repeat this activity using other food-grade liquids (corn oil, milk, olive oil, tea, etc.). Have students make a chart showing the results of each test. Discuss possible causes for different results.

5. If a pollutant enters a stream, it can affect people miles downstream even though no visible trace remains. Based on what they've learned, challenge students to explain this.

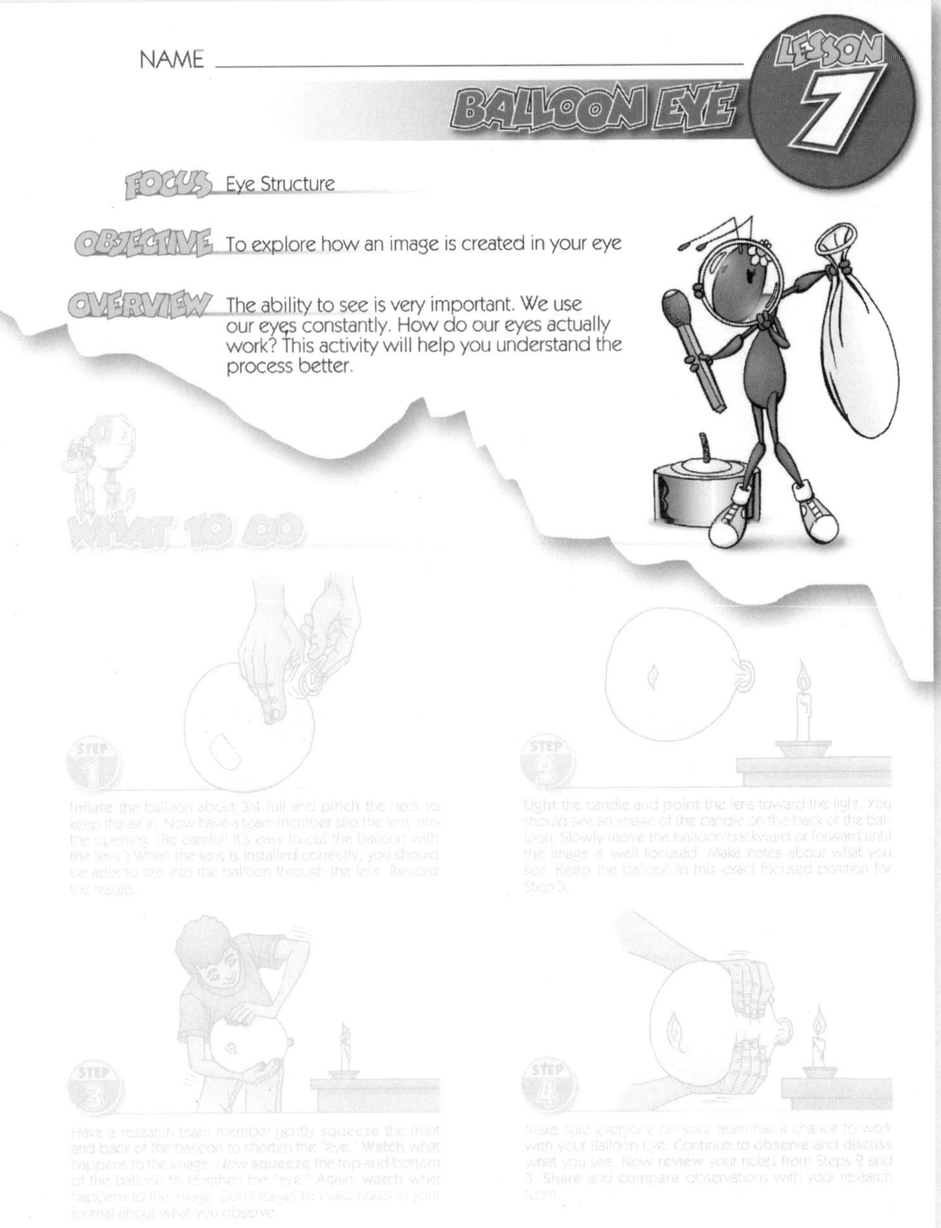
NAME ______________________________

LESSON 7

BALLOON EYE

FOCUS Eye Structure

OBJECTIVE To explore how an image is created in your eye

OVERVIEW The ability to see is very important. We use our eyes constantly. How do our eyes actually work? This activity will help you understand the process better.

WHAT TO DO

STEP 1
Inflate the balloon about 3/4 full and pinch the neck to keep the air in. Now have a team member slip the lens into the opening. (Be careful! It's easy to cut the balloon with the lens.) When the lens is installed correctly, you should be able to see into the balloon through the lens. Record the results.

STEP 2
Light the candle and point the lens toward the light. You should see an image of the candle on the back of the balloon. Slowly move the balloon backward or forward until the image is well focused. Make notes about what you see. Keep the balloon in this exact focused position for Step 3.

STEP 3
Have a research team member gently squeeze the front and back of the balloon to shorten the "eye." Watch what happens to the image. Now squeeze the top and bottom of the balloon to lengthen the "eye." Again, watch what happens to the image. Don't forget to make notes in your journal about what you observe.

STEP 4
Make sure everyone on your team has a chance to work with your Balloon Eye. Continue to observe and discuss what you see. Now review your notes from Steps 2 and 3. Share and compare observations with your research team.

LIFE 35

Category

Life Science

Focus

Eye Structure

Objective

To explore how an image is created in your eye

National Standards

A1, A2, B1, B2, B3, C1, C3, D1, E3, F1, F4, G1

Materials Needed

balloon, large size
lens
candle
match

Safety Concerns

1. Goggles
Goggles are a useful precaution in case of an exploding balloon.

2. Open Flame
Remind students to exercise caution around open flame (loose clothing, long hair, etc.).

Additional Comments

You can avoid students using matches by lighting the candles yourself. When every team is ready to test their balloon eye, darken the room as much as possible. Remind students to be careful moving around! Also, avoid burns and popping balloons by keeping students a safe distance from candles.

Overview

Read the overview aloud to your students. The goal is to create an atmosphere of curiosity and inquiry.

WHAT TO DO

Monitor student research teams as they complete each step.

Step 3

Remind students to squeeze *gently*, using only enough pressure to distort the balloon. Too much pressure could cause the balloon to pop.

NAME

LESSON 7

BALLOON EYE

FOCUS Eye Structure

OBJECTIVE To explore how an image is created in your eye.

OVERVIEW The ability to see is very important. We use our eyes constantly. How do our eyes actually work? This activity will help you understand the process better.

WHAT TO DO

STEP 1

Inflate the balloon about 3/4 full and **pinch** the neck to keep the air in. Now have a team member **slip** the lens into the opening. (Be careful! It's easy to cut the balloon with the lens.) When the lens is installed correctly, you should be able to see into the balloon through the lens. **Record** the results.

STEP 2

Light the candle and **point** the lens toward the light. You should see an image of the candle on the back of the balloon. Slowly **move** the balloon backward or forward until the image is well focused. Make notes about what you see. **Keep** the balloon in this exact focused position for Step 3.

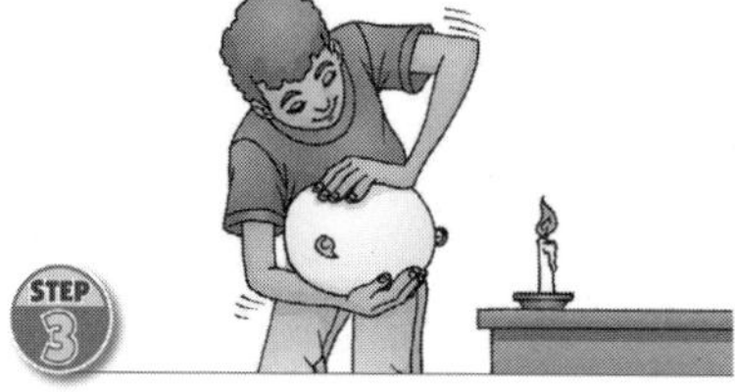

STEP 3

Have a research team member gently **squeeze** the front and back of the balloon to shorten the "eye." **Watch** what happens to the image. Now **squeeze** the top and bottom of the balloon to lengthen the "eye." Again, **watch** what happens to the image. Don't forget to make notes in your journal about what you observe.

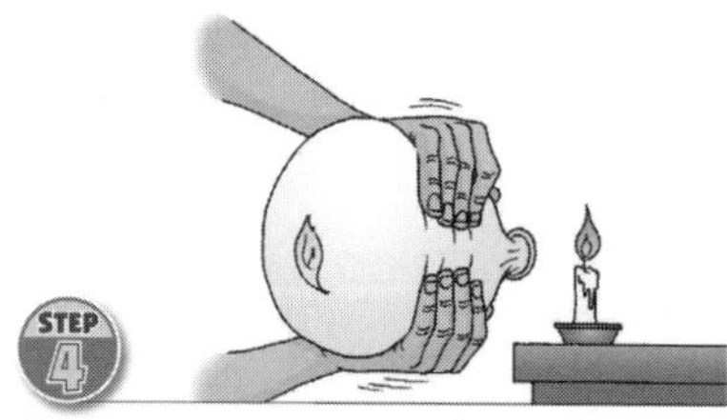

STEP 4

Make sure everyone on your team has a chance to work with your Balloon Eye. Continue to **observe** and **discuss** what you see. Now **review** your notes from Steps 2 and 3. **Share** and **compare** observations with your research team.

LIFE **35**

Teacher to Teacher

The retina is covered with light-sensitive cells called rods and cones. There are three types of cone cells, each with sensitivity to particular wavelengths. Cones function best in bright light and help us see colors. Rod cells have one type of cell. Rods work best in low light conditions. The "blip" in vision you experience when moving from bright sunlight to a dark room is your eyes switching from mostly cones to mostly rods.

What Happened

Review the section with students. Emphasize bold-face words that identify key concepts and introduce new vocabulary.

The lens you put in the neck of the balloon simulates the ***lens*** *of your* ***eye*** *(front of your eye). It helps* ***focus*** *(or concentrate) light onto the* ***retina*** *(back of your eye). The retina is where the* ***image*** *(whatever you're looking at) is reproduced. The shapes you gave the balloon simulate different vision problems that optometrists can usually fix with glasses or contacts.*

Notice the image in the balloon was upside down. That's exactly how images are projected in our eyes! So why don't we "see" everything upside-down? When we're born, our miraculous brain begins learning how to adjust. Ever notice how tiny babies often reach in the wrong place for something they're trying to grab? They're still learning to coordinate their eyes with their brain.

What We Learned

Answers will vary. Suggested responses are shown at left.

What Happened?

The lens you put in the neck of the balloon simulates the lens of your eye (front of your eye). It helps focus (or concentrate) light onto the retina (back of your eye). The retina is where the image (whatever you're looking at) is reproduced. The shapes you gave the balloon simulate different vision problems that optometrists can usually fix with glasses or contacts.

Notice the image in the balloon was upside down. That's exactly how images are projected in our eyes! So why don't we "see" everything upside-down? When we're born, our miraculous brain begins learning how to adjust. Ever notice how tiny babies often reach in the wrong place for something they're trying to grab? They're still learning to coordinate their eyes with their brain.

What We Learned

1. **What did the lens represent in Step 1? What did the back of the balloon represent?**

   a) the lens in your eye

   b) the retina of your eye

2. **In Step 2, what was unusual about the image in the balloon? How does this reflect what happens in your eye?**

   a) it was upside down

   b) the same thing happens in your eye

3. **Describe what happened to the image when you modified the shape of the balloon in Step 3.**

   Answers will vary, but should indicate both times the image was distorted or went out of focus.

4. **Based on what you observed in this lesson, how do contact lenses or glasses help correct vision problems?**

   They correct the distortion caused by an out-of-shape eyeball.

5. **Name three devices (other than glasses or contacts) that use lenses.**

   Answers will vary, but should include devices like microscopes, telescopes, cameras, etc.

Conclusion

Read this section aloud to the class to summarize the concepts learned in this activity.

Food for Thought

Read the Scripture aloud to the class. Talk about how we can avoid being deceived. Focus on the importance of trusting God who knows all things.

Journal

If time permits, have a general class discussion about students' journal entries. Share and compare observations. Be sure to emphasize that "trial and error" is a valuable part of scientific inquiry!

CONCLUSION

The lens of the eye helps focus light onto the retina, creating an image of the object observed. A change in the eye's shape can create vision problems. Optometrists usually fix such problems with glasses or contacts.

Matthew 24:5 This model shows us a lot about the eye and how it works. Just because we see something with our eyes doesn't mean it's true. We can be tricked by optical illusions, models, colors, or other devices.

The opposite is true as well. Just because we don't see something, doesn't mean it doesn't exist! This Scripture talks about a time when many people are going to be deceived. How can you avoid being fooled? By knowing "the real thing." The more time you spend with God, the less likely you are to be fooled by the deceiver. With God, belief isn't based just on our eyesight — it's based on our trust in him!

JOURNAL My Science Notes

38 LIFE

Extended Teaching

1. Have students research the causes of blindness. Discuss ways of preventing blindness, and steps we can take to protect our eyes.

2. Some animals have excellent night vision. Discuss this with students and give examples. Now have teams brainstorm what might account for better night vision. (Their eyes have many more rods!)

3. Take a field trip to an optometrist's office. Discuss types of glasses and contact lenses. Challenge teams to create a poster based on some aspect of this visit.

4. Have students research eye changes that take place with age. Have them compare these changes to the vision problems of older relatives and friends. Have students make lists of problems and possible solutions (if any).

5. Many eye clinics now perform laser vision correction. Invite a clinic representative to visit your classroom. Discuss how this relatively new procedure corrects vision problems, and who can and can't benefit.

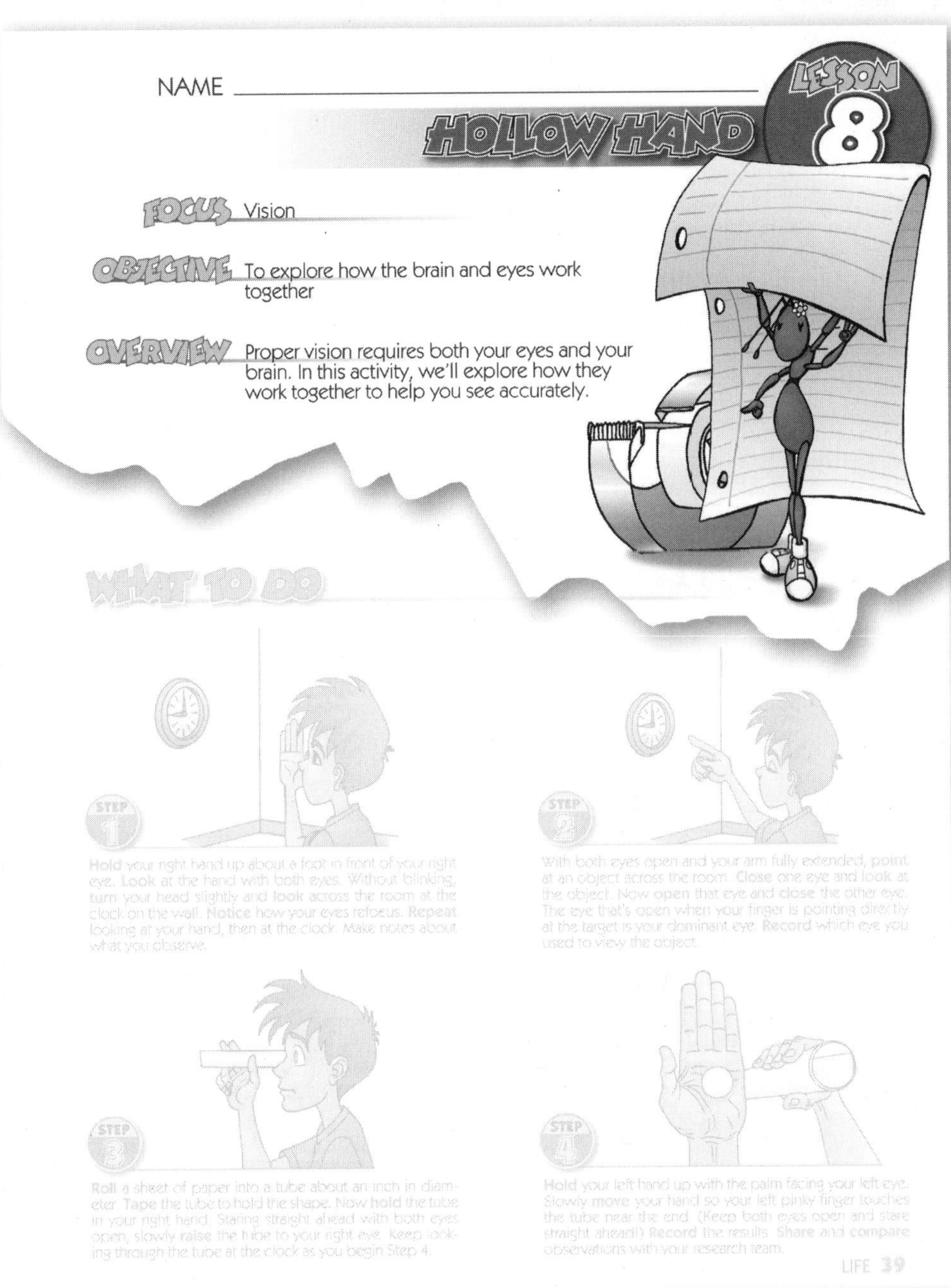

NAME ______________________________

LESSON 8

HOLLOW HAND

FOCUS Vision

OBJECTIVE To explore how the brain and eyes work together

OVERVIEW Proper vision requires both your eyes and your brain. In this activity, we'll explore how they work together to help you see accurately.

WHAT TO DO

STEP 1

Hold your right hand up about a foot in front of your right eye. Look at the hand with both eyes. Without blinking, turn your head slightly and look across the room at the clock on the wall. Notice how your eyes refocus. Repeat looking at your hand, then at the clock. Make notes about what you observe.

STEP 2

With both eyes open and your arm fully extended, point at an object across the room. Close one eye and look at the object. Now open that eye and close the other eye. The eye that's open when your finger is pointing directly at the target is your dominant eye. Record which eye you used to view the object.

STEP 3

Roll a sheet of paper into a tube about an inch in diameter. Tape the tube to hold the shape. Now hold the tube in your right hand. Staring straight ahead with both eyes open, slowly raise the tube to your right eye. Keep looking through the tube at the clock as you begin Step 4.

STEP 4

Hold your left hand up with the palm facing your left eye. Slowly move your hand so your left pinky finger touches the tube near the end. (Keep both eyes open and stare straight ahead!) Record the results. Share and compare observations with your research team.

LIFE 39

Category

Life Science

Focus

Vision

Objective

To explore how the brain and eyes work together

National Standards

A1, A2, B1, B2, B3, C1, C3, D1, E3, F1, F4, G1

Materials Needed

typing paper
tape

Safety Concerns

none

Additional Comments

A great way to begin this activity is to tell students, "I'm going to help you find a big hole in your hand!" Like any optical illusion, some students will get the hang of this quickly, others will need some encouragement. Remind them not to squint, keep both eyes open, and to stare straight ahead.

Overview

Read the overview aloud to your students. The goal is to create an atmosphere of curiosity and inquiry.

WHAT TO DO

Monitor student research teams as they complete each step.

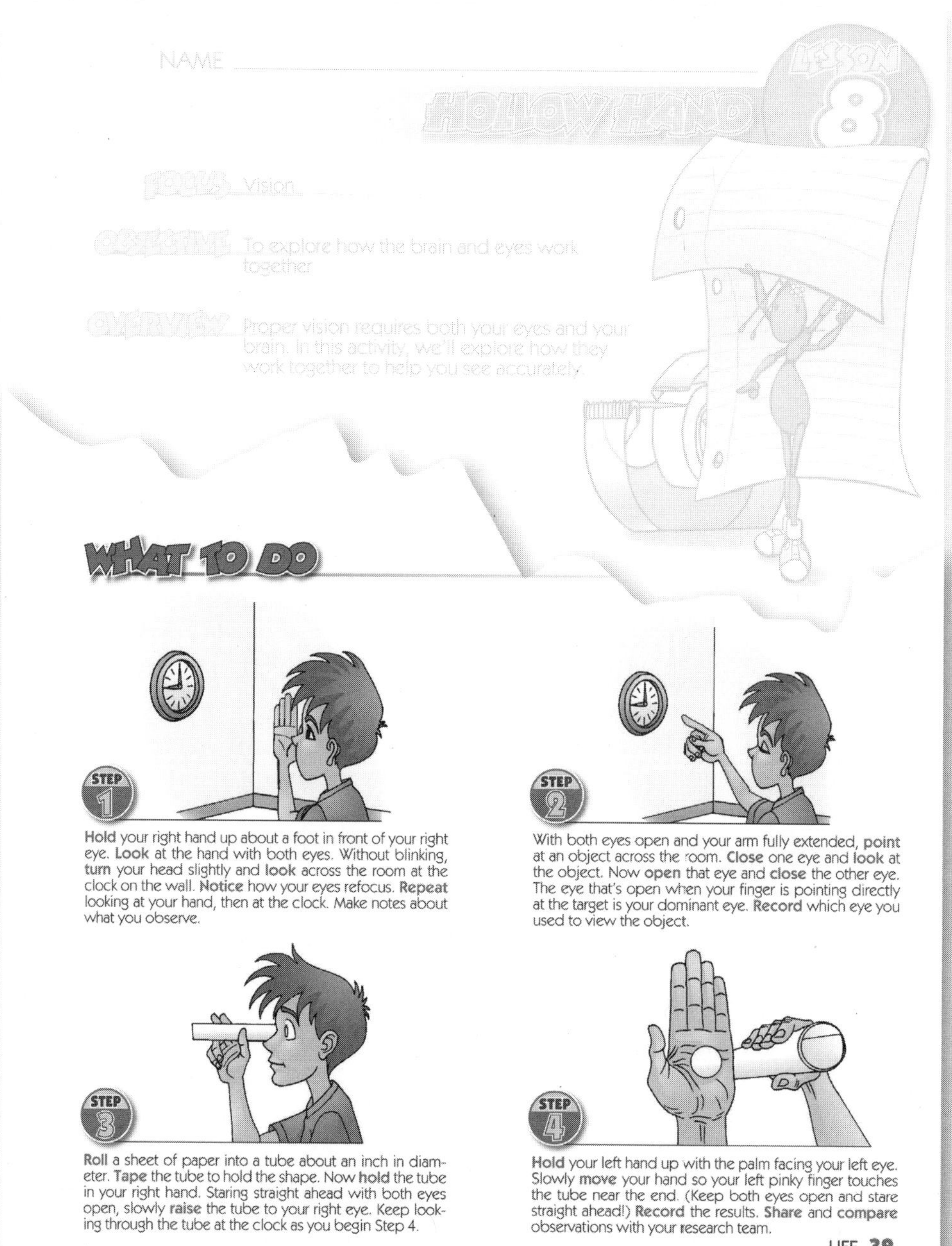

NAME

LESSON 8

HOLLOW HAND

FOCUS Vision

OBJECTIVE To explore how the brain and eyes work together

OVERVIEW Proper vision requires both your eyes and your brain. In this activity, we'll explore how they work together to help you see accurately.

WHAT TO DO

STEP 1

Hold your right hand up about a foot in front of your right eye. **Look** at the hand with both eyes. Without blinking, **turn** your head slightly and **look** across the room at the clock on the wall. **Notice** how your eyes refocus. **Repeat** looking at your hand, then at the clock. Make notes about what you observe.

STEP 2

With both eyes open and your arm fully extended, **point** at an object across the room. **Close** one eye and **look** at the object. Now **open** that eye and **close** the other eye. The eye that's open when your finger is pointing directly at the target is your dominant eye. **Record** which eye you used to view the object.

STEP 3

Roll a sheet of paper into a tube about an inch in diameter. **Tape** the tube to hold the shape. Now **hold** the tube in your right hand. Staring straight ahead with both eyes open, slowly **raise** the tube to your right eye. Keep looking through the tube at the clock as you begin Step 4.

STEP 4

Hold your left hand up with the palm facing your left eye. Slowly **move** your hand so your left pinky finger touches the tube near the end. (Keep both eyes open and stare straight ahead!) **Record** the results. **Share** and **compare** observations with your research team.

LIFE 39

Teacher to Teacher

People who prefer their right eye for viewing something are said to be "right eye dominant." Usually they're right-handed as well. A left eye preference is called "left eye dominance." These people are usually left-handed. A few people are "cross dominant," meaning left eye dominant but right-handed, or vice versa. Cross dominance is rare in the general population, but fairly common in professional baseball players! It allows them to watch the ball while keeping their shoulders square to the plate, making them better hitters.

What Happened?

As we learned in our last lesson, the eye sees an object by focusing light through its lens onto the retina. Identifying signals are sent to your brain through neurons, combining the view from both eyes into a single image.

Normally, both eyes work together and send the same information for your brain to interpret. But in this activity, you tricked your brain by isolating one eye from the other. Each eye got a different image! Since your brain usually gets the same information from both eyes, it was confused. It tried to compensate by blending the two images into one. This resulted in your "seeing" there was a hole through your hand!

What We Learned

1. Describe the way your eyes refocused in Step 1. Did you experience any "double vision"?

Answers will vary, but should reflect the change between blurred and normal vision.

2. How did you discover your dominant eye in Step 2? Which is your dominant eye?

a) by pointing at the clock and closing each eye in turn

b) answers will vary

3. Describe what you observed in Step 3.

Answers will vary, but should reflect the fact that vision was narrowed.

4. Describe what you observed in Step 4. How did this differ from Step 3?

Answers should reflect the "hole in the hand" illusion.

5. What is the common term for what you observed in Step 4? What does the word "illusion" mean?

a) an optical illusion

b) an incorrect perception of reality; something that isn't really there, etc.

What Happened

Review the section with students. Emphasize bold-face words that identify key concepts and introduce new vocabulary.

As we learned in our last lesson, the ***eye*** *sees an object by focusing* ***light*** *through its* ***lens*** *onto the* ***retina****. Identifying signals are sent to your* ***brain*** *through* ***neurons****, combining the view from both eyes into a single* ***image****.*

Normally, both eyes work together and send the same information for your brain to interpret. But in this activity, you tricked your brain by isolating one eye from the other. Each eye got a different image! Since your brain usually gets the same information from both eyes, it was confused. It tried to compensate by blending the two images into one. This resulted in your "seeing" there was a hole through your hand!

What We Learned

Answers will vary. Suggested responses are shown at left.

Conclusion

Read this section aloud to the class to summarize the concepts learned in this activity.

Food for Thought

Read the Scripture aloud to the class. Talk about the temporary nature of life on earth. Discuss ways we can prepare for an eternal future with God.

Journal

If time permits, have a general class discussion about students' journal entries. Share and compare observations. Be sure to emphasize that "trial and error" is a valuable part of scientific inquiry!

Conclusion

Even if our eyes are physically perfect, we can't see without our brain and its connecting neurons. The eyes and brain must work together to provide correct vision.

Food for Thought

2 Corinthians 4:18 Suddenly seeing a hole in your hand was surprising! Nobody would have expected that. Of course, you weren't worried since you knew it was only an illusion! It wasn't something that would last.

This Scripture reminds us not to focus too much on the things we see around us. None of them will last forever. It's much more important to understand what God has planned for you in the future! While the things of this world are temporary, God's Kingdom will last forever. Learn to trust in God, and you will too!

Journal My Science Notes

42 LIFE

Extended Teaching

1. Have students research vision problems. Ask teams to choose a problem (glaucoma, macular degeneration, etc.) and report their findings to the class.

2. Invite a vision specialist to visit your classroom. Discuss how treatments for vision problems have changed over time. Have students write a paragraph about one thing they learned from this visit.

3. Have a volunteer in each team close his/her eyes tightly for 10 seconds, then open them wide. Other team members should watch for changes in the center of the eye (the pupil), and record the results.

4. Have students research a chemical called "rhodopsin," then write a short paper telling how it affects night vision.

5. Challenge students to relate what they've learned in this activity to "magic" tricks. How are they similar? (Sometimes our brain interprets visual information in ways that don't reflect reality!)

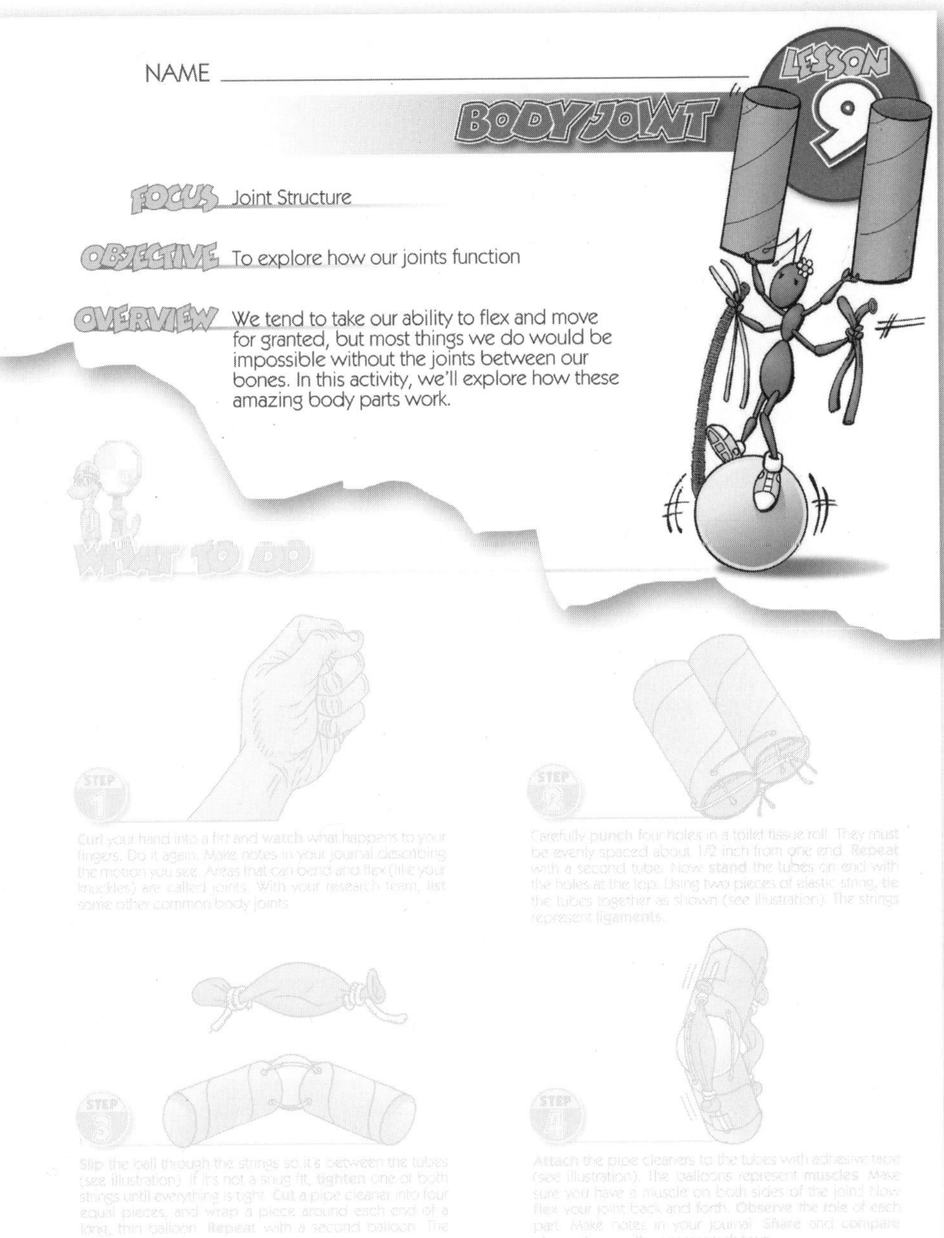

NAME ____________________

LESSON 9

BODY JOINT

FOCUS Joint Structure

OBJECTIVE To explore how our joints function

OVERVIEW We tend to take our ability to flex and move for granted, but most things we do would be impossible without the joints between our bones. In this activity, we'll explore how these amazing body parts work.

WHAT TO DO

STEP 1

Curl your hand into a fist and watch what happens to your fingers. Do it again. Make notes in your journal describing the motion you see. Areas that can bend and flex (like your knuckles) are called joints. With your research team, list some other common body joints.

STEP 2

Carefully punch four holes in a toilet tissue roll. They must be evenly spaced about 1/2 inch from one end. Repeat with a second tube. Now stand the tubes on end with the holes at the top. Using two pieces of elastic string, tie the tubes together as shown (see illustration). The strings represent ligaments.

STEP 3

Slip the ball through the strings so it's between the tubes (see illustration). If it's not a snug fit, tighten one or both strings until everything is tight. Cut a pipe cleaner into four equal pieces, and wrap a piece around each end of a long, thin balloon. Repeat with a second balloon. The pipe cleaners represent tendons.

STEP 4

Attach the pipe cleaners to the tubes with adhesive tape (see illustration). The balloons represent muscles. Make sure you have a muscle on both sides of the joint. Now flex your joint back and forth. Observe the role of each part. Make notes in your journal. Share and compare observations with your research team.

LIFE 43

Category

Life Science

Focus

Joint Structure

Objective

To explore how our joints function

National Standards

A1, A2, B1, B2, B3, C1, C3, D1, E3, F1, F4, G1

Materials Needed

elastic string
rubber ball
pipe cleaner
long, thin balloon pieces - 2
toilet tissue rolls - 2
paper punch
tape
scissors

Safety Concerns

4. Sharp Objects
Remind students to exercise caution when using scissors.

Additional Comments

Assembly can be a little bit tricky. This is a great time to emphasize the "teamwork" aspect of your research teams, since extra hands can make the process go smoother. Be sure to have spare materials on hand incase items break or become lost.

Overview

Read the overview aloud to your students. The goal is to create an atmosphere of curiosity and inquiry.

WHAT TO DO

Monitor student research teams as they complete each step.

Step 2

Encourage students to refer to the illustration for a clear understanding of how the tubes are tied together. This is a critical step in the process!

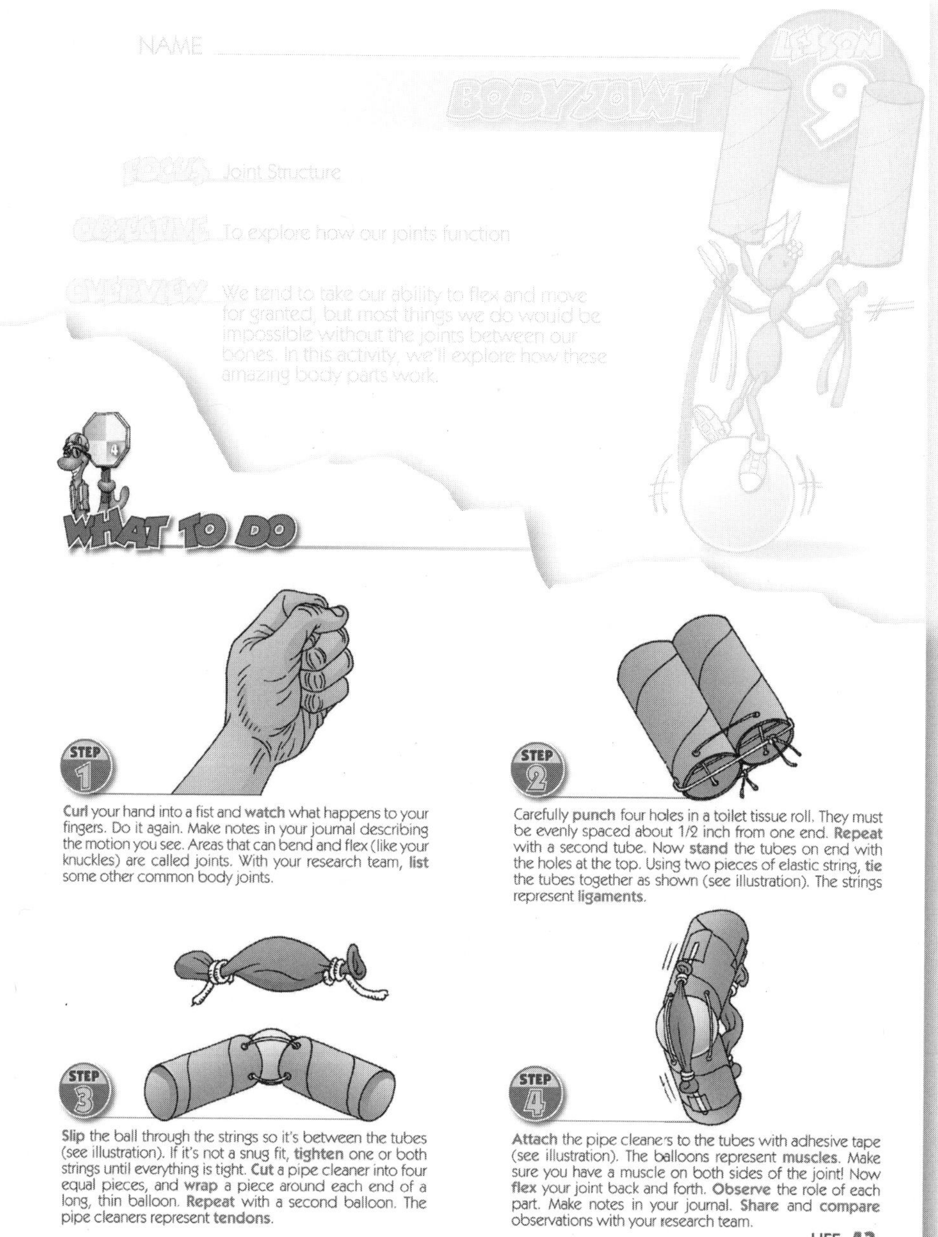

NAME ______________________

LESSON 9

BODY JOINT

FOCUS Joint Structure

OBJECTIVE To explore how our joints function

OVERVIEW We tend to take our ability to flex and move for granted, but most things we do would be impossible without the joints between our bones. In this activity, we'll explore how these amazing body parts work.

WHAT TO DO

STEP 1
Curl your hand into a fist and **watch** what happens to your fingers. Do it again. Make notes in your journal describing the motion you see. Areas that can bend and flex (like your knuckles) are called joints. With your research team, **list** some other common body joints.

STEP 2
Carefully **punch** four holes in a toilet tissue roll. They must be evenly spaced about 1/2 inch from one end. **Repeat** with a second tube. Now **stand** the tubes on end with the holes at the top. Using two pieces of elastic string, **tie** the tubes together as shown (see illustration). The strings represent **ligaments**.

STEP 3
Slip the ball through the strings so it's between the tubes (see illustration). If it's not a snug fit, **tighten** one or both strings until everything is tight. **Cut** a pipe cleaner into four equal pieces, and **wrap** a piece around each end of a long, thin balloon. **Repeat** with a second balloon. The pipe cleaners represent **tendons**.

STEP 4
Attach the pipe cleaners to the tubes with adhesive tape (see illustration). The balloons represent **muscles**. Make sure you have a muscle on both sides of the joint! Now **flex** your joint back and forth. **Observe** the role of each part. Make notes in your journal. **Share** and **compare** observations with your research team.

LIFE **43**

Teacher to Teacher

Joint injuries are very common in sports. These include dislocations, sprains, torn ligaments, and cartilage damage. A dislocation occurs when bones in a joint are separated. A sprain is a minor dislocation. A torn ligament means connecting tissue has been torn, loosening the joint. Cartilage damage involves the cushioning pad between the joints, interfering with normal joint action. In most cases these injuries can be repaired, although in severe cases the joint may never regain full functionality.

WHAT HAPPENED?

A joint is the place where two or more bones come together. Although your skeleton provides you with a strong framework, your joints let this framework flex. This allows you to respond properly when your brain sends a signal through your nervous system saying "Move!"

Muscles provide the force (pull) to make joints flex. Tendons attach the muscles to the bones. Ligaments provide extra support and strength, connecting bones to other bones. As you saw in your model, when movement occurs, all the parts of the joint work together.

WHAT WE LEARNED

1. List at least three common body joints. What is the purpose of each?

   Answers will vary, but common joints include the wrist, elbow, knee, ankle, shoulder, etc.

2. What is the purpose of ligaments in a joint?

   Ligaments connect bones to other bones and provide extra support and strength.

3. What is the purpose of tendons in a joint?

   Tendons attach the muscles to the bones.

4. What is the purpose of the muscles attached to joints?

   Muscles provide the push/pull force to make joints flex and move.

5. Some people have arthritis, a joint inflammation. How might that affect their activities? Be specific.

   Answers will vary, but should include the idea that if a joint is swollen, it can't bend or move easily.

What Happened

Review the section with students. Emphasize bold-face words that identify key concepts and introduce new vocabulary.

*A **joint** is the place where two or more **bones** come together. Although your **skeleton** provides you with a strong **framework**, your joints let this framework **flex**. This allows you to respond properly when your **brain** sends a signal through your **nervous system** saying, "Move!"*

***Muscles** provide the **force** (pull) to make joints flex. **Tendons** attach the muscles to the bones. **Ligaments** provide extra support and strength, connecting bones to other bones. As you saw in your model, when movement occurs, all the parts of the joint work together.*

What We Learned

Answers will vary. Suggested responses are shown at left.

Conclusion

Read this section aloud to the class to summarize the concepts learned in this activity.

Food for Thought

Read the Scripture aloud to the class. Talk about how important it is for church members to work together toward common goals. Discuss ways students can be good parts of "the body."

Journal

If time permits, have a general class discussion about students' journal entries. Share and compare observations. Be sure to emphasize that "trial and error" is a valuable part of scientific inquiry!

CONCLUSION

Joints allow our body's skeleton to flex so that we can move. Muscles provide force to make our joints flex. Tendons attach our muscles to bones. Ligaments hold our bones together at joints.

FOOD FOR THOUGHT

Ephesians 4:16 The parts of joints all work together to make bones move. The ligaments hold the bones together, but they are flexible and strong. The tendons allow the force of the muscles to move the bones and joint around as needed. Without the combined efforts of all the joint parts, the bones would be helpless!

This Scripture tells us that a church is like that, too! All the parts must work together for the good of all. We not only need someone to conduct the services, but also to sweep the floor, mow the grounds, and maintain the buildings. Take time this week to thank all those who make your church run so well!

JOURNAL My Science Notes

46 LIFE

Extended Teaching

1. Have students create a bulletin board showing different body joints and their locations. Use magazine pictures, student drawings, diagrams, and models.

2. Have students research joint replacement surgery (knee, hip, knuckle, etc.). Invite a replacement recipient to visit your class to talk about this procedure. Focus on the benefits of regained mobility.

3. Using the Internet or an encyclopedia, have students research arthritis. Challenge them to find out what's being done to fight arthritis. Have teams present their findings to the class.

4. Start a school campaign for joint injury awareness. Have students create a set of safety posters about helmets, diving safety, and similar topics.

5. If you have an advanced group of students, dissect a whole grocery store chicken. Pay special attention to the joints and how they move. Point out the smooth, shiny, white cartilage which lines the joints.

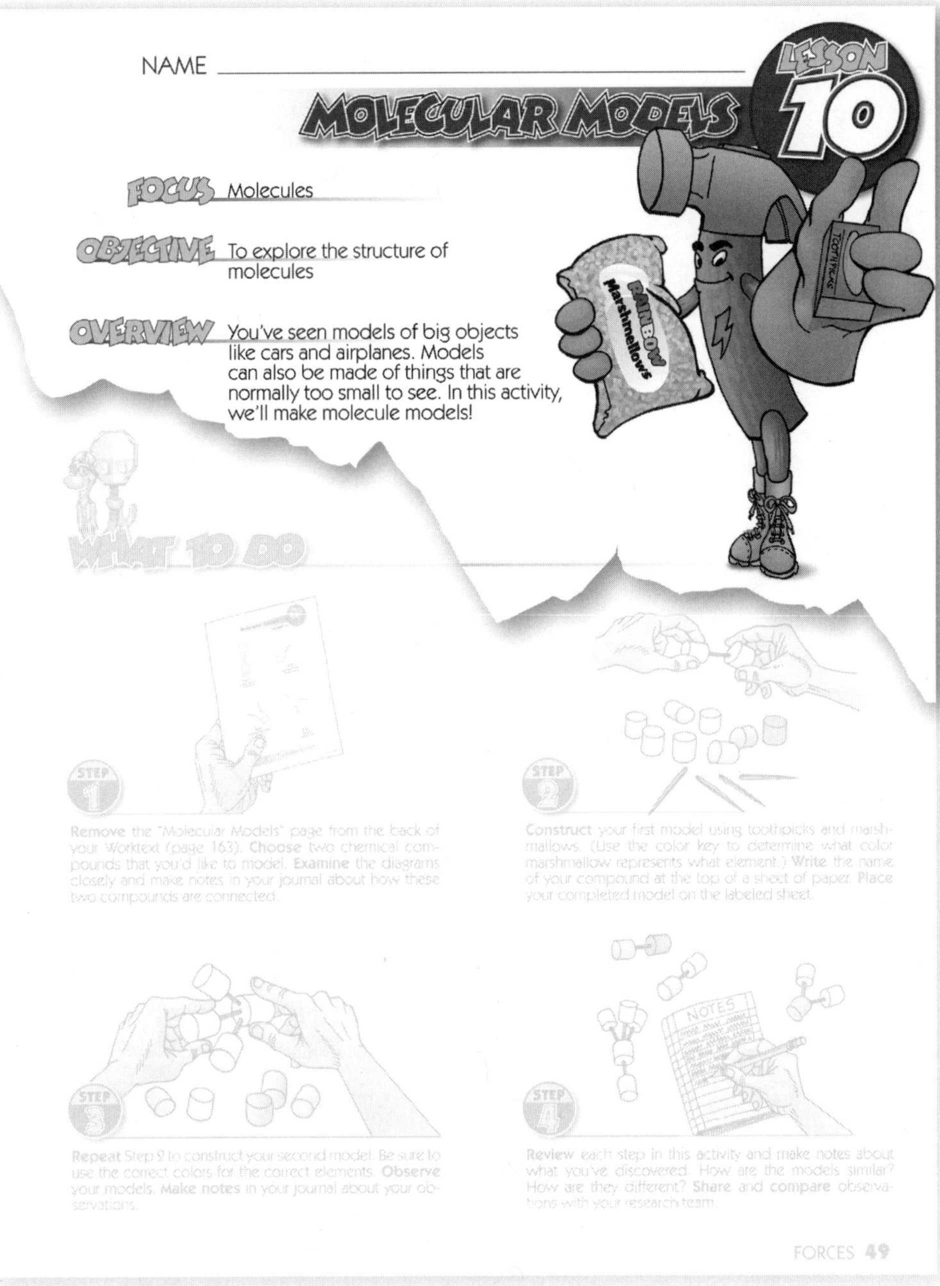

NAME ______________________

MOLECULAR MODELS

LESSON 10

FOCUS Molecules

OBJECTIVE To explore the structure of molecules

OVERVIEW You've seen models of big objects like cars and airplanes. Models can also be made of things that are normally too small to see. In this activity, we'll make molecule models!

WHAT TO DO

STEP 1

Remove the "Molecular Models" page from the back of your Worktext (page 163). **Choose** two chemical compounds that you'd like to model. **Examine** the diagrams closely and make notes in your journal about how these two compounds are connected.

STEP 2

Construct your first model using toothpicks and marshmallows. (Use the color key to detemine what color marshmallow represents what element.) **Write** the name of your compound at the top of a sheet of paper. **Place** your completed model on the labeled sheet.

STEP 3

Repeat Step 2 to construct your second model. Be sure to use the correct colors for the correct elements. **Observe** your models. **Make notes** in your journal about your observations.

STEP 4

Review each step in this activity and make notes about what you've discovered. How are the models similar? How are they different? **Share** and **compare** observations with your research team.

FORCES 49

Category

Physical Science
Forces

Focus

Molecules

Objective

To explore the structure of molecules

National Standards

A1, A2, B1, B2, E1, E2, G1, G2

Materials Needed

Molecular Models worksheet *(student worktext, p. 165)*
toothpicks
colored marshmallows

Safety Concerns

3. Hygiene
Remind students that good scientists don't eat their experiments! No eating marshmallows.

4. Sharp Objects
Remind students to exercise caution when using toothpicks.

Additional Comments

You may wish to sort and bag marshmallows for each team in advance. Caution students to push toothpicks into marshmallows gently. Remind students that even though this activity uses color-coding for better understanding, elements (like oxygen and hydrogen) are colorless.

Overview

Read the overview aloud to the students. Your goal is to create an atmosphere of curiosity and inquiry.

WHAT TO DO

Monitor student research teams as they complete each step.

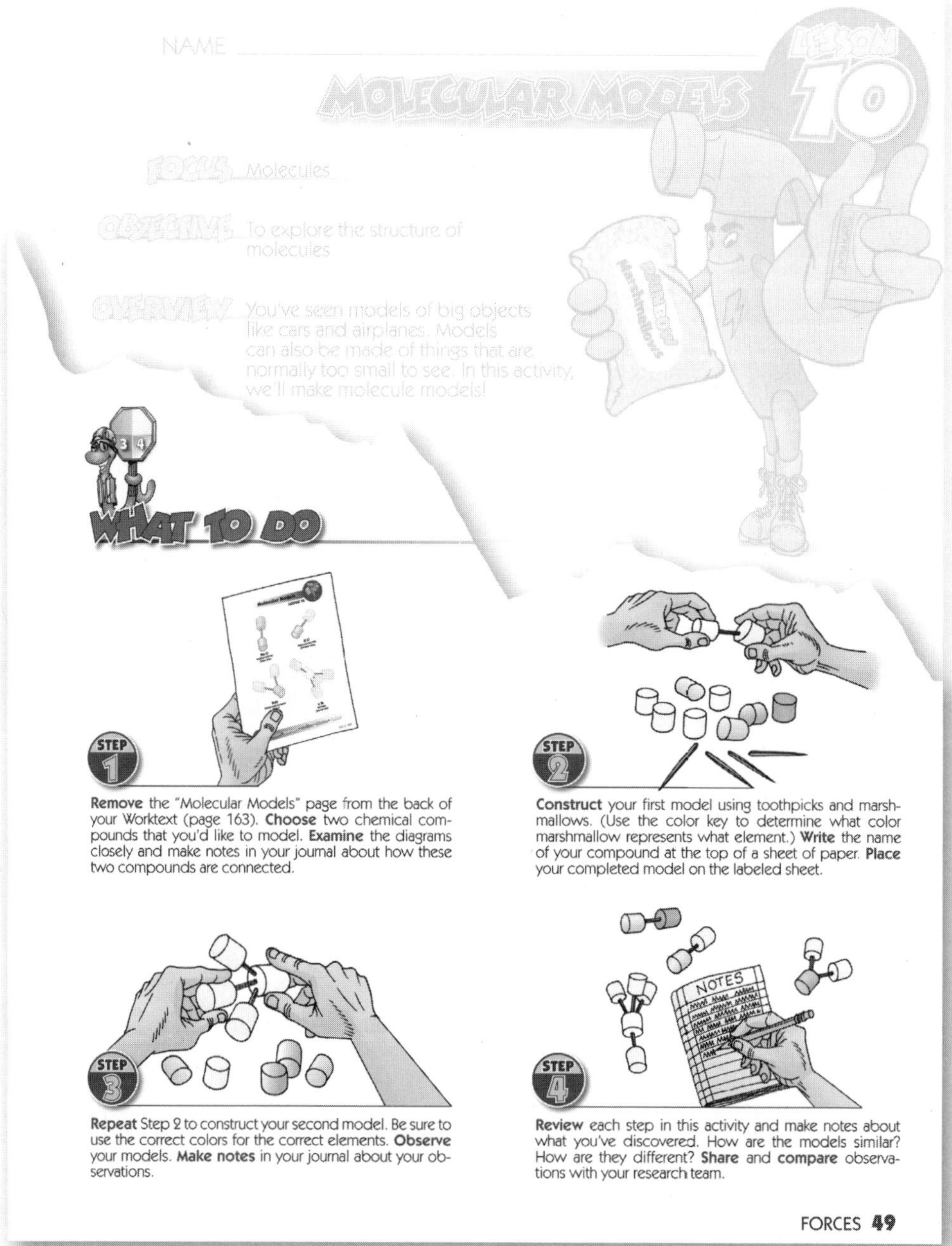

Teacher to Teacher

Here's an analogy to help you understand molecular relationships: Imagine a page printed by an old "dot matrix" printer. Individual "dots" (atoms) combine to make a single alphabet letter (element). The various letters (elements) combine to make words (molecules), and the words (molecules) combine to make sentences (compounds).

What Happened?

You've seen how **magnets** attract each other and stick together. The tiny bits and pieces of our world do something similar. Scientists call the process **bonding**.

Here's how it works: An **atom** is the smallest part of an **element**. Atoms of elements bond together to create **molecules**. A molecule is the smallest part of a **compound**.

Chemical compounds only bond in one way. One sodium atom bonded to one cloride atom always gives you table salt (sodium chloride) and nothing else.

Understanding atoms, elements, molecules, and compounds helps scientists invent new processes and products.

What We Learned

1. **What were the two molecules you chose in Step 1? How were they similar? How were they different?**

   Answers will vary.

2. **What did the marshmallows represent in Step 2? What process did the toothpicks represent?**

   a) atoms

   b) bonding

3. **Describe the difference between an atom, a molecule, and a compound.**

   An atom is the smallest part of an element.

   A molecule is the smallest part of a compound.

4. **Describe one molecule you modeled in Step 2 or 3. What were the elements? How did they fit together?**

   Answers will vary.

5. **Based on what you've learned, what would you need to make a model of a complex compound?**

   A good "map" to follow, plus many more marshmallows and toothpicks.

What Happened

Review the section with students. Emphasize bold-face words that identify key concepts and introduce new vocabulary.

*You've seen how **magnets** attract each other and stick together. The tiny bits and pieces of our world do something similar. Scientists call the process **bonding**.*

*Here's how it works: An **atom** is the smallest part of an **element**. Atoms of elements bond together to create **molecules**. A molecule is the smallest part of a **compound**.*

Chemical compounds only bond in one way. One sodium atom bonded to one chloride atom always gives you table salt (sodium chloride) and nothing else.

Understanding atoms, elements, molecules, and compounds helps scientists invent new processes and products.

What We Learned

Answers will vary. Suggested responses are shown at left.

Conclusion

Read this section aloud to the class to summarize the concepts learned in this activity.

Food for Thought

Read the Scripture aloud to the class. Talk about ways we can "bond together" as followers of Christ. Discuss how a helpful attitude (as opposed to a critical spirit) contributes to this process.

Journal

If time permits, have a general class discussion about notes and drawings various students added to their journal pages. Discuss correct and incorrect predictions, and remind students that this "trial and error" process is part of the scientific process.

CONCLUSION

An atom is the smallest part of an element (like hydrogen or oxygen). The atoms of elements bond together to create molecules (like water). A molecule is the smallest part of a compound.

FOOD FOR THOUGHT

John 13:34-35 It is truly miraculous the way elements hook together to form molecules! Every rock, every plant, every animal (even the air we breathe) is made up of these tiny particles, all working together.

Scripture reminds us that as Jesus' followers we are to bond together, constantly supporting each other. Although we're each unique and we all have different characteristics (like the different elements), when we work together, we can accomplish amazing things. Instead of being critical, learn to look for the good in others, and always strive to be supportive.

JOURNAL **My Science Notes**

52 FORCES

Extended Teaching

1. Invite a chemistry teacher to visit your classroom. Ask him/her to demonstrate one or two interesting chemical reactions. Discuss how an understanding of chemical combinations can lead to new, useful products.

2. Using the Internet, have students research careers that require chemistry. Challenge each team to make a poster depicting one of these professions.

3. Take a field trip to a farming operation. Find out how chemicals are used, and what precautions workers must take when applying them. Have students write a paragraph about one thing they learn.

4. Invite a chemist to visit your classroom. Ask him/her to bring models of complex compounds. Discuss how models help scientists better understand how things work.

5. Using chemistry books or the Internet, have teams find other simple compounds. Challenge them to create a display (including a model) naming this compound and describing its uses.

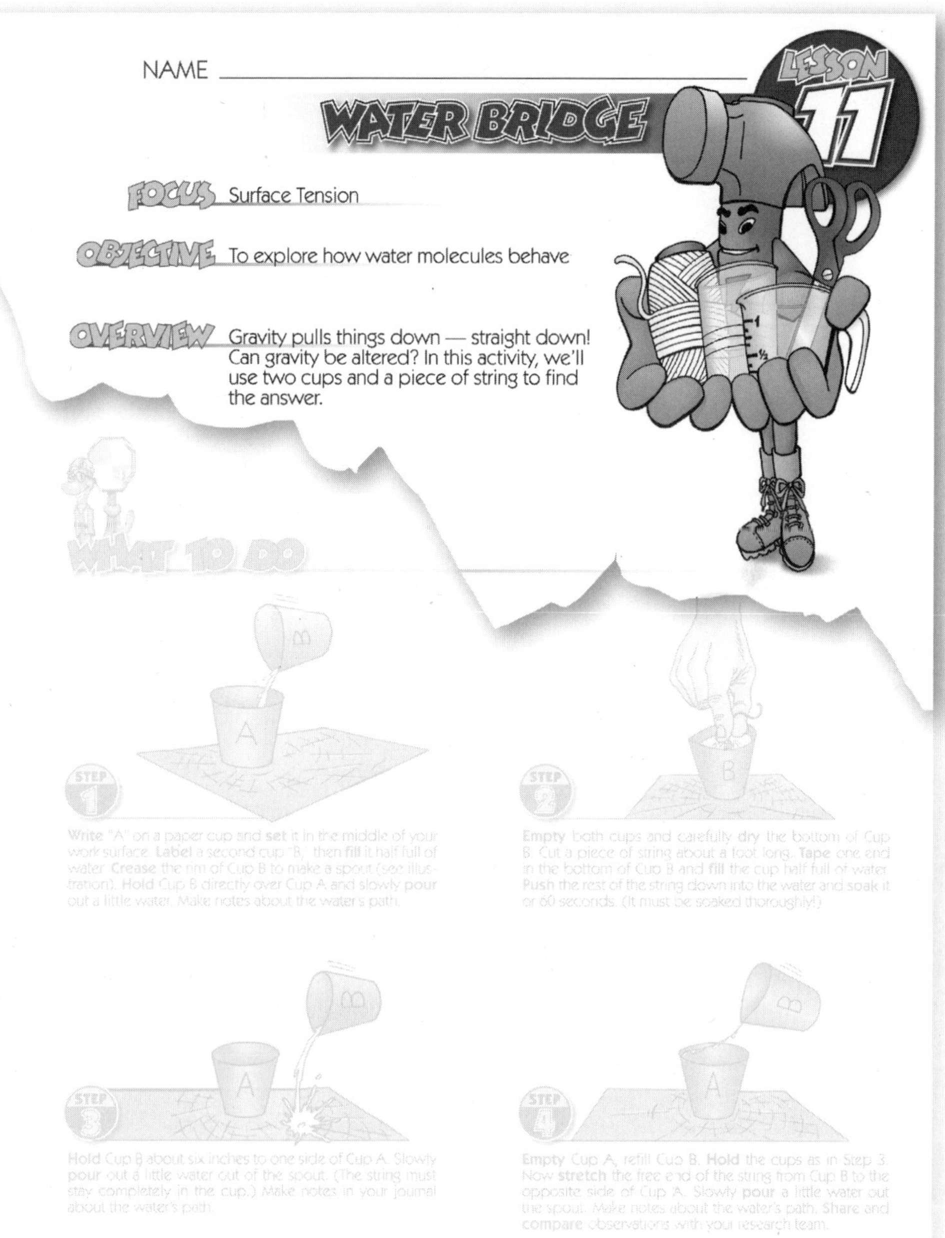

NAME ______________________________

LESSON 11

WATER BRIDGE

FOCUS Surface Tension

OBJECTIVE To explore how water molecules behave

OVERVIEW Gravity pulls things down — straight down! Can gravity be altered? In this activity, we'll use two cups and a piece of string to find the answer.

WHAT TO DO

STEP 1
Write "A" on a paper cup and **set** it in the middle of your work surface. **Label** a second cup "B," then **fill** it half full of water. **Crease** the rim of Cup B to make a spout (see illustration). **Hold** Cup B directly over Cup A and slowly **pour** out a little water. Make notes about the water's path.

STEP 2
Empty both cups and carefully **dry** the bottom of Cup B. Cut a piece of string about a foot long. **Tape** one end in the bottom of Cup B and **fill** the cup half full of water. **Push** the rest of the string down into the water and soak it or 60 seconds. (It must be soaked thoroughly!)

STEP 3
Hold Cup B about six inches to one side of Cup A. Slowly **pour** out a little water out of the spout. (The string must stay completely in the cup.) Make notes in your journal about the water's path.

STEP 4
Empty Cup A, refill Cup B. **Hold** the cups as in Step 3. Now **stretch** the free end of the string from Cup B to the opposite side of Cup A. Slowly **pour** a little water out the spout. Make notes about the water's path. Share and **compare** observations with your research team.

FORCES 53

Category

Physical Science
Forces

Focus

Surface Tension

Objective

To explore how water molecules behave

National Standards

A1, A2, B1, B2, B3, E1, E2, G1, G2

Materials Needed

paper cups - 2
string
water
tape
scissors
paper towels

Safety Concerns

4. Sharp Objects
Remind students to exercise caution when using scissors.

Additional Comments

To minimize clean up, have students place Cup A on a layer of paper towels before beginning Step 3. If you wish, this activity can be done as a teacher demonstration instead. Build curiosity at the start by claiming you can pour water "sideways" from a cup! Be sure to keep extra paper towels handy for clean up.

Overview

Read the overview aloud to your students. The goal is to create an atmosphere of curiosity and inquiry.

WHAT TO DO

Monitor student research teams as they complete each step.

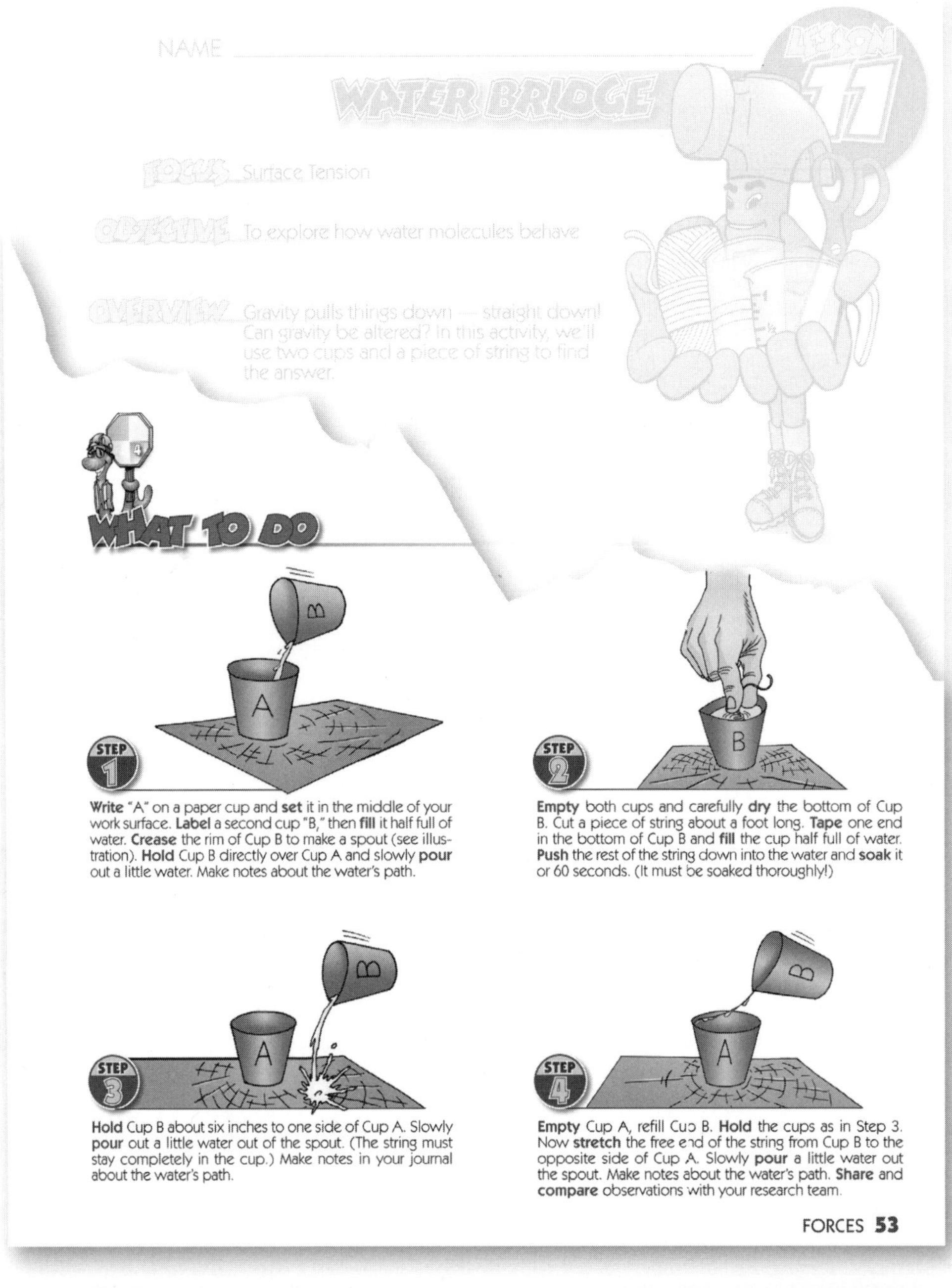

NAME

WATER BRIDGE

LESSON 11

FOCUS Surface Tension

OBJECTIVE To explore how water molecules behave

OVERVIEW Gravity pulls things down — straight down! Can gravity be altered? In this activity, we'll use two cups and a piece of string to find the answer.

WHAT TO DO

STEP 1

Write "A" on a paper cup and **set** it in the middle of your work surface. **Label** a second cup "B," then **fill** it half full of water. **Crease** the rim of Cup B to make a spout (see illustration). **Hold** Cup B directly over Cup A and slowly **pour** out a little water. Make notes about the water's path.

STEP 2

Empty both cups and carefully **dry** the bottom of Cup B. Cut a piece of string about a foot long. **Tape** one end in the bottom of Cup B and **fill** the cup half full of water. **Push** the rest of the string down into the water and **soak** it or 60 seconds. (It must be soaked thoroughly!)

STEP 3

Hold Cup B about six inches to one side of Cup A. Slowly **pour** out a little water out of the spout. (The string must stay completely in the cup.) Make notes in your journal about the water's path.

STEP 4

Empty Cup A, refill Cup B. **Hold** the cups as in Step 3. Now **stretch** the free end of the string from Cup B to the opposite side of Cup A. Slowly **pour** a little water out the spout. Make notes about the water's path. **Share** and **compare** observations with your research team.

FORCES 53

Teacher to Teacher

When hydrogen is bonded to oxygen (also nitrogen or fluorine), it can create what scientists call a "hydrogen bond." Even though there's no place for additional hydrogen to attach to the original atom, the compound still exerts a strong pull on hydrogen in other molecules. This strong pull is what creates the phenomenon of surface tension.

WHAT HAPPENED?

Yes, the drops of water seemed to break the **law of gravity!** Instead of falling straight down to the work surface, they moved sideways and into the other cup. Why did this happen?

Water **molecules** have a characteristic called **surface tension**. This causes them to stick to things (including each other). In this activity, the water molecules formed a path from one cup to the other along the string. As you tipped the top cup and the water ran out, each molecule followed the others along this path.

Although the drops appeared to be breaking the law of gravity, they still went "down" from one cup to the other. The law wasn't broken at all. We just took advantage of a characteristic of surface tension to modify the way the drops fell.

WHAT WE LEARNED

1. **Describe how the water poured out of the cup in Step 1. What path did it take as it fell?**

   It poured smoothly and fell almost straight down.

2. **Why do you think it was important to soak the string in Step 2?**

   So water would already be on the string, otherwise the first drops might just fall off.

3. **Describe Step 3. What path did the water take as it fell?**

   Same as in Step 1, only the cup wasn't underneath the flow of water.

4. **Describe Step 4. How was this step different from previous steps? How was it the same?**

   a) water followed string

   b) different: string from cup to cup

   c) same: same cups, same pouring motion

5. **What characteristic affected the water's behavior in Step 4? Describe how surface tension works.**

   a) surface tension

   b) water molecules "hold hands" and stick together

What Happened

Review the section with students. Emphasize bold-face words that identify key concepts and introduce new vocabulary.

*Yes, the drops of water seemed to break the **law of gravity!** Instead of falling straight down to the work surface, they moved sideways and into the other cup. Why did this happen?*

*Water **molecules** have a characteristic called **surface tension.** This causes them to stick to things (including each other). In this activity, the water molecules formed a path from one cup to the other along the string. As you tipped the top cup and the water ran out, each molecule followed the others along this path.*

Although the drops appeared to be breaking the law of gravity, they still went "down" from one cup to the other. The law wasn't broken at all. We just took advantage of a characteristic of surface tension to modify the way the drops fell.

What We Learned

Answers will vary. Suggested responses are shown at left.

Conclusion

Read this section aloud to the class to summarize the concepts learned in this activity.

Food for Thought

Read the Scripture aloud to the class. Talk about the importance of rules and responsibility. Discuss ways we can learn to follow "the path of righteousness."

Journal

If time permits, have a general class discussion about notes and drawings various students added to their journal pages. Discuss correct and incorrect predictions, and remind students that this "trial and error" process is part of the scientific process.

Water molecules have a characteristic called surface tension that helps bind them together. Gravity is a constant force. While gravity itself can't be changed, sometimes its effects can be modified.

Proverbs 22:6 With a little effort, you were able to train those little water drops to follow the right path. Gravity, the string, and surface tension were your partners in the training process.

From time to time, it may seem like the adults in your life are being a little hard on you. It's their job to teach you to follow the right path! And don't forget, they have rules and responsibilities that they need to follow, too. As followers of Jesus, we all must "stick together" and support each other on the path of righteousness.

JOURNAL **My Science Notes**

56 FORCES

Extended Teaching

1. Repeat this activity using waxed string, dental floss, and a thin rubber band. Have students compare the results created by each material with the original activity.

2. Repeat this activity, but first add a drop of liquid soap to the water in the cup. Have students compare the results with the original activity.

3. Show a video clip of astronauts playing with liquids in a weightless environment. (NASA quest is a great starting point for space videos.) Discuss similarities and differences to water's behavior on Earth.

4. Have students research creatures which use surface tension to "walk on water." Challenge each team to create a poster depicting one of these creatures.

5. Take a field trip to a municipal water treatment plant. Tour the facility and find out how it works. Have students write a paragraph about one thing they learn.

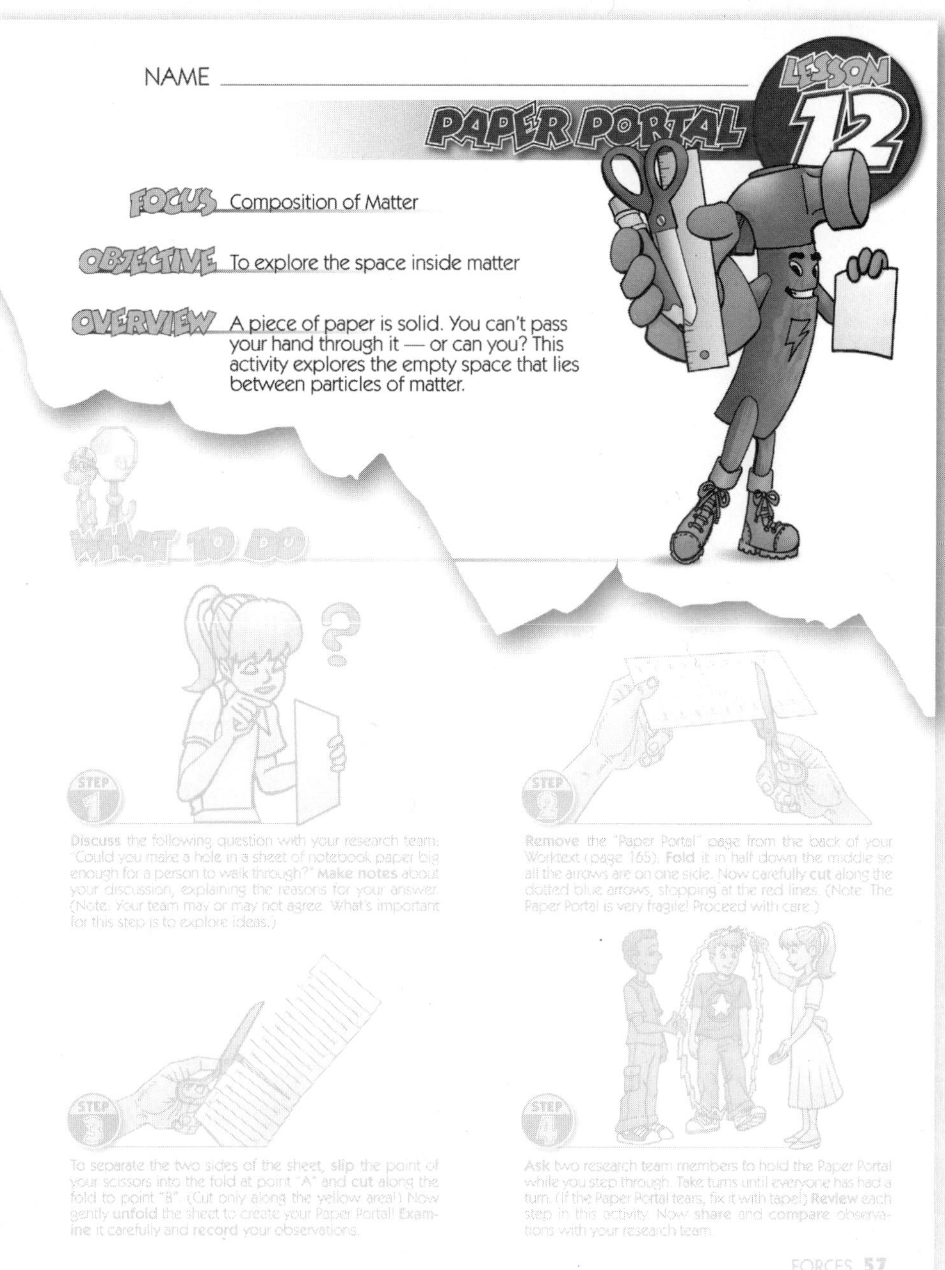

NAME ______________________

LESSON 12

PAPER PORTAL

FOCUS Composition of Matter

OBJECTIVE To explore the space inside matter

OVERVIEW A piece of paper is solid. You can't pass your hand through it — or can you? This activity explores the empty space that lies between particles of matter.

WHAT TO DO

STEP 1 **Discuss** the following question with your research team: "Could you make a hole in a sheet of notebook paper big enough for a person to walk through?" **Make notes** about your discussion, explaining the reasons for your answer. (Note: Your team may or may not agree. What's important for this step is to explore ideas.)

STEP 2 **Remove** the "Paper Portal" page from the back of your Worktext (page 165). **Fold** it in half down the middle so all the arrows are on one side. Now carefully **cut** along the dotted blue arrows, stopping at the red lines. (Note: The Paper Portal is very fragile! Proceed with care.)

STEP 3 To separate the two sides of the sheet, **slip** the point of your scissors into the fold at point "A" and **cut** along the fold to point "B". (Cut only along the yellow area!) Now gently **unfold** the sheet to create your Paper Portal! **Examine** it carefully and **record** your observations.

STEP 4 **Ask** two research team members to hold the Paper Portal while you step through. Take turns until everyone has had a turn. (If the Paper Portal tears, fix it with tape!) **Review** each step in this activity. Now **share** and **compare** observations with your research team.

FORCES 57

Category

Physical Science
Forces

Focus

Composition of Matter

Objective

To explore the space inside matter

National Standards

A1, A2, B1, E1, E2, G1, G2

Materials Needed

Paper Portal worksheet *(student worktext, p. 167)*
scissors

Safety Concerns

4. Sharp Objects
Remind students to exercise caution when using scissors.

Additional Comments

A great option is to have a class discussion following team discussions in Step 1. Focus on student's reasons for their viewpoints. (Don't try to come to a consensus.) Then follow Step 4 with a similar discussion. Focus on how viewpoints have changed with additional information. If a Paper Portal tears beyond repair, simply use one from another student's worktext.

Overview

Read the overview aloud to your students. The goal is to create an atmosphere of curiosity and inquiry.

WHAT TO DO

Monitor student research teams as they complete each step.

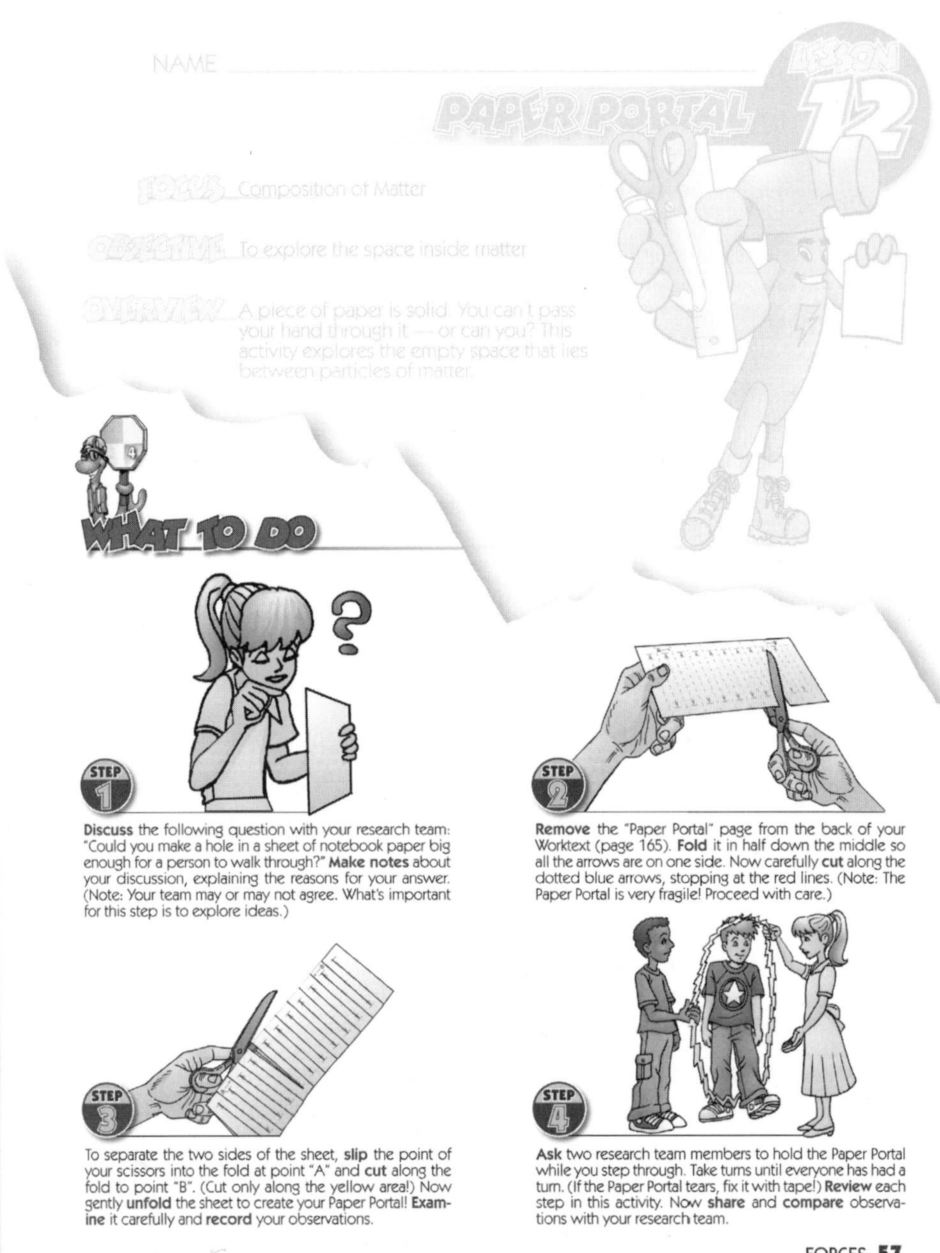

NAME

PAPER PORTAL

LESSON 12

FOCUS Composition of Matter

OBJECTIVE To explore the space inside matter

OVERVIEW A piece of paper is solid. You can't pass your hand through it — or can you? This activity explores the empty space that lies between particles of matter.

WHAT TO DO

STEP 1

Discuss the following question with your research team: "Could you make a hole in a sheet of notebook paper big enough for a person to walk through?" **Make notes** about your discussion, explaining the reasons for your answer. (Note: Your team may or may not agree. What's important for this step is to explore ideas.)

STEP 2

Remove the "Paper Portal" page from the back of your Worktext (page 165). **Fold** it in half down the middle so all the arrows are on one side. Now carefully **cut** along the dotted blue arrows, stopping at the red lines. (Note: The Paper Portal is very fragile! Proceed with care.)

STEP 3

To separate the two sides of the sheet, **slip** the point of your scissors into the fold at point "A" and **cut** along the fold to point "B". (Cut only along the yellow area!) Now gently **unfold** the sheet to create your Paper Portal! **Examine** it carefully and **record** your observations.

STEP 4

Ask two research team members to hold the Paper Portal while you step through. Take turns until everyone has had a turn. (If the Paper Portal tears, fix it with tape!) **Review** each step in this activity. Now **share** and **compare** observations with your research team.

FORCES **57**

Teacher to Teacher

Atoms are incredibly tiny, yet still filled with unimaginable space! If the proton of an atom were the size of a ping-pong ball, the electron of the same atom would be about the size of a tennis ball — but be located over a mile away! The only reason objects seem solid is there are billions and billions of atoms in every square inch.

What Happened?

As we learned in Lesson 2, **matter** (everything around you) is made of tiny bits and pieces (like **atoms**). But the major ingredient in matter is **space** — lots of space! In a way, objects are only solid in relationship to your body. In other words, if the **density** (how tight the atoms are packed) of an object is equal to or greater than the density of your body, then the object seems solid. But if an object is less dense than your body, then it's not very solid. That's why we can walk through fog (little density), but not through a brick wall (very dense)!

However, the Paper Portal you made shows that even so-called solid objects are mostly empty space. In fact, if you could cut the slices thin enough (maybe down to the **molecular** level), you might be able to fit your entire school inside the loop of a single sheet of notebook paper! Amazing, isn't it?

What We Learned

1 **What did your team predict in Step 1? How does this reflect what happened in Step 4?**

Answers will vary.

2 **When you began to cut the paper in Step 2, what were you doing to the molecules?**

Cutting the paper separated the molecules.

3 **How large was the hole you created in Step 3? How could you have made it bigger?**

a) big enough to walk through

b) cut more slices, making them even thinner

4 **Compare the paper after Step 4 with the paper in Step 1. How were they similar? How were they different?**

a) same paper

b) paper opened up a lot in Step 4

5 **What does density mean? List three very dense objects and three objects that are not very dense.**

a) how tightly something is packed together

b) dense: bricks, books, humans, etc.
less dense: fog, smoke, tissue paper, etc.

What Happened

Review the section with students. Emphasize bold-face words that identify key concepts and introduce new vocabulary.

*As we learned in Lesson 10, **matter** (everything around you) is made of tiny bits and pieces (like **atoms**). But the major ingredient in matter is **space** — lots of space! In a way, objects are only solid in relationship to your body. In other words, if the **density** (how tight the atoms are packed) of an object is equal to or greater than the density of your body, then the object seems solid. But if an object is less dense than your body, then it's not very solid. That's why we can walk through fog (little density), but not through a brick wall (very dense)!*

*However, the Paper Portal you made shows that even so-called solid objects are mostly empty space. In fact, if you could cut the slices thin enough (maybe down to the **molecular** level), you might be able to fit your entire school inside the loop of a single sheet of notebook paper! Amazing, isn't it?*

What We Learned

Answers will vary. Suggested responses are shown at left.

Conclusion

Read this section aloud to the class to summarize the concepts learned in this activity.

Food for Thought

Read the Scripture aloud to the class. Talk about "baggage" that could interfere with our relationship with God. Discuss how staying close to God helps "equip" us for life's journey.

Journal

If time permits, have a general class discussion about notes and drawings various students added to their journal pages. Discuss correct and incorrect predictions, and remind students that this "trial and error" process is part of the scientific process.

Although all matter is composed of atoms and molecules, the primary component of matter is empty space.

FOOD FOR THOUGHT

Matthew 19:24 Getting through a hole in a piece of paper wasn't easy! Scripture talks about another difficult passage. It was a door in Jerusalem's wall called the "eye of the needle." It was barely big enough to lead an unloaded camel through. A rich traveler with a huge load just wouldn't fit! The only way they could get through was to completely unload the camel first.

Jesus told this story to remind us not to burden ourselves with the baggage of this world. The things we need for God's Kingdom can't be loaded on a camel! But if you trust God, he'll equip you with just what you need for the journey!

JOURNAL My Science Notes

60 FORCES

Extended Teaching

1. Repeat this activity with a 3" by 5" index card. Follow the same basic pattern as the worksheet, only use 1/4" between the lines and edges instead of 1/2". Have students compare the results with the original activity.

2. Have teams compute the approximate area of a worksheet in square inches (8" x 11" = 88 sq. in.). Now have them lay the paper portal on the floor and compute its approximate area. Compare the results.

3. Discuss surface area. Remind students that grinding, chopping, and similar actions all increase an object's surface area. Challenge teams to make a poster that illustrates "before and after" examples.

4. Discuss why increased surface area can be helpful (splitting firewood to make it burn easier, spreading paint thin to let it dry, etc.). Have teams make posters illustrating one aspect of this.

5. A scientist named Rutherford did a famous experiment with the atoms in gold. Research this experiment as a class, then discuss your findings. Have students write a paragraph about one thing they learn.

NAME

SPINNING STEEL

LESSON 13

FOCUS Velocity

OBJECTIVE To explore how gravity can be defeated

OVERVIEW Gravity is constantly pulling everything down. In Lesson 2, we discovered its effects can sometimes be modified. This activity explores that concept again using a different force.

WHAT TO DO

STEP 1

First, **check** to make sure gravity is still working! **Hold** the metal ball in one hand. Put your other hand underneath it. **Drop** the ball. **Record** the results in your journal.

STEP 2

Hold a clear plastic cup in one hand. Gently **drop** the ball into the cup. Now slowly **swirl** the cup around in a circular motion. **Record** what happens to the ball.

STEP 3

Leave the ball in the cup. **Place** another cup upside down on the first cup. **Line up** the rims and **tape** the cups together securely. Slowly **swirl** the cups, then gradually increase speed until you're swirling them rapidly. **Record** what happens to the ball.

STEP 4

Review your notes for each step in this activity. What conclusions can you draw? **Share** and **compare** your observations with your research team.

FORCES 61

Category

Physical Science
Forces

Focus

Velocity

Objective

To explore how gravity can be defeated

National Standards

A1, A2, B2, B3, E1, E2, F5, G1, G2

Materials Needed

metal ball
clear plastic cups - 2
tape

Safety Concerns

1. Goggles
Students should wear goggles in Step 3 in case the cups come apart.

Additional Comments

It takes a degree of coordination to control the ball's velocity so that it climbs up the cup. You may wish to practice this in advance so you can demonstrate for any team that is having difficulty. Make sure all team members get a turn. Cups must be taped securely in Step 3, or the ball will fly out!

Overview

Read the overview aloud to your students. The goal is to create an atmosphere of curiosity and inquiry.

WHAT TO DO

Monitor student research teams as they complete each step.

NAME ____________________

LESSON 13

SPINNING STEEL

FOCUS Velocity

OBJECTIVE To explore how gravity can be defeated

OVERVIEW Gravity is constantly pulling everything down. In Lesson 2, we discovered its effects can sometimes be modified. This activity explores that concept again using a different force.

WHAT TO DO

STEP 1

First, **check** to make sure gravity is still working! **Hold** the metal ball in one hand. Put your other hand underneath it. **Drop** the ball. **Record** the results in your journal.

STEP 2

Hold a clear plastic cup in one hand. Gently **drop** the ball into the cup. Now slowly **swirl** the cup around in a circular motion. **Record** what happens to the ball.

STEP 3

Leave the ball in the cup. **Place** another cup upside down on the first cup. **Line up** the rims and **tape** the cups together securely. Slowly **swirl** the cups, then gradually increase speed until you're swirling them rapidly. **Record** what happens to the ball.

STEP 4

Review your notes for each step in this activity. What conclusions can you draw? **Share** and **compare** your observations with your research team.

FORCES **61**

Teacher to Teacher

Scientists call the timed addition of energy "resonance." Such inputs can greatly increase an object's velocity. Pumping a playground swing is a good example. An "atom smasher" (synchrotron) uses this type of resonance to accelerate tiny particles to enormous speeds, causing atoms to break up — in some cases, even forming new elements!

WHAT HAPPENED?

Each time you flicked your wrist, you gave the ball some **energy**. If you timed it right, the increased energy made the ball go even faster. (Adding energy at just the right time is called **resonance**.) As the ball went faster and faster, it gained **velocity** (speed).

A bullet fired from a gun has **linear velocity** — it speeds away in a straight path. Since your ball was confined by the sloping sides of the cup, the increased energy gave it **angular velocity** — it sped along in a curved path. In this case, the angular velocity was enough to overcome **gravity** and move the ball up the wall of the cups. Of course, as soon as you quit providing energy, gravity took over again and the ball fell back to the bottom of the cup.

WHAT WE LEARNED

1. **What did you do to test gravity in Step 1? What was the result?**

a) dropped the metal ball

b) it fell straight down

2. **What did the ball do in Step 2? How was this different from its movement in Step 1? Why?**

a) went round and round

b) answers should describe linear vs. angular velocity

c) the cup confined the ball

3. **Why was the top cup important in Step 3? What might have happened without it when you added force?**

a) to keep the ball in the cup

b) the ball would have flown out

4. **Was gravity still present in Step 3? Why did the ball go up, not down?**

a) yes

b) angular velocity was strong enough to overcome gravity

5. **Think about riding a bike. Compare the type of velocity shown by your body with the type of velocity shown by the wheels.**

Your body has linear velocity (straight line); the wheels have angular velocity (round and round).

What Happened

Review the section with students. Emphasize bold-face words that identify key concepts and introduce new vocabulary.

Each time you flicked your wrist, you gave the ball some ***energy.*** *If you timed it right, the increased energy made the ball go even faster. (Adding energy at just the right time is called* ***resonance.****) As the ball went faster and faster, it gained* ***velocity*** *(speed).*

A bullet fired from a gun has ***linear velocity*** *— it speeds away in a straight path. Since your ball was confined by the sloping sides of the cup, the increased energy gave it* ***angular velocity*** *— it sped along in a curved path. In this case, the angular velocity was enough to overcome* ***gravity*** *and move the ball up the wall of the cups. Of course, as soon as you quit providing energy, gravity took over again and the ball fell back to the bottom of the cup.*

What We Learned

Answers will vary. Suggested responses are shown at left.

Conclusion

Read this section aloud to the class to summarize the concepts learned in this activity.

Food for Thought

Read the Scripture aloud to the class. Talk about the amazing power of God and the importance of letting God into our hearts.

Journal

If time permits, have a general class discussion about notes and drawings various students added to their journal pages. Discuss correct and incorrect predictions, and remind students that this "trial and error" process is part of the scientific process.

Conclusion

Gravity is a constant force. While it can't be changed, sometimes its effects can be modified. To overcome gravity, there must be a stronger force present. If you achieve enough velocity, you can temporarily defeat gravity.

Food for Thought

John 5:28-29 In this activity, you supplied enough force to make the ball climb up the walls of the cup — even against the powerful force of gravity! For this to happen, there had to be a greater force than the one opposing it.

Death is a powerful force, yet this Scripture talks about people rising from their graves! Obviously, there has to be a more powerful force at work here — and that force is the power of God. Never forget that no matter how things appear (and sometimes they can appear pretty hopeless), God is the most powerful force in the universe. After all, he's the one who created it in the first place!

Journal **My Science Notes**

64 FORCES

Extended Teaching

1. Repeat this activity using one or two BBs. Have students compare the results to the original activity. How were they similar? How were they different?

2. Have teams list common objects that demonstrate angular velocity (a top, a wheel, a pulley, etc.). Challenge each team to create a poster depicting at least three such items. Label posters "Angular Velocity."

3. Have teams list common objects that demonstrate linear velocity (a moving car, a thrown ball, a javelin, etc.). Challenge each team to create a poster depicting at least three such items. They should label posters "Linear Velocity."

4. Increasing velocity at the sub-atomic level can release enormous power. Have teams research the "Manhattan Project." Ask students to write a short paper about what they learn.

5. If there is one near your area, take a field trip to a nuclear power plant. Find out how these massive facilities operate. Discuss safety concerns and environmental issues. Have students write a paragraph about one thing they learn.

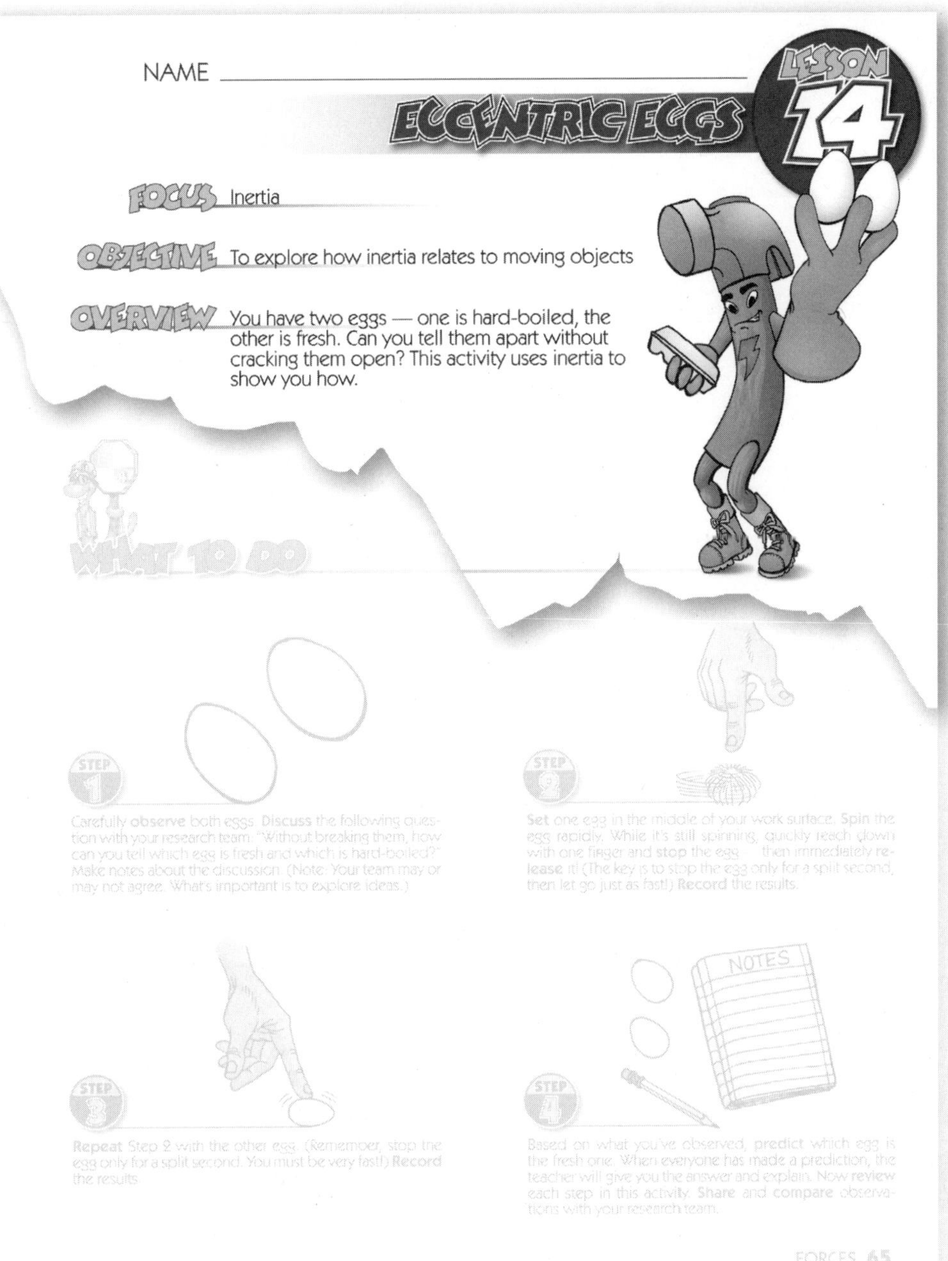

NAME ____________________

LESSON 14

ECCENTRIC EGGS

FOCUS Inertia

OBJECTIVE To explore how inertia relates to moving objects

OVERVIEW You have two eggs — one is hard-boiled, the other is fresh. Can you tell them apart without cracking them open? This activity uses inertia to show you how.

WHAT TO DO

STEP 1

Carefully **observe** both eggs. **Discuss** the following question with your research team: "Without breaking them, how can you tell which egg is fresh and which is hard-boiled?" Make notes about the discussion. (Note: Your team may or may not agree. What's important is to explore ideas.)

STEP 2

Set one egg in the middle of your work surface. **Spin** the egg rapidly. While it's still spinning, quickly reach down with one finger and **stop** the egg — then immediately **release** it! (The key is to stop the egg only for a split second, then let go just as fast!) **Record** the results.

STEP 3

Repeat Step 2 with the other egg. (Remember, stop the egg only for a split second. You must be very fast!) **Record** the results.

STEP 4

Based on what you've observed, **predict** which egg is the fresh one. When everyone has made a prediction, the teacher will give you the answer and explain. Now **review** each step in this activity. **Share** and **compare** observations with your research team.

FORCES 65

Category

Physical Science
Forces

Focus

Inertia

Objective

To explore how inertia relates to moving objects

National Standards

A1, A2, B2, B3, E1, E2, F5, G1, G2

Materials Needed

fresh egg
hard-boiled egg

Safety Concerns

4.Breakage/Slipping
Raw eggs have the potential to break and create slippery surfaces.

Additional Comments

Most people define inertia this way: "When something is not moving, it stays at rest until a force acts upon it." That's true, but there's a second part to Newton's first law: "When something is moving, it *keeps* moving until a force acts on it." This second part of the Law of Inertia is demonstrated in this activity.

Overview

Read the overview aloud to your students. The goal is to create an atmosphere of curiosity and inquiry.

WHAT TO DO

Monitor student research teams as they complete each step.

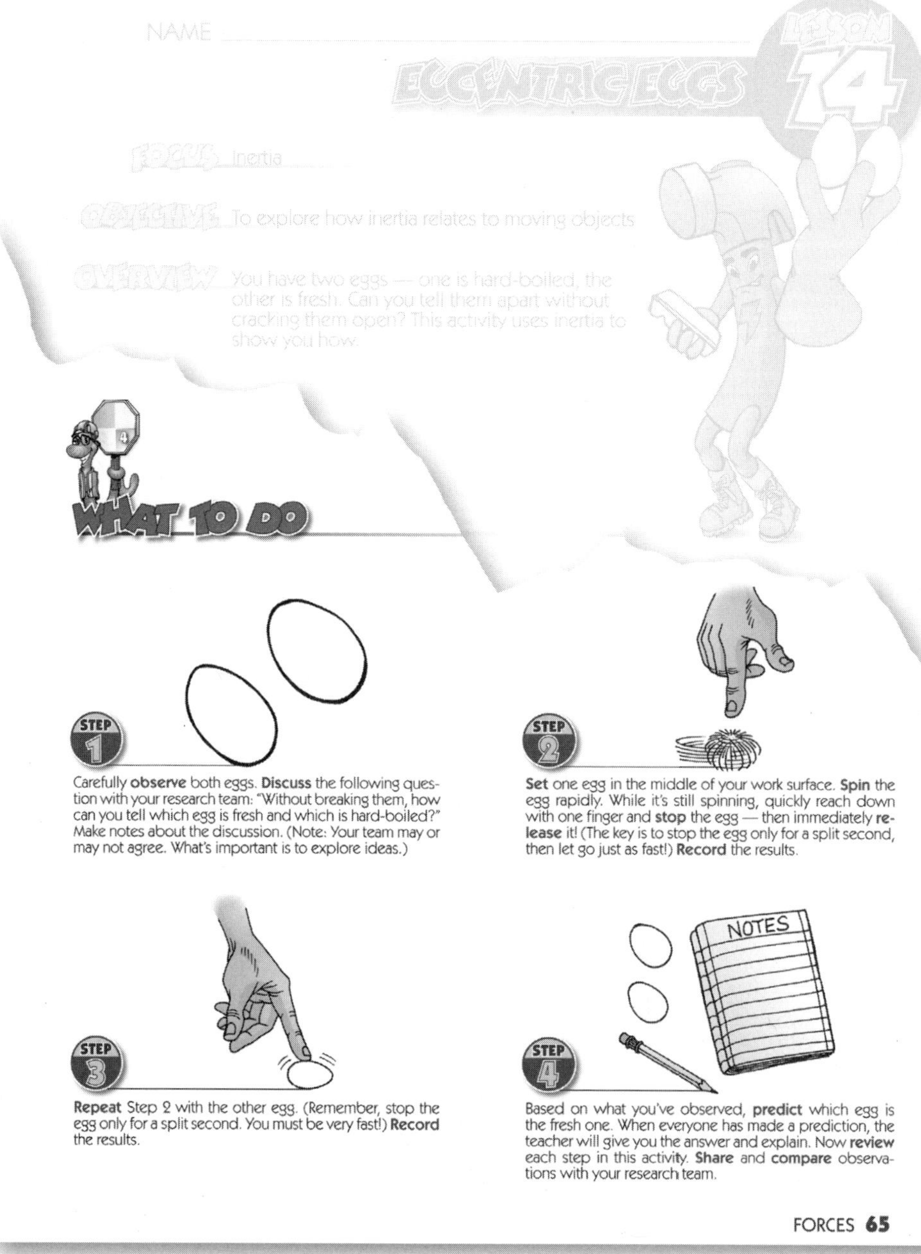

NAME

LESSON 14

ECCENTRIC EGGS

FOCUS Inertia

OBJECTIVE To explore how inertia relates to moving objects

OVERVIEW You have two eggs — one is hard-boiled, the other is fresh. Can you tell them apart without cracking them open? This activity uses inertia to show you how.

WHAT TO DO

STEP 1

Carefully **observe** both eggs. **Discuss** the following question with your research team: "Without breaking them, how can you tell which egg is fresh and which is hard-boiled?" Make notes about the discussion. (Note: Your team may or may not agree. What's important is to explore ideas.)

STEP 2

Set one egg in the middle of your work surface. **Spin** the egg rapidly. While it's still spinning, quickly reach down with one finger and **stop** the egg — then immediately **release** it! (The key is to stop the egg only for a split second, then let go just as fast!) **Record** the results.

STEP 3

Repeat Step 2 with the other egg. (Remember, stop the egg only for a split second. You must be very fast!) **Record** the results.

STEP 4

Based on what you've observed, **predict** which egg is the fresh one. When everyone has made a prediction, the teacher will give you the answer and explain. Now **review** each step in this activity. **Share** and **compare** observations with your research team.

FORCES **65**

Teacher to Teacher

The Law of Inertia says that when something is at rest it stays motionless unless a force acts on it. But the second (less familiar) part of the law says that when something is moving, it keeps moving unless a force acts on it. This was demonstrated by the behavior of the raw egg in this activity.

WHAT HAPPENED?

Newton's first law is the law of **inertia**. It says that an object sitting still remains still until a **force** is applied to it. But it also says that a moving object stays moving until a force stops it. This second part of the law explains what happened in this activity.

The hard-boiled egg was **solid** all the way through. When your fingers stopped the shell, the entire egg stopped. But the fresh egg was really two parts — the shell, and the **liquid** inside. When you stopped the shell, the liquid didn't stop since it wasn't attached to the shell. When you quickly removed the **force**, the liquid was still moving and it **transferred** some of its motion back to the shell.

WHAT WE LEARNED

1. **From what you observed and were told, how were the eggs in Step 1 similar? How were they different?**

   a) looked the same on the outside

   b) one was fresh, one was hard-boiled

2. **Describe how each egg reacted to the "spin and release" procedure.**

   One stopped completely; the other kept moving a little after the release.

66 FORCES

3. **Explain why the two eggs reacted differently. What was different about their structures? Be specific.**

   Fresh egg was liquid inside, separate from shell; hard-boiled egg was solid inside, same as shell.

4. **What did you predict in Step 4? Why? How did your prediction reflect the final answer?**

   Answers will vary, but should reflect logical comparisons.

5. **Based on what you learned, why are seatbelts important? Which egg is somewhat like a person wearing a seatbelt?**

   a) so that you stop when the car stops

   b) the hard-boiled egg since it was "attached" to the shell

FORCES 67

What Happened

Review the section with students. Emphasize bold-face words that identify key concepts and introduce new vocabulary.

Newton's first law is the law of ***inertia****. It says that an object sitting still remains still until a* ***force*** *is applied to it. But it also says that a moving object stays moving until a force stops it. This second part of the law explains what happened in this activity.*

The hard-boiled egg was ***solid*** *all the way through. When your fingers stopped the shell, the entire egg stopped. But the fresh egg was really two parts – the shell, and the* ***liquid*** *inside. When you stopped the shell, the liquid didn't stop since it wasn't attached to the shell. When you quickly removed the* ***force****, the liquid was still moving and it* ***transferred*** *some of its motion back to the shell.*

What We Learned

Answers will vary. Suggested responses are shown at left.

Conclusion

Read this section aloud to the class to summarize the concepts learned in this activity.

Food for Thought

Read the Scripture aloud to the class. Often people seem to think that religion is just rules — "don't do this" and "don't do that!" Discuss how a relationship with Christ actually sets us free.

Journal

If time permits, have a general class discussion about notes and drawings various students added to their journal pages. Discuss correct and incorrect predictions, and remind students that this "trial and error" process is part of the scientific process.

An object at rest remains at rest unless a force acts on it. An object in motion remains in motion unless a force acts on it. This is Newton's first law.

FOOD FOR THOUGHT

Romans 15:13 In this activity, the fresh egg had enough freedom inside to keep on going even when it hit an obstacle. When the hard-boiled egg encountered resistance, it stopped dead in its tracks.

Like the hard-boiled egg, sometimes our hearts can be hard and unyielding. Just like the egg, when we run into a problem, it stops us completely. When Jesus is in our hearts, guiding our lives, we can keep on going even when we're faced with tough obstacles. The fresh egg was free to keep on moving because it was free inside. In the same way, the freedom of Jesus' love will keep us going strong!

JOURNAL **My Science Notes**

68 FORCES

Extended Teaching

1. Challenge teams to use what they've learned in this activity to develop safety posters showing the importance of using seatbelts. Post the best ones around your school.

2. Most schools have a rule against running in the hallways. Have teams discuss how the law of inertia relates to this rule. Ask students to write a paragraph or two explaining the connection.

3. Take a field trip to a local car dealer. Ask them to demonstrate or discuss various safety features on different models. Have students write a paragraph about one thing they learn.

4. Watch a safety film on the importance of seatbelts. Have a class discussion about how inertia played a role in the film.

5. Challenge each team to create a bulletin board about inertia. Use pictures cut from magazines or student drawings for illustrations.

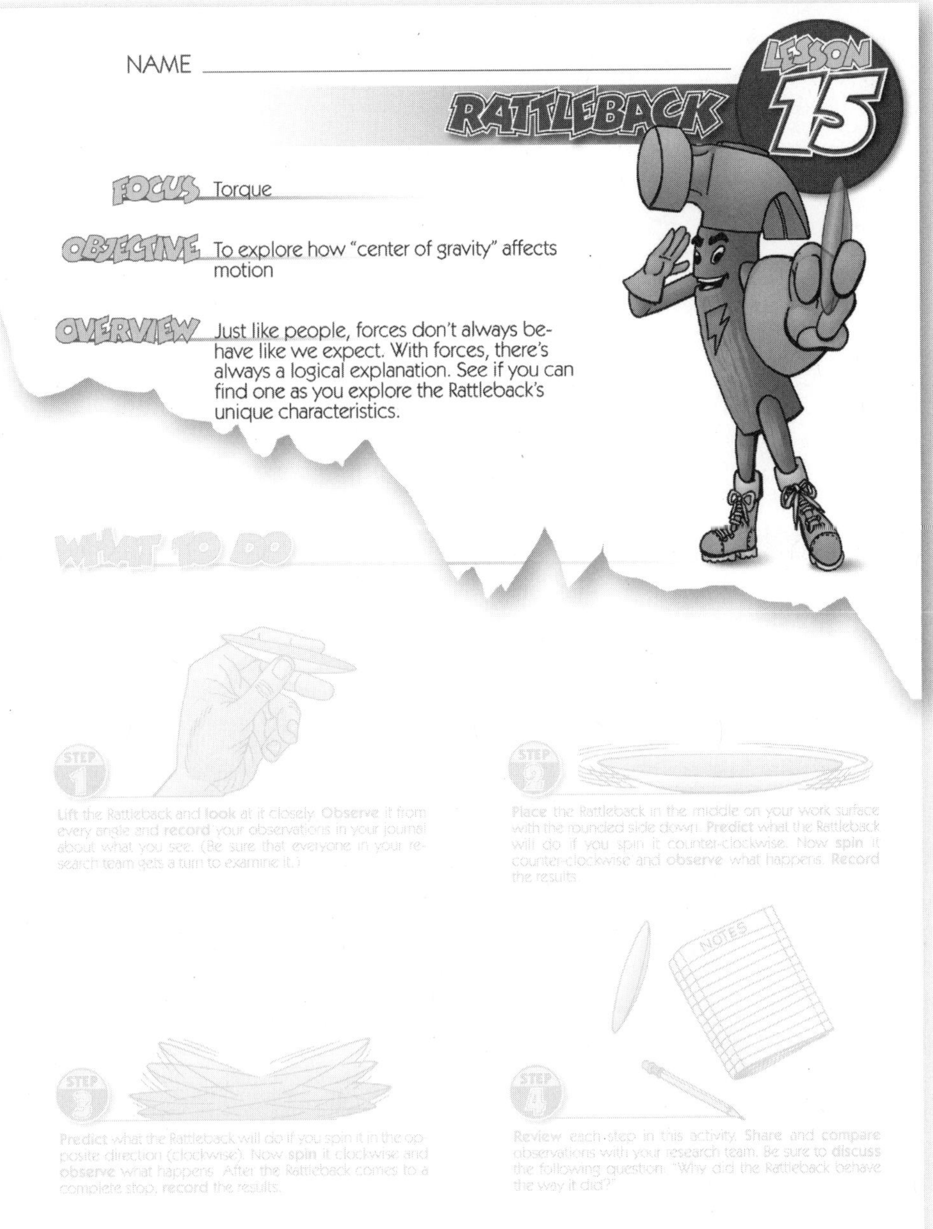

NAME ______________________

LESSON 15

RATTLEBACK

FOCUS Torque

OBJECTIVE To explore how "center of gravity" affects motion

OVERVIEW Just like people, forces don't always behave like we expect. With forces, there's always a logical explanation. See if you can find one as you explore the Rattleback's unique characteristics.

WHAT TO DO

STEP 1

Lift the Rattleback and **look** at it closely. **Observe** it from every angle and **record** your observations in your journal about what you see. (Be sure that everyone in your research team gets a turn to examine it.)

STEP 2

Place the Rattleback in the middle on your work surface with the rounded side down. **Predict** what the Rattleback will do if you spin it counter-clockwise. Now **spin** it counter-clockwise and **observe** what happens. **Record** the results.

STEP 3

Predict what the Rattleback will do if you spin it in the opposite direction (clockwise). Now **spin** it clockwise and **observe** what happens. After the Rattleback comes to a complete stop, **record** the results.

STEP 4

Review each step in this activity. **Share** and **compare** observations with your research team. Be sure to **discuss** the following question: "Why did the Rattleback behave the way it did?"

FORCES 69

Category

Physical Science
Forces

Focus

Torque

Objective

To explore how "center of gravity" affects motion

National Standards

A1, A2, B2, B3, E1, E2, F5, G1, G2

Materials Needed

rattleback

Safety Concerns

none

Additional Comments

A good way to introduce this activity is to tell students this toy "has a mind of its own!" Challenge them to find out how.

Overview

Read the overview aloud to your students. The goal is to create an atmosphere of curiosity and inquiry.

WHAT TO DO

Monitor student research teams as they complete each step.

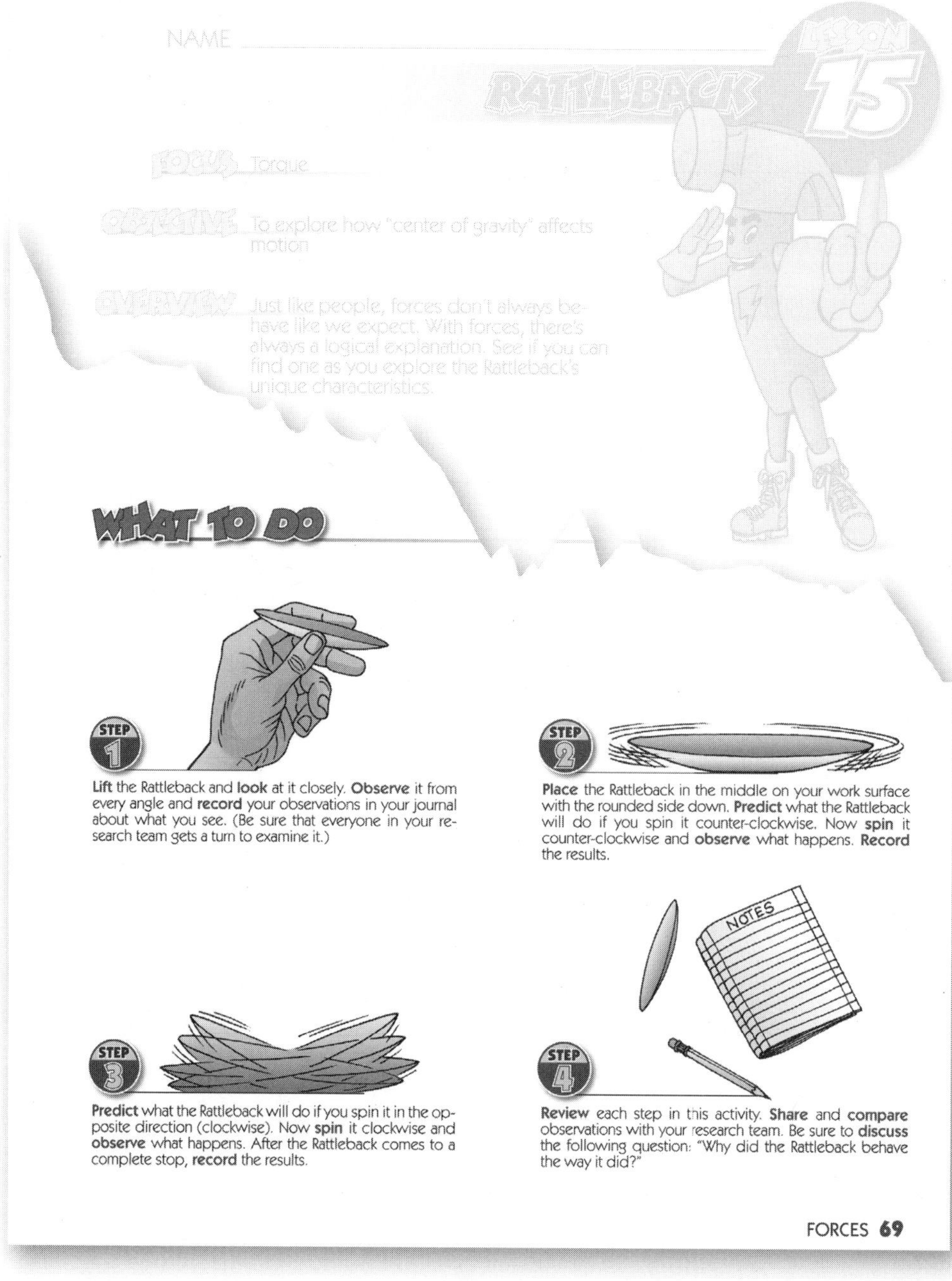

NAME

LESSON 15

RATTLEBACK

FOCUS Torque

OBJECTIVE To explore how "center of gravity" affects motion

OVERVIEW Just like people, forces don't always behave like we expect. With forces, there's always a logical explanation. See if you can find one as you explore the Rattleback's unique characteristics.

WHAT TO DO

STEP 1

Lift the Rattleback and **look** at it closely. **Observe** it from every angle and **record** your observations in your journal about what you see. (Be sure that everyone in your research team gets a turn to examine it.)

STEP 2

Place the Rattleback in the middle on your work surface with the rounded side down. **Predict** what the Rattleback will do if you spin it counter-clockwise. Now **spin** it counter-clockwise and **observe** what happens. **Record** the results.

STEP 3

Predict what the Rattleback will do if you spin it in the opposite direction (clockwise). Now **spin** it clockwise and **observe** what happens. After the Rattleback comes to a complete stop, **record** the results.

STEP 4

Review each step in this activity. **Share** and **compare** observations with your research team. Be sure to **discuss** the following question: "Why did the Rattleback behave the way it did?"

FORCES **69**

Teacher to Teacher

Preferential spin bias is created by the shape of an object and its center of gravity. Since the mass of the rattleback isn't evenly distributed, its center of gravity is not in the "middle." This accounts for its strange behavior. When a mechanic "balances" your tires, he's actually adding little weights to make the center of gravity the point where the wheel bolts to your car. Keep in mind that when an object is symmetrical, spinning makes it travel straighter. A quarterback spins the football as he releases a pass. The rifling in a gun barrel makes a bullet spin. Generally the faster a balanced object spins, the straighter its path.

WHAT HAPPENED?

Torque is a **turning** or **twisting** force. A spinning top, a swinging bat, a rolling wheel — all demonstrate the force of torque.

During the examination in Step 1, you may have noticed that the Rattleback is not a uniform shape. In fact, it's kind of lopsided. This unusual shape causes the Rattleback's **center of gravity** to be off center! And as you observed, an object with an off-center **balance point** always spins more easily in one direction. Scientists call this **preferential spin bias**. Torque applied in the opposite direction may cause it to "rattle back."

Friction was the **opposing force** that stopped the Rattleback at the end of each spin. Whenever two things rub together, friction eventually stops them. Friction is also a very important force in science — but we'll save that for another lesson!

WHAT WE LEARNED

1. **Look at the Rattleback from one end. Draw and describe the shape you see.**

   Drawing and description should show a lopsided cross-section.

2. **What did you predict in Step 2? How did your prediction reflect what actually happened?**

   Answers will vary, but should reflect logical comparisons.

3. **What did you predict in Step 3? How did your prediction reflect what actually happened?**

   Answers will vary, but should reflect logical comparisons.

4. **Explain "preferencial spin bias." (Hint: Look at the root word of "preferencial" and the definition of "bias.")**

   When an object spins more easily in one direction; when something prefers to spin in one direction.

5. **Give three examples of how the force of friction stops things.**

   A rolling ball slows down, brakes stopping a bicycle, a runner sliding into home plate, etc.

What Happened

Review the section with students. Emphasize bold-face words that identify key concepts and introduce new vocabulary.

Torque *is a* ***turning*** *or* ***twisting*** *force. A spinning top, a swinging bat, a rolling wheel — all demonstrate the force of torque.*

During the examination in Step 1, you may have noticed that the Rattleback is not a uniform shape. In fact, it's kind of lopsided. This unusual shape causes the Rattleback's ***center of gravity*** *to be off center! And as you observed, an object with an off-center* ***balance point*** *always spins more easily in one direction. Scientists call this* ***preferential spin bias****. Torque applied in the opposite direction may cause it to "rattle back."*

Friction *was the* ***opposing force*** *that stopped the Rattleback at the end of each spin. Whenever two things rub together, friction eventually stops them. Friction is also a very important force in science — but we'll save that for another lesson!*

What We Learned

Answers will vary. Suggested responses are shown at left.

Conclusion

Read this section aloud to the class to summarize the concepts learned in this activity.

Food for Thought

Read the Scripture aloud to the class. Talk about the life of Samson. Discuss how his life might have been different if he'd always followed God.

Journal

If time permits, have a general class discussion about notes and drawings various students added to their journal pages. Discuss correct and incorrect predictions, and remind students that this "trial and error" process is part of the scientific process.

Sometimes forces don't do what we expect, but there's always a logical explanation. An object's preferencial spin bias depends on its center of gravity, also known as its balance point. Applying torque in the opposite direction may cause the object to "rattle back" as it did in this activity.

Hebrews 11:32 The Rattleback started in one direction, wobbled around a bit, then took off in the other direction! Some powerful force drew it back to the direction it was supposed to go.

Sometimes people can go spinning off in the wrong direction, too. Samson started off as one of God's mighty men, but then he took off down the wrong path. His life became a series of bumps, bruises, and pain. In the end, the power of God drew him back again. In fact, you'll find that he's even listed with other great men of faith (like Enoch, Moses, and Abraham) in Hebrews 11.

JOURNAL **My Science Notes**

72 FORCES

Extended Teaching

1. Make a bulletin board of athletes in action. Challenge teams to determine the athlete's center of gravity in each picture. Discuss how center of gravity is important to athletes.

2. Have each team construct a mobile with wire and string using different size objects. Ask them to show their mobile to the class and describe challenges they faced getting it to balance.

3. Repeat this activity placing tiny pieces of clay at various points on the Rattleback. Challenge teams to find a combination that will overcome the Rattleback's preferential spin bias. Discuss the results.

4. Take a field trip to a tire shop. Ask the technicians to demonstrate how wheels are balanced, and show what can happen to a tire that's not properly balanced. Have students write a paragraph about one thing they learn.

5. Invite a college quarterback or pitcher to visit your school. Have him/her throw a ball with and without spinning. Compare the difference. Discuss how spins affect the balls performance.

NAME

BERNOULLI BALL

LESSON 16

FOCUS Bernoulli Principle

OBJECTIVE To explore air pressure and lift

OVERVIEW As we learned in Lesson 6, forces don't always behave as we expect them to. But then, there's always a logical explanation. See if you can solve the mystery in this activity.

WHAT TO DO

STEP 1

Discuss the following question with your research team: "If you put a ping-pong ball in a funnel and blow straight up, what will happen?" **Make notes** in your journal about the discussion. (Note: Your team may or may not agree. What's important is to explore ideas.)

STEP 2

Tilt your head back and **put** the funnel in your mouth. **Place** the ping-pong ball in the funnel. Take a deep breath, then **blow** through the funnel as hard as you can. **Record** the results. Be sure everyone on your team gets a turn. (Use an antiseptic wipe to clean the funnel between turns!)

STEP 3

Discuss the following question with your research team. "If you put a ping-pong ball in a funnel and blow straight down, what will happen?" **Make notes** about the discussion. (Just like Step 1, your team may or may not agree. What's important is to explore ideas.)

STEP 4

Turn the funnel upside down with the ball held tightly inside. Now **blow** through the funnel as hard as you can. As soon as the air is escaping really fast, **release** the ball. **Record** the results. Be sure everyone gets a turn. **Share** and **compare** observations with your research team.

FORCES 73

Category

Physical Science
Forces

Focus

The Bernoulli Principle

Objective

To explore air pressure and lift

National Standards

A1, A2, B1, B2, B3, E1, E2, G1, G2

Materials Needed

funnel
ping-pong ball
antiseptic wipes

Safety Concerns

4. Hygiene
Carefully disinfect funnels and balls between uses.

Additional Comments

You can make inexpensive funnels from the top section of 20 ounce soft drink bottles. Remind students not to blow too hard or too long or they will get dizzy! After the activity is complete, disinfect funnels and balls carefully, then store for use next year.

Overview

Read the overview aloud to your students. The goal is to create an atmosphere of curiosity and inquiry.

WHAT TO DO

Monitor student research teams as they complete each step.

NAME

BERNOULLI BALL

LESSON 16

FOCUS Bernoulli Principle

OBJECTIVE To explore air pressure and lift

OVERVIEW As we learned in Lesson 6, forces don't always behave as we expect them to. But then, there's always a logical explanation. See if you can solve the mystery in this activity.

WHAT TO DO

STEP 1

Discuss the following question with your research team: "If you put a ping-pong ball in a funnel and blow straight up, what will happen?" **Make notes** in your journal about the discussion. (Note: Your team may or may not agree. What's important is to explore ideas.)

STEP 2

Tilt your head back and **put** the funnel in your mouth. **Place** the ping-pong ball in the funnel. Take a deep breath, then **blow** through the funnel as hard as you can. **Record** the results. Be sure everyone on your team gets a turn. (Use an antiseptic wipe to clean the funnel between turns!)

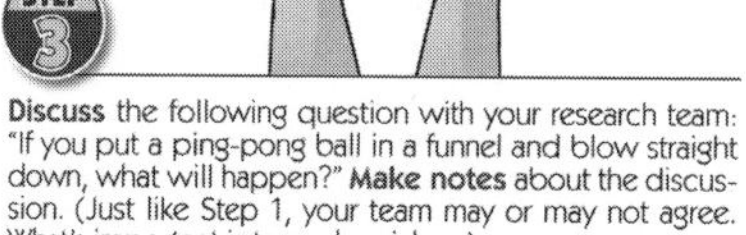

STEP 3

Discuss the following question with your research team: "If you put a ping-pong ball in a funnel and blow straight down, what will happen?" **Make notes** about the discussion. (Just like Step 1, your team may or may not agree. What's important is to explore ideas.)

STEP 4

Turn the funnel upside down with the ball held tightly inside. Now **blow** through the funnel as hard as you can. As soon as the air is escaping really fast, **release** the ball. **Record** the results. Be sure everyone gets a turn. **Share** and **compare** observations with your research team.

FORCES **73**

Teacher to Teacher

All forces come in pairs. If you're sitting in a chair, gravity will hold you in place until you exert a greater force (your leg muscles) to lift you out of it. In Step 2, the ping-pong ball couldn't fly out because fast moving air kept the air pressure in the funnel lower than the air pressure outside. This held true even when the funnel was inverted in Step 4!

WHAT HAPPENED?

To understand what happened, you have to know two facts. First, nothing moves unless more **force** is **pushing** (or **pulling**) in one direction than in the other. Second, fast moving air has lower **air pressure** than slow moving air. This is called the **Bernoulli Principle**, named after the scientist who discovered this.

Even in Step 4, the ball couldn't get out until the pressure inside the funnel was greater than the pressure outside. The fast moving air was creating a pocket of low pressure! The harder you blew, the lower the pressure and the tighter the ball was held. **Gravity** couldn't defeat this low pressure until the air speed moving through the funnel dropped.

When you ran out of air, the fast moving air stopped, and gravity became the victor.

WHAT WE LEARNED

1. **What did you predict in Step 1? How did your prediction reflect what happened in Step 2?**

   Answers will vary, but should reflect logical comparisons.

2. **What did you predict in Step 3? How did your prediction reflect what happened in Step 4?**

   Answers will vary, but should reflect logical comparisons.

74 FORCES

3. **Describe the Bernoulli Principle.**

   Fast moving air has lower air pressure than slow moving air.

4. **In Step 4, what finally caused the ball to drop out of the funnel? What forces were competing?**

   a) the air slowed down

   b) gravity and the Bernoulli principle

5. **Air flows over an airplane wing faster than under it. Based on the Bernoulli Principle, what might happen?**

   The faster air on top of the wing causes lower air pressure, creating lift to make the plane fly.

FORCES 75

What Happened

Review the section with students. Emphasize bold-face words that identify key concepts and introduce new vocabulary.

*To understand what happened, you have to know two facts. First, nothing moves unless more **force** is **pushing** (or **pulling**) in one direction than in the other. Second, fast moving air has lower **air pressure** than slow moving air. This is called the **Bernoulli Principle**, named after the scientist who discovered this.*

*Even in Step 4, the ball couldn't get out until the pressure inside the funnel was greater than the pressure outside. The fast moving air was creating a pocket of low pressure! The harder you blew, the lower the pressure and the tighter the ball was held. **Gravity** couldn't defeat this low pressure until the air speed moving through the funnel dropped.*

When you ran out of air, the fast moving air stopped, and gravity became the victor.

What We Learned

Answers will vary. Suggested responses are shown at left.

Conclusion

Read this section aloud to the class to summarize the concepts learned in this activity.

Food for Thought

Read the Scripture aloud to the class. Talk about ways to spend time with God. Discuss how time is an important component in developing any relationship.

Journal

If time permits, have a general class discussion about notes and drawings various students added to their journal pages. Discuss correct and incorrect predictions, and remind students that this "trial and error" process is part of the scientific process.

Conclusion

Fast-moving air has lower air pressure than slow-moving air. This is called the Bernoulli Principle. Faster-moving air on top of an airplane wing produces lift, causing the airplane to rise.

Food for Thought

Psalm 46:1-2 Your breath created a pressure difference that caused the ball to be supported in the funnel — just the opposite of what you probably thought would happen! As we've discovered this year, no matter whether we walk, sail, ride, or fly, there is some kind of force supporting us.

This Psalm reminds us of the greatest force of all, the one that supports us no matter what other forces surround us. When we spend time getting to know God, learning to trust him, then we can rely on his ever-present power. When our problems seem too much to bear, we can turn to the most powerful support ever known!

Journal My Science Notes

76 FORCES

Extended Teaching

1. Sometimes it hard to get enough air for Step 4. Repeat this step, only this time attach the funnel to the exhaust hose of a powerful vacuum cleaner. Have students compare the results with the original activity.

2. Take a field trip to an air museum. Find out how lift affects the wings, rudders, flaps, and other surfaces on aircraft. Have students write a paragraph about one thing they learn.

3. Invite a high school or college baseball pitcher to visit your classroom. Ask him/her to explain how they use the ridges on the ball to make it fly differently. Have students write a paragraph about one thing they learn.

4. Using the Internet, have teams research different kinds of airplane wings. Compare gliders, fighter jets, stunt planes, and more. Challenge each team to create a poster comparing at least two types of wings.

5. Using the Internet, have teams research different kinds of bird wings. Compare eagles, penguins, hummingbirds, and more. Challenge each team to create a poster comparing at least two types of wings.

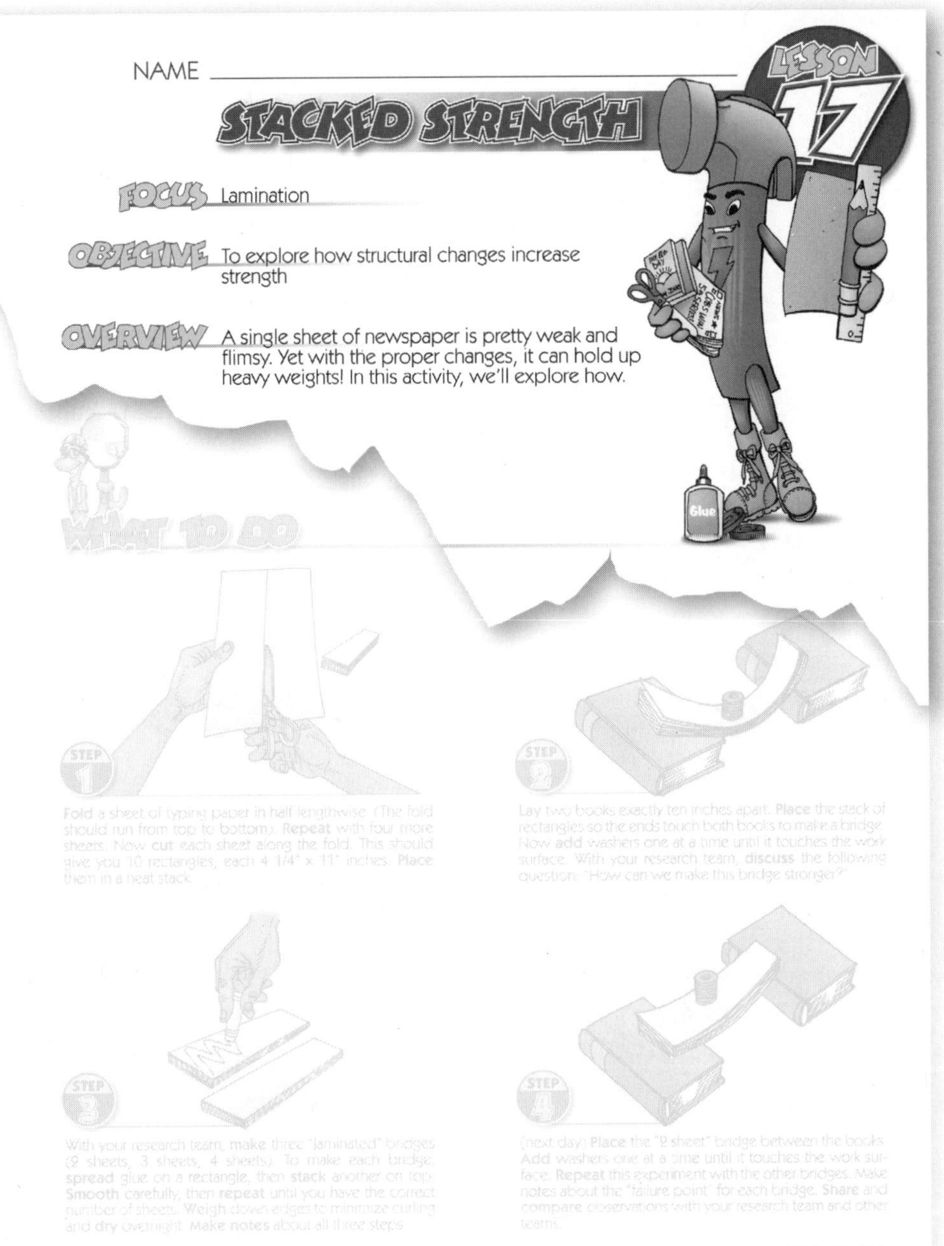

NAME ______________________

LESSON 17

STACKED STRENGTH

FOCUS Lamination

OBJECTIVE To explore how structural changes increase strength

OVERVIEW A single sheet of newspaper is pretty weak and flimsy. Yet with the proper changes, it can hold up heavy weights! In this activity, we'll explore how.

WHAT TO DO

STEP 1 **Fold** a sheet of typing paper in half lengthwise. (The fold should run from top to bottom). **Repeat** with four more sheets. Now **cut** each sheet along the fold. This should give you 10 rectangles, each 4 1/4" x 11" inches. **Place** them in a neat stack.

STEP 2 Lay two books exactly ten inches apart. **Place** the stack of rectangles so the ends touch both books to make a bridge. Now **add** washers one at a time until it touches the work surface. With your research team, **discuss** the following question: "How can we make this bridge stronger?"

STEP 3 With your research team, **make** three "laminated" bridges (2 sheets, 3 sheets, 4 sheets). To make each bridge, **spread** glue on a rectangle, then **stack** another on top. **Smooth** carefully, then **repeat** until you have the correct number of sheets. **Weigh** down edges to minimize curling and **dry** overnight. **Make notes** about all three steps.

STEP 4 (next day) **Place** the "2 sheet" bridge between the books. **Add** washers one at a time until it touches the work surface. **Repeat** this experiment with the other bridges. Make notes about the "failure point" for each bridge. **Share** and **compare** observations with your research team and other teams.

FORCES 77

Category

Physical Science
Forces

Focus

Lamination

Objective

To explore how structural changes increase strength

National Standards

A1, A2, B1, B2, B3, E1, E2, F5, G1, G2

Materials Needed

washers - 10
typing paper - 5 sheets
books - 2
glue stick
scissors
ruler

Safety Concerns

4. Sharp Objects
Remind students to exercise caution when using scissors.

Additional Comments

Be sure the glued sheets have at least 24 hours to dry — longer if possible. A great math connection is to challenge teams to create graphs comparing the performance of the three laminated "bridges" they create, then comparing those results with the results of other teams.

Overview

Read the overview aloud to your students. The goal is to create an atmosphere of curiosity and inquiry.

WHAT TO DO

Monitor student research teams as they complete each step.

Step 4

Drying time, type and amount of glue, etc., will impact the results. However, usually a "2 sheet bridge" supports about 2 washers; a "3 sheet bridge" supports about 6 washers; and a "4 sheet bridge" supports about 12 washers.

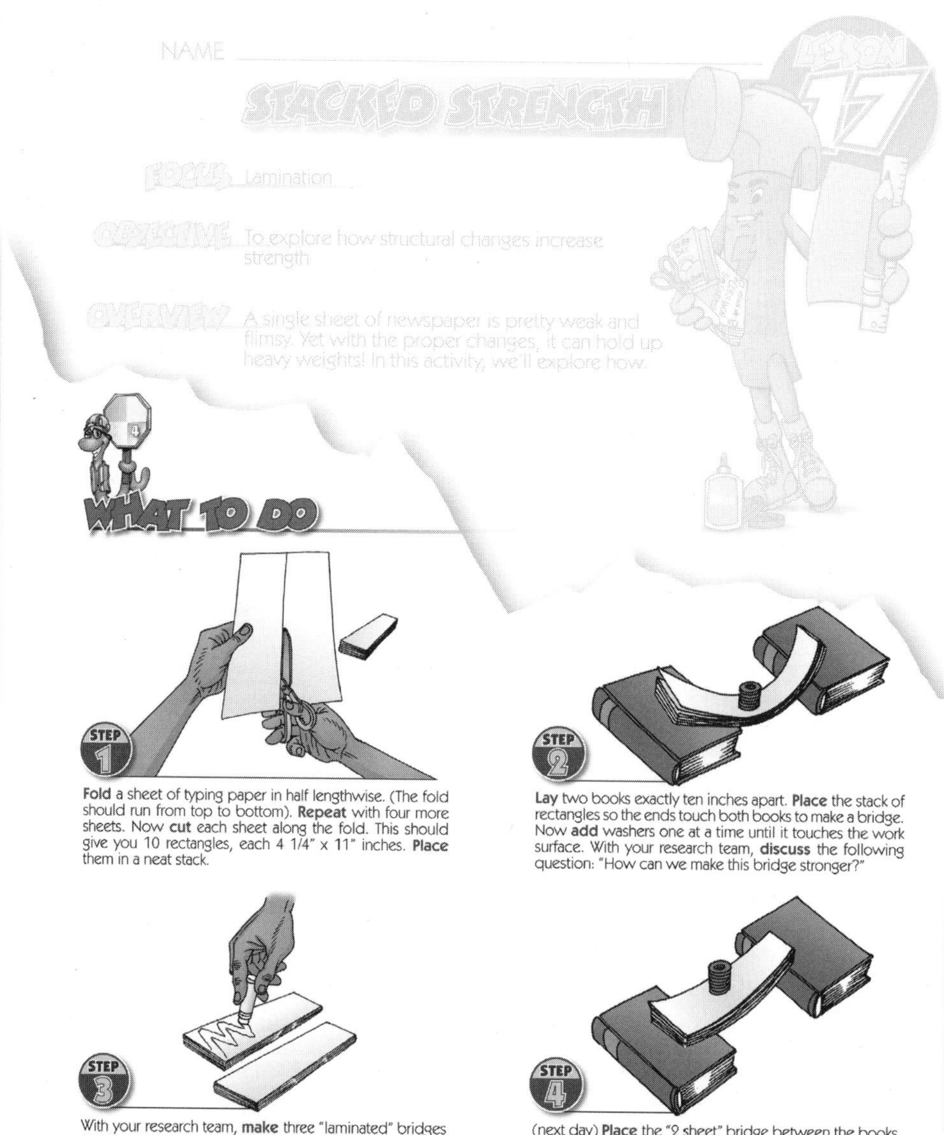

NAME

LESSON 17

STACKED STRENGTH

FOCUS Lamination

OBJECTIVE To explore how structural changes increase strength

OVERVIEW A single sheet of newspaper is pretty weak and flimsy. Yet with the proper changes, it can hold up heavy weights! In this activity, we'll explore how.

WHAT TO DO

STEP 1

Fold a sheet of typing paper in half lengthwise. (The fold should run from top to bottom). **Repeat** with four more sheets. Now **cut** each sheet along the fold. This should give you 10 rectangles, each 4 1/4" x 11" inches. **Place** them in a neat stack.

STEP 2

Lay two books exactly ten inches apart. **Place** the stack of rectangles so the ends touch both books to make a bridge. Now **add** washers one at a time until it touches the work surface. With your research team, **discuss** the following question: "How can we make this bridge stronger?"

STEP 3

With your research team, **make** three "laminated" bridges (2 sheets, 3 sheets, 4 sheets). To make each bridge, **spread** glue on a rectangle, then **stack** another on top. **Smooth** carefully, then **repeat** until you have the correct number of sheets. **Weigh** down edges to minimize curling and **dry** overnight. **Make notes** about all three steps.

STEP 4

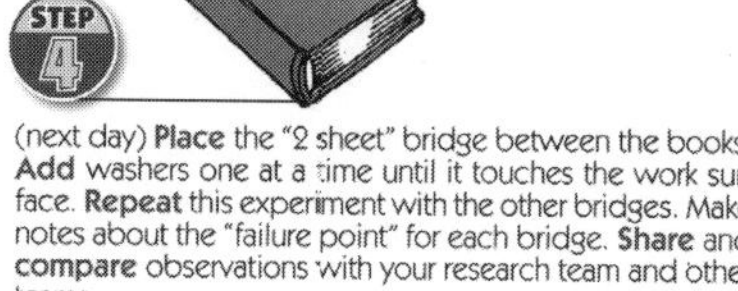

(next day) **Place** the "2 sheet" bridge between the books. **Add** washers one at a time until it touches the work surface. **Repeat** this experiment with the other bridges. Make notes about the "failure point" for each bridge. **Share** and **compare** observations with your research team and other teams.

FORCES **77**

Teacher to Teacher

Scientists call liquid material used to attach one material to another "adhesive." There are thousands of specialized adhesives designed for specific surfaces and materials. Some are as basic as wallpaper paste. Others are used for complex tasks like fabricating airplane parts. There are even adhesives designed for huge tasks like repairing highway bridges!

WHAT HAPPENED?

Fastening layers of material together to make them stronger is called **lamination**. Many building materials, like plywood and structural beams, are manufactured this way for special strength! The reason lamination is so strong is because any **force** applied to a laminated object is spread out evenly through the layers, rather than putting all the **stress** on one spot.

Lamination can be seen in many living things, too. (That's probably where people got the idea!) For instance, all tall trees grow in layers. Look closely at the **cross-section** of a tree trunk and you'll see the layers that scientists call **growth rings**. You can also see lamination in shells and in the antlers and horns of many animals. Just as in man-made products, lamination in God's natural world is there to provide strength.

WHAT WE LEARNED

1. **What are some of the ideas your research team had for making a stronger bridge in Step 2?**

   Answers will vary.

2. **What was the purpose of the glue in Step 3? Why was it important to let it dry thoroughly?**

   a) to join the layers together

   b) it doesn't reach full strength until it's dry

3. **Compare the "2 sheet," "3 sheet," and "4 sheet" bridges. How many washers did each bridge hold?**

   Answers will vary (see note under "What To Do").

4. **Based on your observations, how many washers would a "5 sheet" bridge hold? Why?**

   a) answers will vary, but should reflect exponential growth in strength

   b) each layer makes the bridge much stronger

5. **Name one man-made and one natural object that shows a form of lamination.**

   a) man-made: plywood, structural beams, etc.

   b) trees, shells, horns, etc.

What Happened

Review the section with students. Emphasize bold-face words that identify key concepts and introduce new vocabulary.

Fastening layers of material together to make them stronger is called ***lamination****. Many building materials, like plywood and structural beams, are manufactured this way for special strength! The reason lamination is so strong is because any* ***force*** *applied to a laminated object is spread out evenly through the layers, rather than putting all the* ***stress*** *on one spot.*

Lamination can be seen in many living things, too. (That's probably where people got the idea!) For instance, all tall trees grow in layers. Look closely at the ***cross-section*** *of a tree trunk and you'll see the layers that scientists call* ***growth rings****. You can also see lamination in shells and in the antlers and horns of many animals. Just as in man-made products, lamination in God's natural world is there to provide strength.*

What We Learned

Answers will vary. Suggested responses are shown at left.

Conclusion

Read this section aloud to the class to summarize the concepts learned in this activity.

Food for Thought

Read the Scripture aloud to the class. Talk about how working together makes a church stronger. Discuss ways we can support one another.

Journal

If time permits, have a general class discussion about notes and drawings various students added to their journal pages. Discuss correct and incorrect predictions, and remind students that this "trial and error" process is part of the scientific process.

Lamination combines materials so the end product is stronger than the individual pieces. Lamination helps spread the load or force evenly through all the parts.

FOOD FOR THOUGHT

1 Peter 3:8 None of the strips you used to make your laminated bridge were very strong. It was only when they worked together that they were able to bear the weight and successfully span the gap.

Just as the strips of the laminated bridge had to stick together to get the job done, so we must also work together in unity. Scripture reminds us that a church full of willing, helpful people can accomplish much more than any one individual. A classroom full of students that support one another can have more fun and learn much more. Ask God to help you learn to always be kind, helpful, and supportive.

JOURNAL **My Science Notes**

80 FORCES

Extended Teaching

1. Have teams list various natural things that are laminated. Compare lists and discuss how lamination makes these things strong. Challenge each team to make a poster showing some aspect of natural lamination.

2. Enlarge the back of a penny and show it on the overhead. Point out the words "E Pluribus Unum." Explain that this is latin for "of many, one." Discuss how the relatively weak colonies combined to form a strong nation.

3. Using the Internet, have teams research building materials that use lamination. Challenge each team to create a poster depicting one of these materials and describing its use.

4. Take a field trip to a lumber mill. Find out how plywood is made. Discuss how the various layers add strength. Have students write a paragraph about one thing they learn.

5. Invite a carpenter to visit your classroom. Ask him/her to bring small samples of laminated materials (plywood, beams, countertops, doors, etc.). Have students write a paragraph about one thing they learn.

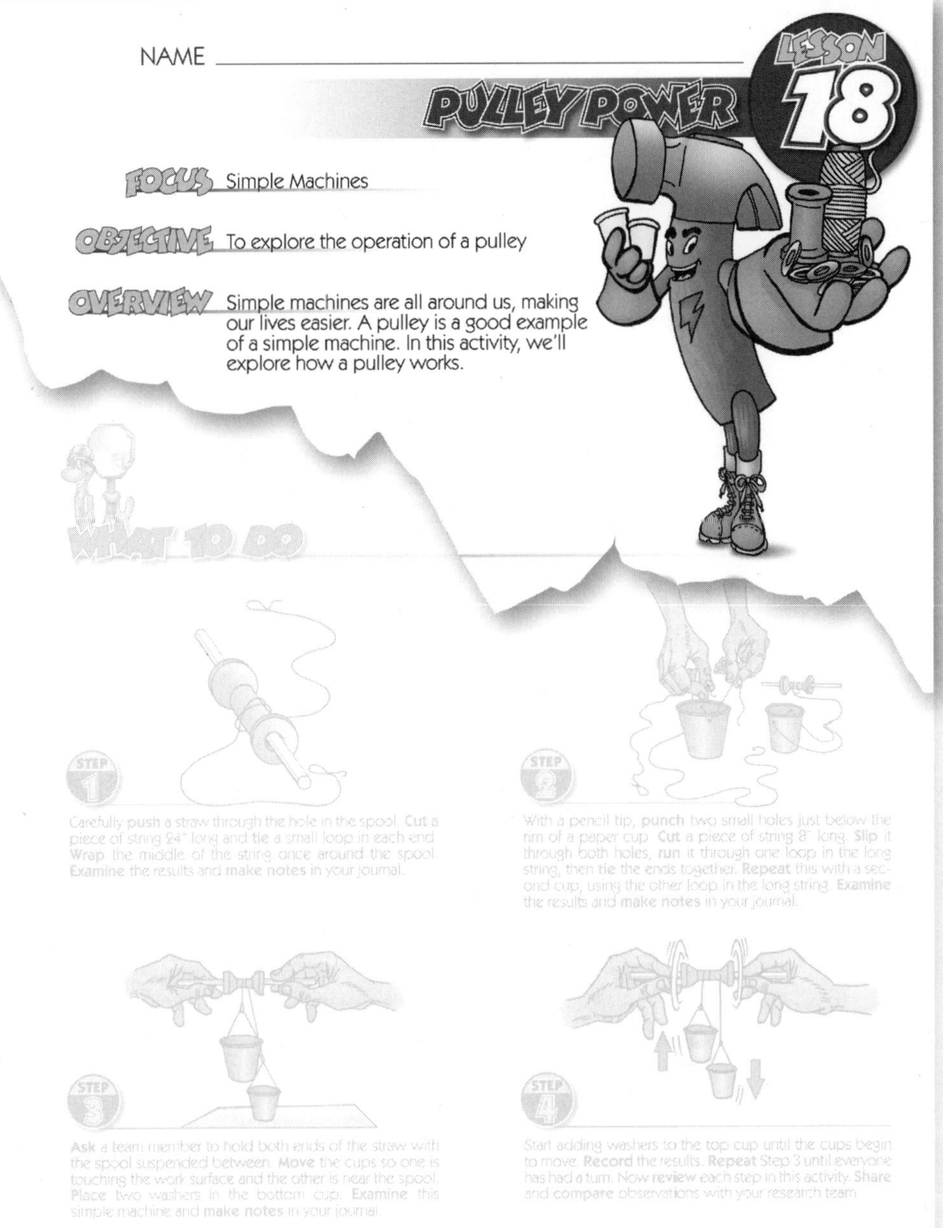
NAME ______________________________

LESSON 18

PULLEY POWER

FOCUS Simple Machines

OBJECTIVE To explore the operation of a pulley

OVERVIEW Simple machines are all around us, making our lives easier. A pulley is a good example of a simple machine. In this activity, we'll explore how a pulley works.

WHAT TO DO

STEP 1: Carefully **push** a straw through the hole in the spool. **Cut** a piece of string 24" long and **tie** a small loop in each end. **Wrap** the middle of the string once around the spool. **Examine** the results and **make notes** in your journal.

STEP 2: With a pencil tip, **punch** two small holes just below the rim of a paper cup. **Cut** a piece of string 8" long. **Slip** it through both holes, **run** it through one loop in the long string, then **tie** the ends together. **Repeat** this with a second cup, using the other loop in the long string. **Examine** the results and **make notes** in your journal.

STEP 3: **Ask** a team member to hold both ends of the straw with the spool suspended between. **Move** the cups so one is touching the work surface and the other is near the spool. **Place** two washers in the bottom cup. **Examine** this simple machine and **make notes** in your journal.

STEP 4: Start adding washers to the top cup until the cups begin to move. **Record** the results. **Repeat** Step 3 until everyone has had a turn. Now **review** each step in this activity. **Share** and **compare** observations with your research team.

FORCES 81

Category

Physical Science
Forces

Focus

Simple Machines

Objective

To explore the operation of a pulley

National Standards

A1, A2, B2, B3, E1, E2, F5, G1, G2

Materials Needed

soda straw
spool
string
paper cups - 2
washers - 8
scissors
pencil

Safety Concerns

4. Sharp Objects
Remind students to exercise caution when using scissors.

Additional Comments

Focus on the fact that a pulley is a simple machine. There are five additional simple machines: the wheel, the axle, the inclined plane, the wedge, and the screw.

Overview

Read the overview aloud to your students. The goal is to create an atmosphere of curiosity and inquiry.

WHAT TO DO

Monitor student research teams as they complete each step.

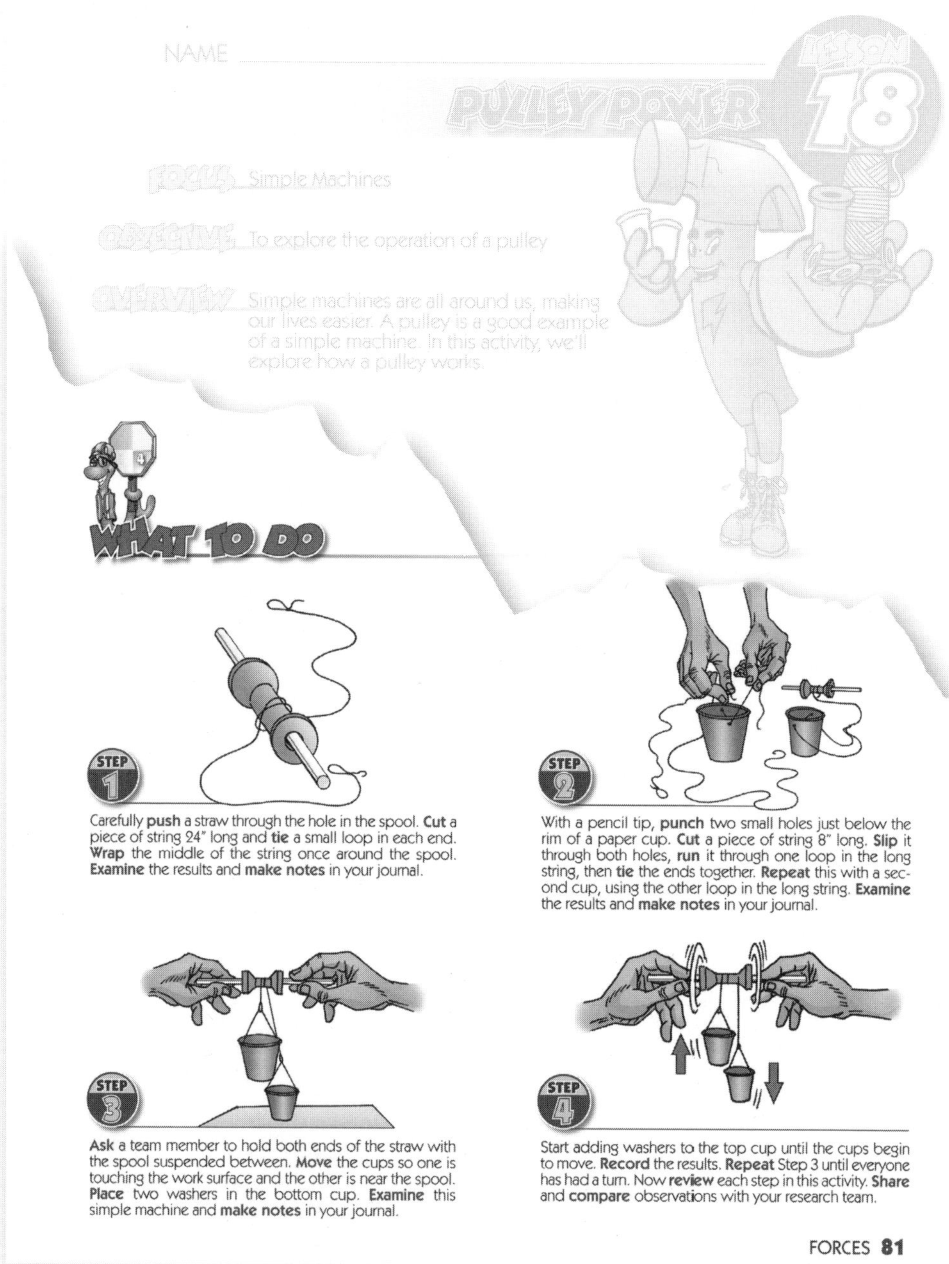

Teacher to Teacher

Efficiency is the amount of work you get out of a machine compared to how much energy you put into it. In this activity, lifting two washers was the work output. The energy input was the number of washers added to the second cup. Due to losses caused by friction and other things, no simple machine is 100% efficient — so the number of washers added was always higher than the number of washers lifted.

A **pulley** is a **simple machine** containing at least one **wheel** and one **axle**. (In this activity, the spool is the wheel; the straw inside the spool is the axle.)

One important function of a machine is to change the direction of a **force**. When you use a screwdriver to open a can of paint, you **push** down, but the lid goes up. The screwdriver works as a simple machine called a **lever**. In this activity, the pulley changed the downward force of the washers in the top cup to an upward motion of the bottom cup. Pulleys are used in factory assembly lines, in car engines, as hoists in hay barns — even as parts in some toys!

WHAT WE LEARNED

1 **What part of a simple machine is the spool by itself? Give three examples of wheels you might find in other machines.**

a) a wheel

b) wheels on a bicycle, a shopping cart, farm equipment, etc.

2 **What part of a simple machine is the straw by itself? Give three examples of axles you might find in other machines.**

a) an axle

b) axles on a car, a wagon, a trailer, etc.

82 FORCES

3 **What kind of machine did you get when you combined the spool and straw? Give three examples of a wheel and axle combination.**

a) a pulley or a wheel and axle

b) pulleys in factories, in car engines, in toys, etc.

4 **How did the pulley change the downward force of the cup in Step 4? What happened to the bottom cup?**

As the top cup began to fall, the pulley and string made the bottom cup rise.

5 **Name three simple machines. Tell how each one might change the direction of a force.**

a) any of the following: pulley, wheel, axle, inclined plane (or lever), wedge, screw

b) answers will vary

FORCES 83

What Happened

Review the section with students. Emphasize bold-face words that identify key concepts and introduce new vocabulary.

*A **pulley** is a **simple machine** containing at least one **wheel** and one **axle**. (In this activity, the spool is the wheel; the straw inside the spool is the axle.)*

*One important function of a machine is to change the direction of a **force**. When you use a screwdriver to open a can of paint, you **push** down, but the lid goes up. The screwdriver works as a simple machine called a **lever**. In this activity, the pulley changed the downward force of the washers in the top cup to an upward motion of the bottom cup. Pulleys are used in factory assembly lines, in car engines, as hoists in hay barns — even as parts in some toys!*

What We Learned

Answers will vary. Suggested responses are shown at left.

Conclusion

Read this section aloud to the class to summarize the concepts learned in this activity.

Food for Thought

Read the Scripture aloud to the class. Discuss how our relationship with God can help us become more thoughtful and caring. (Hint: It's hard to get water from an empty well!)

Journal

If time permits, have a general class discussion about notes and drawings various students added to their journal pages. Discuss correct and incorrect predictions, and remind students that this "trial and error" process is part of the scientific process.

A pulley is a simple machine. Machines can make work easier to do. One important role of simple machines is to change the direction of an applied force.

FOOD FOR THOUGHT

John 12:32 When you're working with forces, there are only two choices — push and pull. The pulley system you built did a great job of pulling the weight up against the pull of gravity. That's the purpose of a machine.

As followers of Jesus, we also have two choices when it comes to dealing with the people around us. We can push them away by being proud, judgmental, or critical. Or we can help pull them toward Jesus by being kind, thoughtful, and caring. What kind of example are you? Are you a pusher or puller when it comes to people you meet?

JOURNAL **My Science Notes**

84 FORCES

Extended Teaching

1. Repeat this activity, only lubricate the straw "axle" with cooking oil. Have teams compare the results with the original activity. Discuss how friction plays a role.

2. Have teams research historical uses for pulleys (to lift water from a well, to lift hay into a barn, etc.). Challenge each team to create a poster depicting one historic use for a pulley, describing how it worked.

3. Invite an engineer to visit your classroom. Ask him/her to talk about how engineers increase efficiency. Encourage him/her to give examples or show samples. Have students write a paragraph about one thing they learn.

4. Take a field trip to a local factory. Look for ways wheels, axles, and pulleys are used on an assembly line. Discuss what you have seen, then have students write a paragraph about one thing they learned.

5. Sponsor a "Simple Solutions" week. Have each team compile a list of simple machines they find at home and school. At the end of the week, compare lists to see how many "simple solutions" these machines provide.

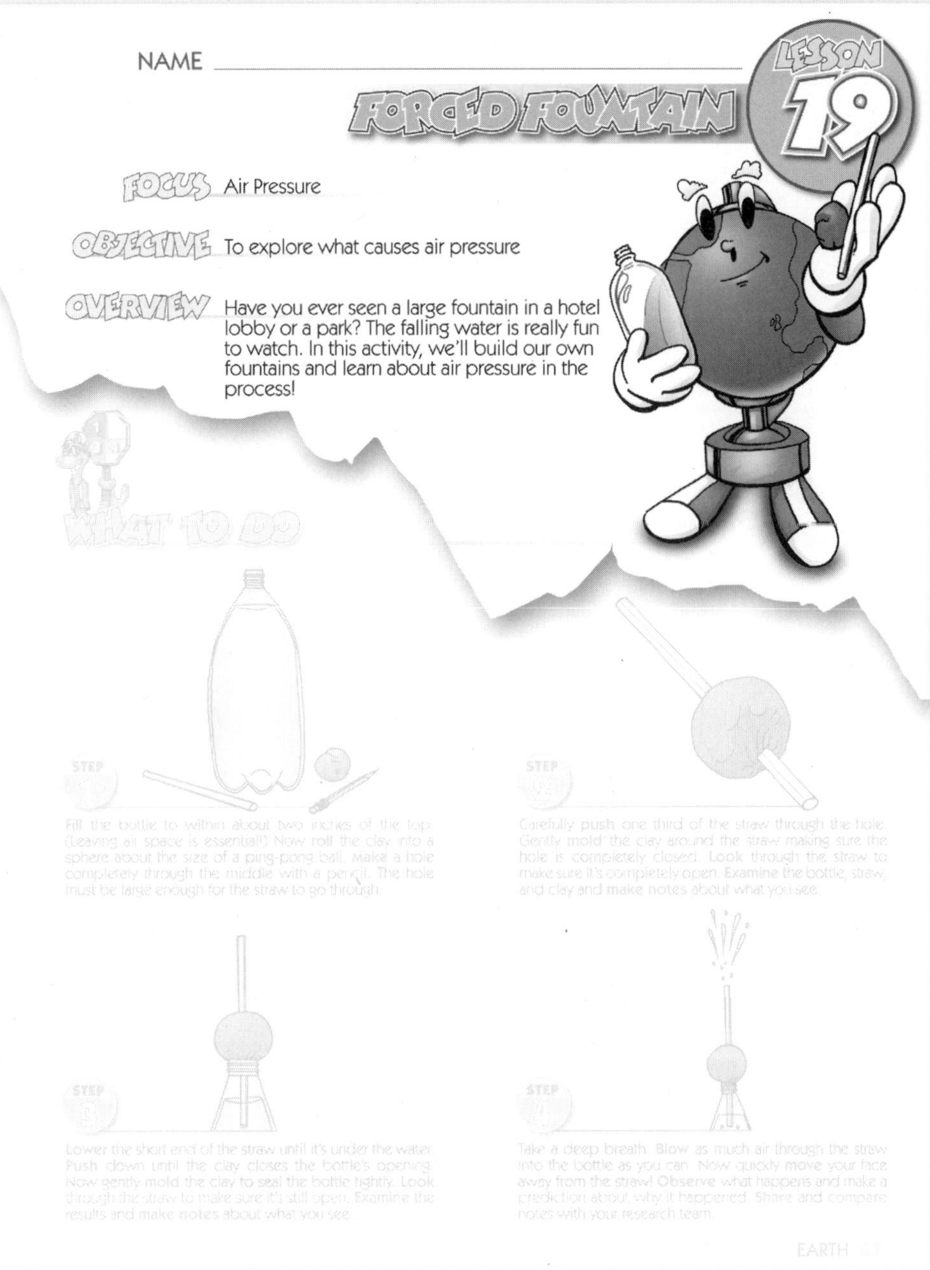
NAME

FORCED FOUNTAIN

LESSON 19

FOCUS Air Pressure

OBJECTIVE To explore what causes air pressure

OVERVIEW Have you ever seen a large fountain in a hotel lobby or a park? The falling water is really fun to watch. In this activity, we'll build our own fountains and learn about air pressure in the process!

WHAT TO DO

STEP 1 Fill the bottle to within about two inches of the top. (Leaving air space is essential!) Now roll the clay into a sphere about the size of a ping-pong ball. Make a hole completely through the middle with a pencil. The hole must be large enough for the straw to go through.

STEP 2 Carefully push one third of the straw through the hole. Gently mold the clay around the straw making sure the hole is completely closed. Look through the straw to make sure it's completely open. Examine the bottle, straw, and clay and make notes about what you see.

STEP 3 Lower the short end of the straw until it's under the water. Push down until the clay closes the bottle's opening. Now gently mold the clay to seal the bottle tightly. Look through the straw to make sure it's still open. Examine the results and make notes about what you see.

STEP 4 Take a deep breath. Blow as much air through the straw into the bottle as you can. Now quickly move your face away from the straw! Observe what happens and make a prediction about why it happened. Share and compare notes with your research team.

EARTH

Additional Comments

To minimize the mess, move this activity outdoors. Remind teams that the clay must seal the bottle and the straw must be below the water surface (see illustration) or the activity will not work. Keep plenty of paper towels on hand for cleanup.

Overview

Read the overview aloud to your students. The goal is to create an atmosphere of curiosity and inquiry.

Category

Earth Science

Focus

Air Pressure

Objective

To explore what causes air pressure

National Standards

A1, A2, B1, B2, B3, D1, G1, G2

Materials Needed

clay
soda straw
soft drink bottle - 2 liter
water
pencil

Safety Concerns

1. Goggles
Goggles are a reasonable precaution for this activity.

3. Hygiene
If students take turns, disinfect or replace straw for each student.

4. Slipping
There is a potential for spills with this activity. Remind students to exercise caution.

WHAT TO DO

Monitor student research teams as they complete each step.

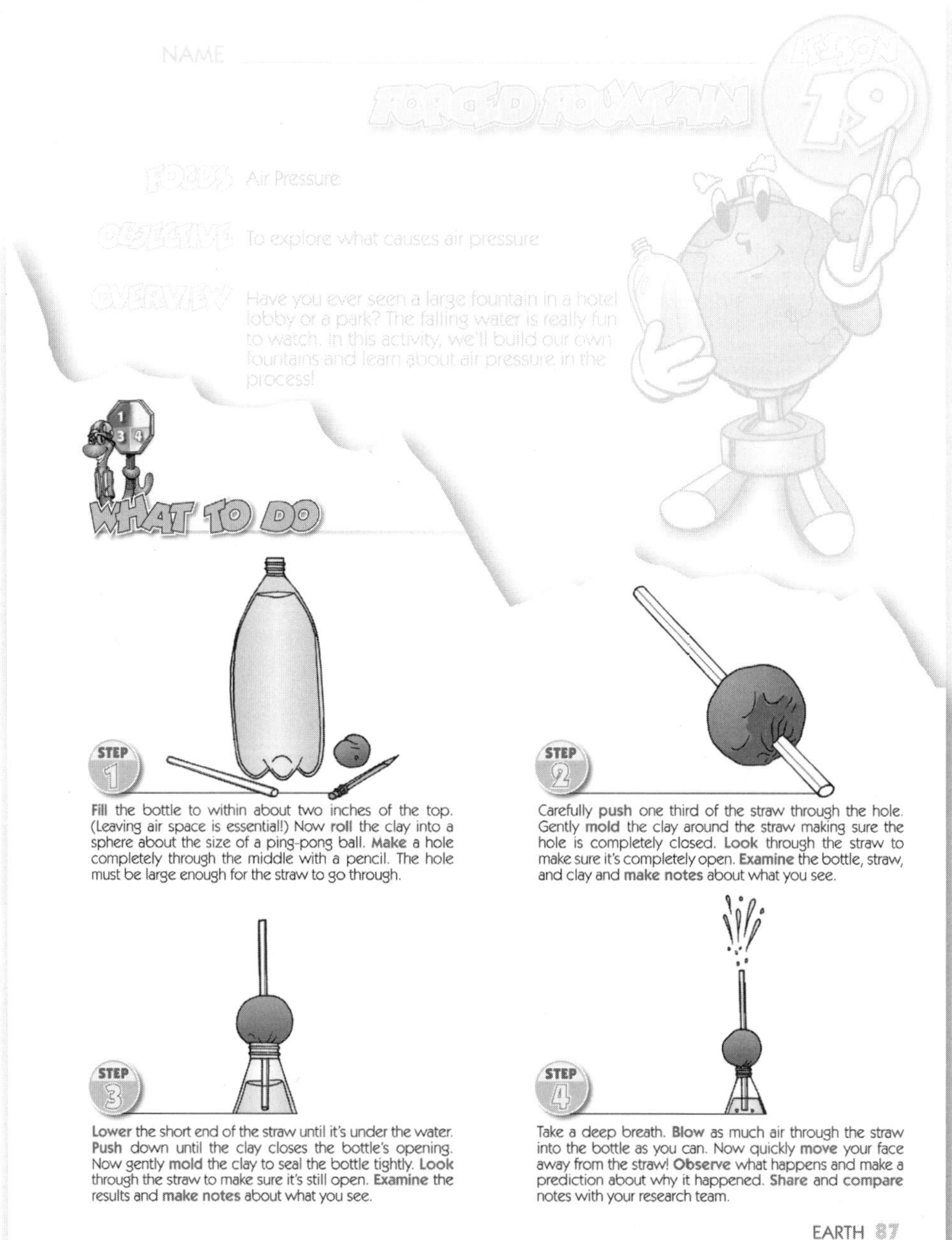

NAME

LESSON 19

FORCED FOUNTAIN

FOCUS Air Pressure

OBJECTIVE To explore what causes air pressure

OVERVIEW Have you ever seen a large fountain in a hotel lobby or a park? The falling water is really fun to watch. In this activity, we'll build our own fountains and learn about air pressure in the process!

WHAT TO DO

STEP 1

Fill the bottle to within about two inches of the top. (Leaving air space is essential!) Now **roll** the clay into a sphere about the size of a ping-pong ball. **Make** a hole completely through the middle with a pencil. The hole must be large enough for the straw to go through.

STEP 2

Carefully **push** one third of the straw through the hole. Gently **mold** the clay around the straw making sure the hole is completely closed. **Look** through the straw to make sure it's completely open. **Examine** the bottle, straw, and clay and **make notes** about what you see.

STEP 3

Lower the short end of the straw until it's under the water. **Push** down until the clay closes the bottle's opening. Now gently **mold** the clay to seal the bottle tightly. **Look** through the straw to make sure it's still open. **Examine** the results and **make notes** about what you see.

STEP 4

Take a deep breath. **Blow** as much air through the straw into the bottle as you can. Now quickly **move** your face away from the straw! **Observe** what happens and make a prediction about why it happened. **Share** and **compare** notes with your research team.

EARTH 87

Teacher to Teacher

Gasses (like air) can be squeezed into a smaller space, creating pressure. Scientists call this compression. Car tires, air tools, and aerosol cans are all examples of compression in action. Liquids (like water) cannot be compressed, which makes them ideal for transmitting forces. Scientists call this process hydraulics. Your circulatory system, a car's power steering, and the plumbing in your house are all forms of hydraulics at work.

Force is needed to make anything move. There's no exception to this rule! In this activity, the force of your lungs was what **pushed** the air. Since your lungs hold more air than there was space for in the bottle, the force **compressed** more **molecules** into less space — something like squeezing an entire football team into a tiny car instead of a large school bus!

Squeezing all those extra molecules into the air space created **pressure**. (Note: The air space in the bottle was necessary because **liquids** like water don't compress like air does.) This made the **air pressure** in the bottle much greater than the pressure outside. As soon as you quit blowing (removing the force), the air pressure quickly shoved the water through the straw and out of the bottle — creating your Forced Fountain!

 **What is needed to make things move? What provided the force for this activity?**

a) force

b) the force of someone's lungs pushing air

 **What was the purpose of the clay? What might have happened without it?**

a) to seal the bottle

b) air would have escaped and no pressure would have built up

 **What might have happened if you completely filled the bottle with water? Why?**

a) answers should reflect the fact that the activity wouldn't work

b) because liquids can't compress

4 **Describe what happened in Step 4. What caused this to occur?**

a) water flew out of the bottle

b) blowing increased pressure in the bottle; releasing the straw let that pressure force water out of the bottle

 **How is pressure on a liquid or gas helpful? Give two examples. What provides the force to create the pressure?**

a) it can create movement

b) car tires, air tools, aerosol cans, household plumbing, power steering, etc.

c) compressed air, your heart beat, etc.

What Happened

Review the section with students. Emphasize bold-face words that identify key concepts and introduce new vocabulary.

Force *is needed to make anything move. There's no exception to this rule! In this activity, the force of your lungs was what* ***pushed*** *the air. Since your lungs hold more air than there was space for in the bottle, the force* ***compressed*** *more* ***molecules*** *into less space — something like squeezing an entire football team into a tiny car instead of a large school bus!*

Squeezing all those extra molecules into the air space created ***pressure****. (Note: The air space in the bottle was necessary because* ***liquids*** *like water don't compress like air does.) This made the* ***air pressure*** *in the bottle much greater than the pressure outside. As soon as you quit blowing (removing the force), the air pressure quickly shoved the water through the straw and out of the bottle — creating your Forced Fountain!*

What We Learned

Answers will vary. Suggested responses are shown at left.

Conclusion

Read this section aloud to the class to summarize the concepts learned in this activity.

Food for Thought

Read the Scripture aloud to the class. Talk about God's great power and abundant goodness. Discuss ways we can share God's love with others.

Journal

If time permits, have a general class discussion about notes and drawings various students added to their journal pages. Discuss correct and incorrect predictions, and remind students that this "trial and error" process is part of the scientific process.

Force can be used to compress air. Compressed air has pressure. Liquids like water can't be compressed, but they can help transfer force from one place to another.

Psalm 23:5 Sometimes something is so full that it just can't contain itself. With a little help from your lungs, your Forced Fountain had an abundance of air, and the pressure made it overflow!

Scripture reminds us of God's great power and abundant goodness. Just like the fountain, God's blessings fill us with more than we can contain. All the many blessings in our lives come from God. Just like your overflowing fountain, you should share your abundant blessings with others!

JOURNAL **My Science Notes**

90 EARTH

Extended Teaching

1. Repeat this activity, but try starting with different amounts of air space in the bottle. Have teams compare the results with the original activity.

2. Using the Internet, have teams research aerosol cans to discover how pressure helps them function. Challenge each team to create a poster depicting and describing how they work, and some of the products they contain.

3. Discuss environmental hazards from traditional aerosol cans. Take a field trip to a grocery store. Challenge teams to find products that are available in both aerosol and pump versions. Compare prices.

4. Have each team make a list of common items with trapped air. Share and compare lists and discuss how air pressure can be helpful.

5. Take a field trip to a construction site. Ask the contractor to demonstrate various air tools and how they work. Have students write a paragraph about one thing they learn.

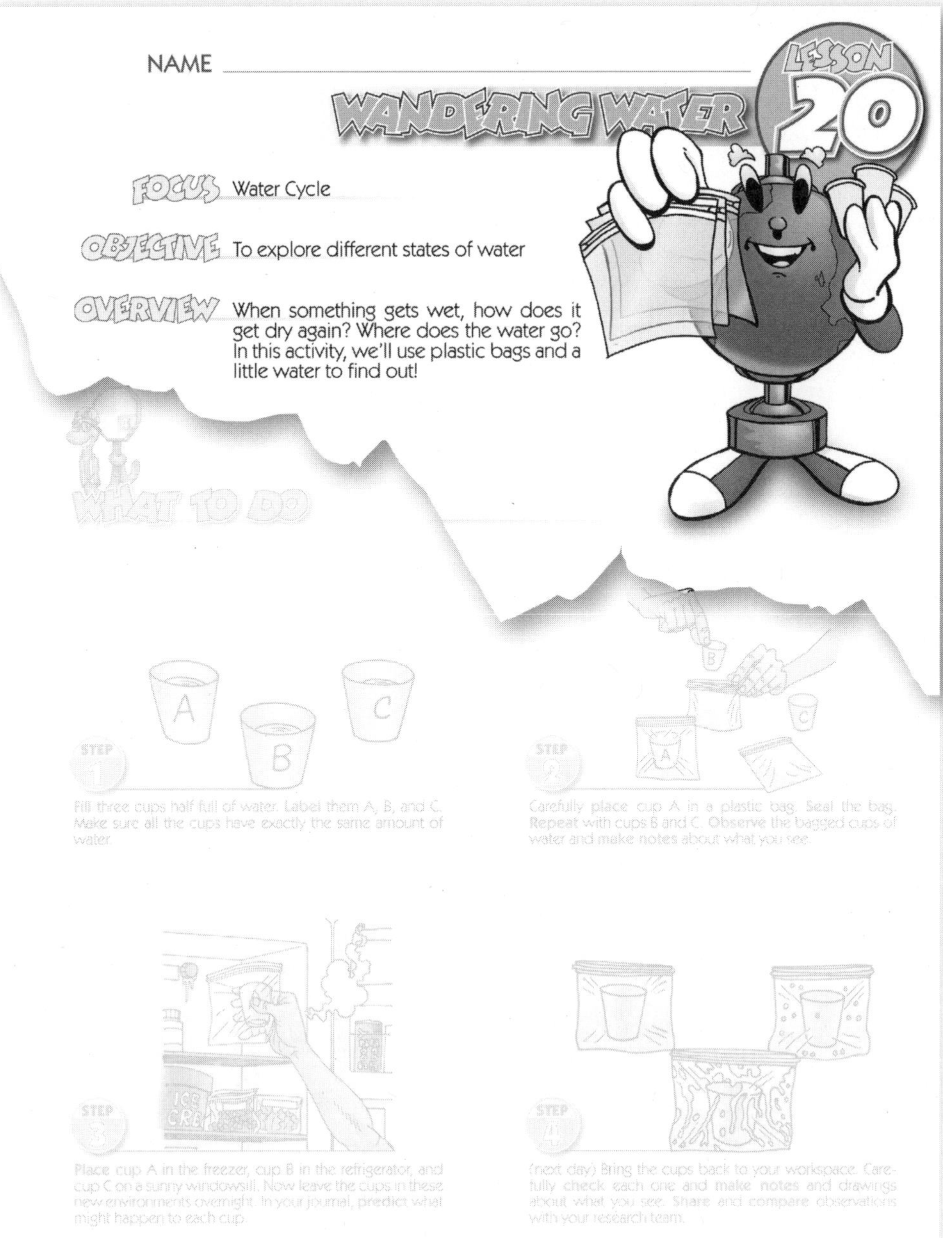

NAME

WANDERING WATER

LESSON 20

FOCUS Water Cycle

OBJECTIVE To explore different states of water

OVERVIEW When something gets wet, how does it get dry again? Where does the water go? In this activity, we'll use plastic bags and a little water to find out!

WHAT TO DO

STEP 1 Fill three cups half full of water. Label them A, B, and C. Make sure all the cups have exactly the same amount of water.

STEP 2 Carefully place cup A in a plastic bag. Seal the bag. Repeat with cups B and C. Observe the bagged cups of water and make notes about what you see.

STEP 3 Place cup A in the freezer, cup B in the refrigerator, and cup C on a sunny windowsill. Now leave the cups in these new environments overnight. In your journal, predict what might happen to each cup.

STEP 4 (next day) Bring the cups back to your workspace. Carefully check each one and make notes and drawings about what you see. Share and compare observations with your research team.

EARTH

Category

Earth Science

Focus

Water Cycle

Objective

To explore different states of water

National Standards

A1, A2, B1, B2, B3, D1, G1, G2

Materials Needed

paper cups - 3
plastic bags (sealable)
marker
water
refrigerator/freezer

Safety Concerns

4. Slipping
There is a potential for spills with this activity. Remind students to exercise caution.

Additional Comments

Make sure cups don't spill as bags are moved to their locations. To avoid accidents, you may want to place the bags in the freezer. Each sealed bag models a miniature atmosphere. The processes are similar to what happens in the "sea of air" that surrounds us on Earth.

Overview

Read the overview aloud to your students. The goal is to create an atmosphere of curiosity and inquiry.

WHAT TO DO

Monitor student research teams as they complete each step.

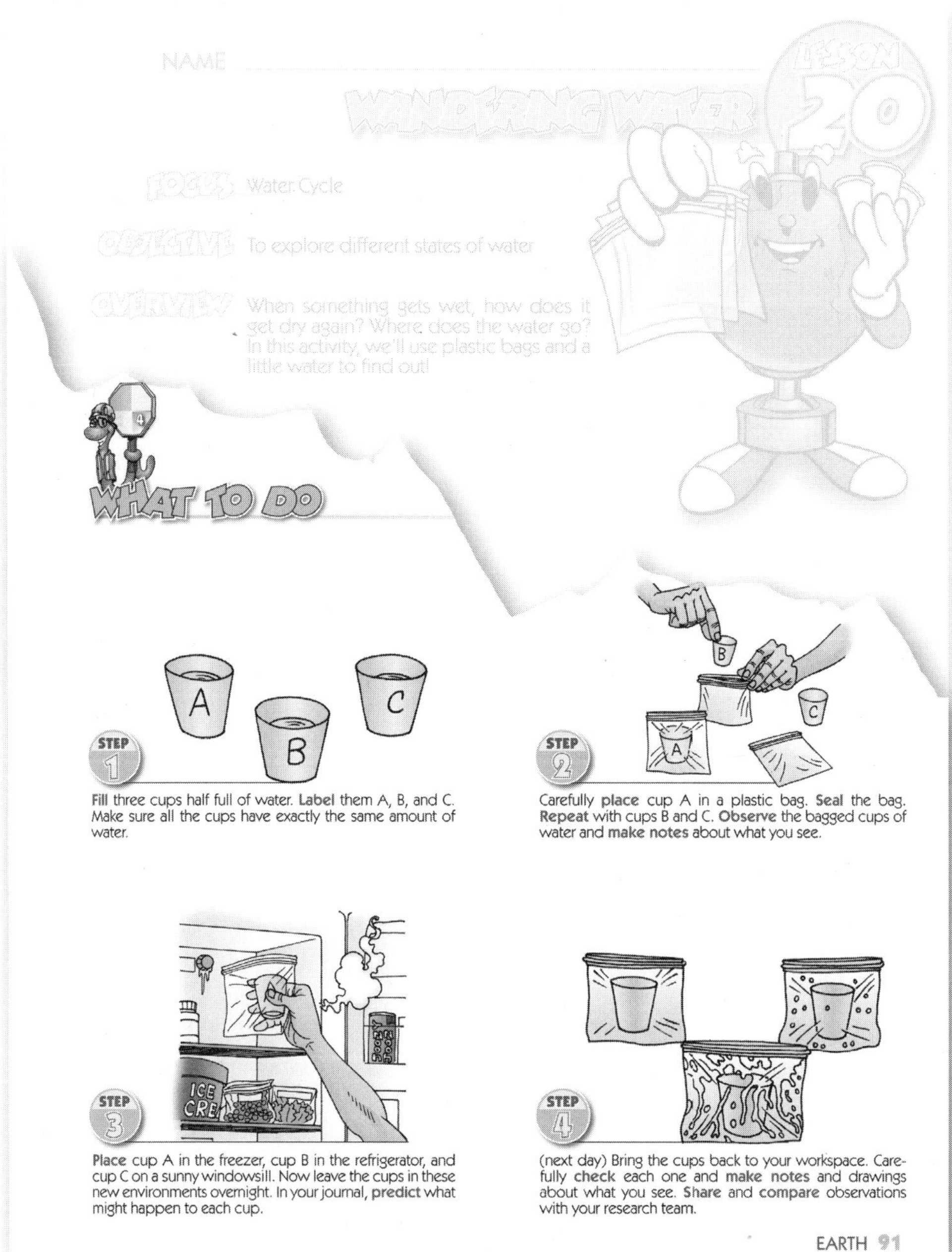

NAME

WANDERING WATER

LESSON 20

FOCUS Water Cycle

OBJECTIVE To explore different states of water

OVERVIEW When something gets wet, how does it get dry again? Where does the water go? In this activity, we'll use plastic bags and a little water to find out!

WHAT TO DO

STEP 1

Fill three cups half full of water. **Label** them A, B, and C. Make sure all the cups have exactly the same amount of water.

STEP 2

Carefully **place** cup A in a plastic bag. **Seal** the bag. **Repeat** with cups B and C. **Observe** the bagged cups of water and **make notes** about what you see.

STEP 3

Place cup A in the freezer, cup B in the refrigerator, and cup C on a sunny windowsill. Now leave the cups in these new environments overnight. In your journal, **predict** what might happen to each cup.

STEP 4

(next day) Bring the cups back to your workspace. Carefully **check** each one and **make notes** and drawings about what you see. **Share** and **compare** observations with your research team.

EARTH 91

Teacher to Teacher

Earth's water cycle helps keep water and energy balanced around the planet. Solar energy is intense near the equator. Without wind and ocean currents to disperse this energy, the tropics would experience constant, violent hurricanes, and the rest of Earth would be left with little or no rain!

Your bags of water **simulated** what happens to the water in Earth's **atmosphere** under different conditions. Cup C received lots of **energy** from the sun. This caused the water to **evaporate**, changing the water **molecules** from a **liquid** to a **gas**. Some of these gas particles bumped the bag's cooler sides, causing them to slow down, lose energy, and turn back into a liquid. (Scientists call this process **condensation**.) Eventually enough water molecules condensed to form a drop of water, and some of these drops fell as a result of **gravity**. This is a good model of the **water cycle** of Earth.

Notice that this cycle wasn't nearly as active in the bag holding Cup B. There was almost no condensation at all with Cup A! So what was missing? The energy force driving the entire process — **heat** and **light energy** from the sun! The process is similar on Earth's surface. Colder air is usually dryer since the water cycle isn't nearly as active.

Why was labeling the cups important? Why do scientists carefully label their experiments?

a) to keep the cups from getting mixed up

b) so their evaluations are precise and accurate

2 Why was it important to keep all the bags shut tightly? What problems might a leak have caused?

a) so each bag was a sealed environment

b) it might allow outside air in the bag and vice versa

Describe your predictions in Step 3. How did they reflect what happened in Step 4?

Answers will vary, but should reflect logical comparisons.

Describe any physical changes you noticed in each bag in Step 4. How were they similar? How were they different?

Cup A: block of ice in cup
Cup B: a few water drops on the bag
Cup C: bag filled with water drops

What were the three states of water shown in this activity? Give an everyday example of each.

a) solid, liquid, gas

b) solid: ice cubes; liquid: a lake or stream; gas: fog or clouds (or similar examples)

What Happened

Review the section with students. Emphasize bold-face words that identify key concepts and introduce new vocabulary.

Your bags of water ***simulated*** *what happens to the water in Earth's* ***atmosphere*** *under different conditions. Cup C received lots of* ***energy*** *from the sun. This caused the water to* ***evaporate****, changing the water* ***molecules*** *from a* ***liquid*** *to a* ***gas****. Some of these gas particles bumped the bag's cooler sides, causing them to slow down, lose energy, and turn back into a liquid. (Scientists call this process* ***condensation****.) Eventually enough water molecules condensed to form a drop of water, and some of these drops fell as a result of* ***gravity****. This is a good model of the* ***water cycle*** *of Earth.*

Notice that this cycle wasn't nearly as active in the bag holding Cup B. There was almost no condensation at all with Cup A! So what was missing? The energy force driving the entire process — ***heat*** *and* ***light energy*** *from the sun! The process is similar on the Earth's surface. Colder air is usually drier since the water cycle isn't nearly as active.*

What We Learned

Answers will vary. Suggested responses are shown at left.

Conclusion

Read this section aloud to the class to summarize the concepts learned in this activity.

Food for Thought

Read the Scripture aloud to the class. Talk about how our souls need God's "living water" to survive. Discuss ways we can "drink" this living water every day.

Journal

If time permits, have a general class discussion about notes and drawings various students added to their journal pages. Discuss correct and incorrect predictions, and remind students that this "trial and error" process is part of the scientific process.

Water evaporates and condenses, freezes and thaws. These physical changes are part of the water cycle that distributes life-sustaining water around the planet. The energy for this process is provided by the sun.

John 4:4-10 As we saw in this activity, water on Earth is constantly moving in an ongoing recycling process. Since water is essential to our survival, it's a process that helps keep us alive!

In this Scripture, Jesus talks about a different kind of water that's also essential for survival. In fact, it's so essential that he called it "living" water! Just as our bodies can't survive without physical water, so our souls can't survive without this living water which is the power of God in our lives. Remember, you take a big drink of God's living water every time you study and follow his Word.

JOURNAL **My Science Notes**

94 EARTH

Extended Teaching

1. Repeat this activity using salt water. Have teams compare the results with the original activity. What conclusions can be drawn?

2. Repeat the "sunshine" portion of this activity with two bags: one clear, one black. Open the bags after a day in the sun. Compare the results. What conclusions can be drawn?

3. Conduct a "cycle safari." Have teams watch for and record examples of evaporation and condensation at home and school. At the end of the week have each team share their findings. Discuss the results.

4. Invite a greenhouse operator to visit your classroom. Discuss the role evaporation and condensation play in proper greenhouse management. Have students write a paragraph about one thing they learn.

5. Take a field trip to a local television station. Ask the meteorologist to explain how the water cycle affects local weather patterns. Challenge teams to create a poster depicting one thing they learn.

NAME

MINIATURE GLACIER

LESSON 21

FOCUS Glaciers

OBJECTIVE To explore one way glaciers affect Earth's surface

OVERVIEW Some glaciers are miles long and hundreds of feet thick! What effect do these huge blocks of ice have on land? In this activity, you may find some surprising answers!

WHAT TO DO

STEP 1 Fill the container with water to within one inch of the top. Now write "North America" on the top surface of the board. Predict what might happen when you set the board in the water.

STEP 2 Gently set the board on the surface of the water (label up). As it floats, observe how much is above the surface of the water and how much is below. Record the results. Now remove the board and mark the water line. Dry the board overnight.

STEP 3 (next day) Carefully set two ice cubes on top of the board. Gently set the board in the water again. As it floats, observe how much is above the surface of the water and how much is below. Compare this to yesterday's level.

STEP 4 Predict what might happen as the ice melts. Observe the block at the end of the day to check your prediction. Make notes about what you see. Share and compare observations with your research team tomorrow.

EARTH 93

Category
Earth Science

Focus
Glaciers

Objective
To explore one way glaciers affect Earth's surface

National Standards
A1, A2, B1, B2, B3, D1, D2, G1, G2

Materials Needed
block of wood
bucket
water
waterproof marker
ice cubes - 2

Safety Concerns
4. Slipping
There is a potential for spills with this activity. Remind students to exercise caution.

Additional Comments
Placing the ice cubes in the center of the board requires a study hand. You may need to assist some teams. A large rubber band can also be helpful. Temperature and humidity will affect how long it takes the ice to melt. The difference in the two marks (with and without ice) will be small, but should still be noticeable.

Overview
Read the overview aloud to your students. The goal is to create an atmosphere of curiosity and inquiry.

WHAT TO DO

Monitor student research teams as they complete each step.

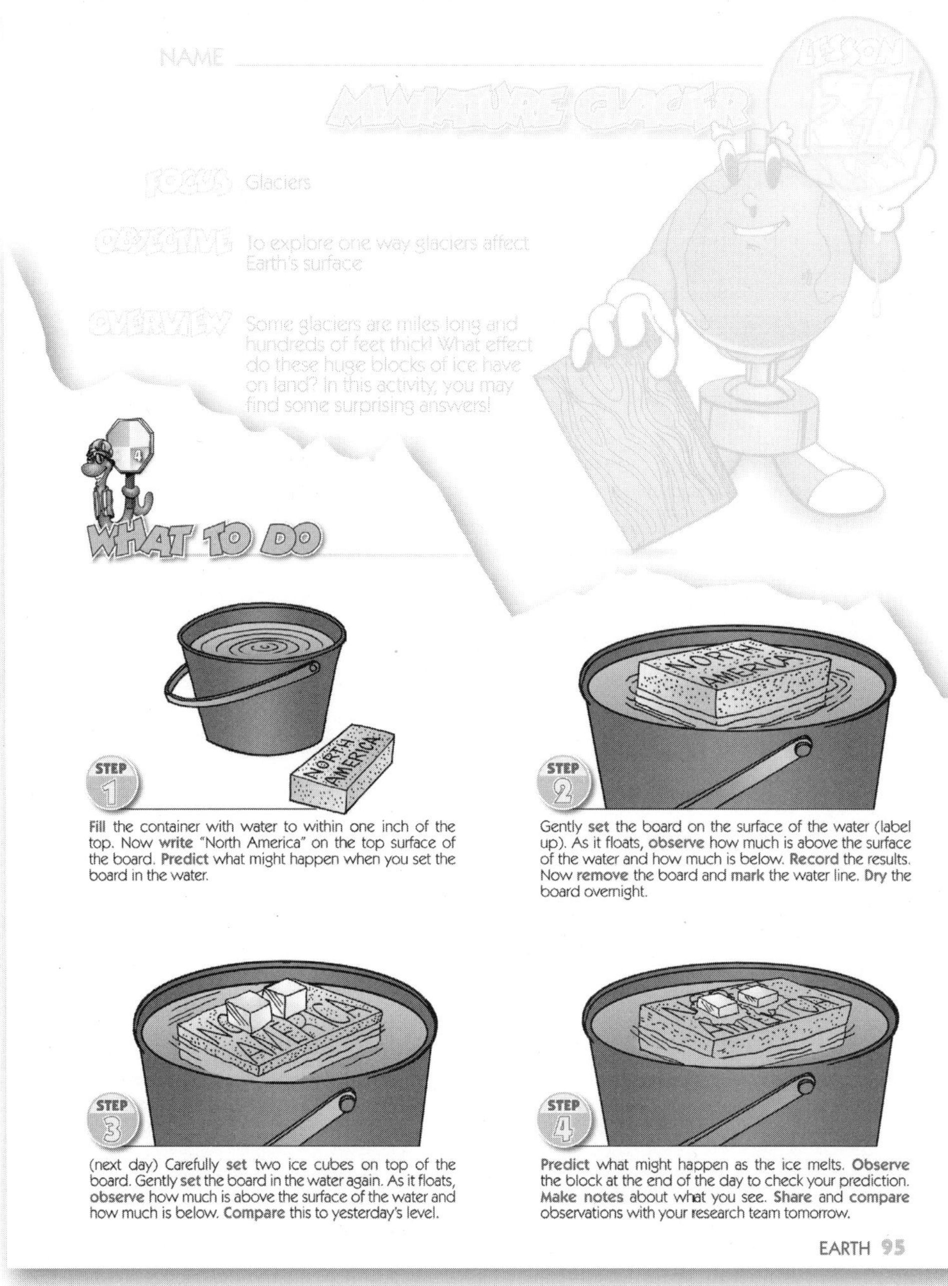

NAME ______________________

LESSON 21

MINIATURE GLACIER

FOCUS Glaciers

OBJECTIVE To explore one way glaciers affect Earth's surface

OVERVIEW Some glaciers are miles long and hundreds of feet thick! What effect do these huge blocks of ice have on land? In this activity, you may find some surprising answers!

WHAT TO DO

STEP 1
Fill the container with water to within one inch of the top. Now **write** "North America" on the top surface of the board. **Predict** what might happen when you set the board in the water.

STEP 2
Gently **set** the board on the surface of the water (label up). As it floats, **observe** how much is above the surface of the water and how much is below. **Record** the results. Now **remove** the board and **mark** the water line. **Dry** the board overnight.

STEP 3
(next day) Carefully **set** two ice cubes on top of the board. Gently **set** the board in the water again. As it floats, **observe** how much is above the surface of the water and how much is below. **Compare** this to yesterday's level.

STEP 4
Predict what might happen as the ice melts. **Observe** the block at the end of the day to check your prediction. **Make notes** about what you see. **Share** and **compare** observations with your research team tomorrow.

EARTH 95

Teacher to Teacher

Glacier science has its own unique vocabulary. The transition between snow and glacier ice is called "firn." A growing glacier has "a positive budget," while a shrinking glacier has "a negative budget." When a glacier reaches the sea, its erosion is called "ablation." For more vocabulary fun, challenge students to research the term "galloping glacier"!

The average block of ice (the kind convenience stores sell) weighs about fifteen pounds. Imagine the **weight** of a block of ice almost a mile square! Currently **glaciers** cover about 10 percent of the Earth's land area. In one spot, the ice mass in Antarctica is over two and a half miles thick! Scientists tell us the weight of all that ice has pushed part of Antarctica's land over a mile below sea level.

But how can anything (even a heavy glacier) **push** down solid land? The **crust** (outer layer) of Earth is actually "floating" on the **mantle** (layer beneath it) which is made of hot, semi-melted rock. Look at your model: Water in your pool (mantle) held the board up (crust) but your mini-glacier (ice cubes) pushed the board down. As the "glacier" melted, losing weight, the board (crust) began to rise. This is what happens with glaciers and continents, too!

WHAT WE LEARNED

1. **Which layer of the Earth do you think the water represents in step 1?**

The water represents Earth's mantle, a layer of hot, semi-melted rock.

2. **Which layer of the Earth do you think the board represents in step 2? Why does the board float higher in step 2 than step 3?**

a) the board represents the crust

b) in Step 3, the board has the added weight of the ice

3. **What were your predictions in step 3 for the block of ice and board?**

Answers will vary, but should reflect logical comparisons.

4. **What did you observe happening to the block of ice and the board in step 4?**

As the ice melted, the board floated higher.

5. **What do you think caused the changes you observed in step 4? On a map, locate a glacier. What is the glacier you found called?**

a) answers should reflect factors like temperature, buoyancy, etc.

b) answers will vary

What Happened

Review the section with students. Emphasize bold-face words that identify key concepts and introduce new vocabulary.

*The average block of ice (the kind convenience stores sell) weighs about fifteen pounds. Imagine the **weight** of a block of ice almost a square mile! Currently **glaciers** cover about 10% of the Earth's land area. In one spot, the ice mass in Antarctica is over two and a half miles thick! Scientists tell us the weight of all that ice has pushed part of Antarctica's land over a mile below sea level.*

*But how can anything (even a heavy glacier) **push** down solid land? The **crust** (outer layer) of Earth is actually "floating" on the **mantle** (layer beneath it) which is made of hot, semi-melted rock. Look at your model: Water in your pool (mantle) held the board up (crust), but your mini-glacier (ice cubes) pushed the board down. As the "glacier" melted, losing weight, the board (crust) began to rise. This is what happens with glaciers and continents, too!*

What We Learned

Answers will vary. Suggested responses are shown at left.

Conclusion

Read this section aloud to the class to summarize the concepts learned in this activity.

Food for Thought

Read the Scripture aloud to the class. Talk about how God is always there for us, no matter how difficult the circumstances. Discuss ways we can learn to trust God more fully.

Journal

If time permits, have a general class discussion about notes and drawings various students added to their journal pages. Discuss correct and incorrect predictions, and remind students that this "trial and error" process is part of the scientific process.

Glaciers are huge blocks of ice. Their massive weight forces the crust of the Earth downward into the mantle. As glaciers melt, the land beneath them begins to rise.

James 4:10 It's hard to imagine the massive weight of a glacier — something so huge and heavy that it is literally pushing the ground down beneath it!

Yet some days our problems seem a lot like that. We feel like the weight of the whole world is resting on our shoulders. Like a heavy glacier, we sink deeper into the dark pit of despair.

But Scripture reminds us that God is there to lift us up. As we get to know God and learn to trust him, he will encourage us and give us the help we need.

JOURNAL **My Science Notes**

98 EARTH

Extended Teaching

1. Repeat this activity outdoors using a 2x8 and ice block made in a milk carton. Float your glacier in a wading pool. Have students compare the results with the original activity.

2. Have students research glaciers around the world. Challenge each team to "adopt" a specific glacier, then create a poster with its name, a map of its location, and information that describes it.

3. Visit an ice plant. Find out how ice is made and its various uses. Have students write a paragraph about one thing they learn.

4. Invite a geologist to visit your classroom. Talk about the impact ancient glaciers had on America's landscape. (If you live in the Northern U.S., visit some of these spots!) Have students write a paragraph about one thing they learn.

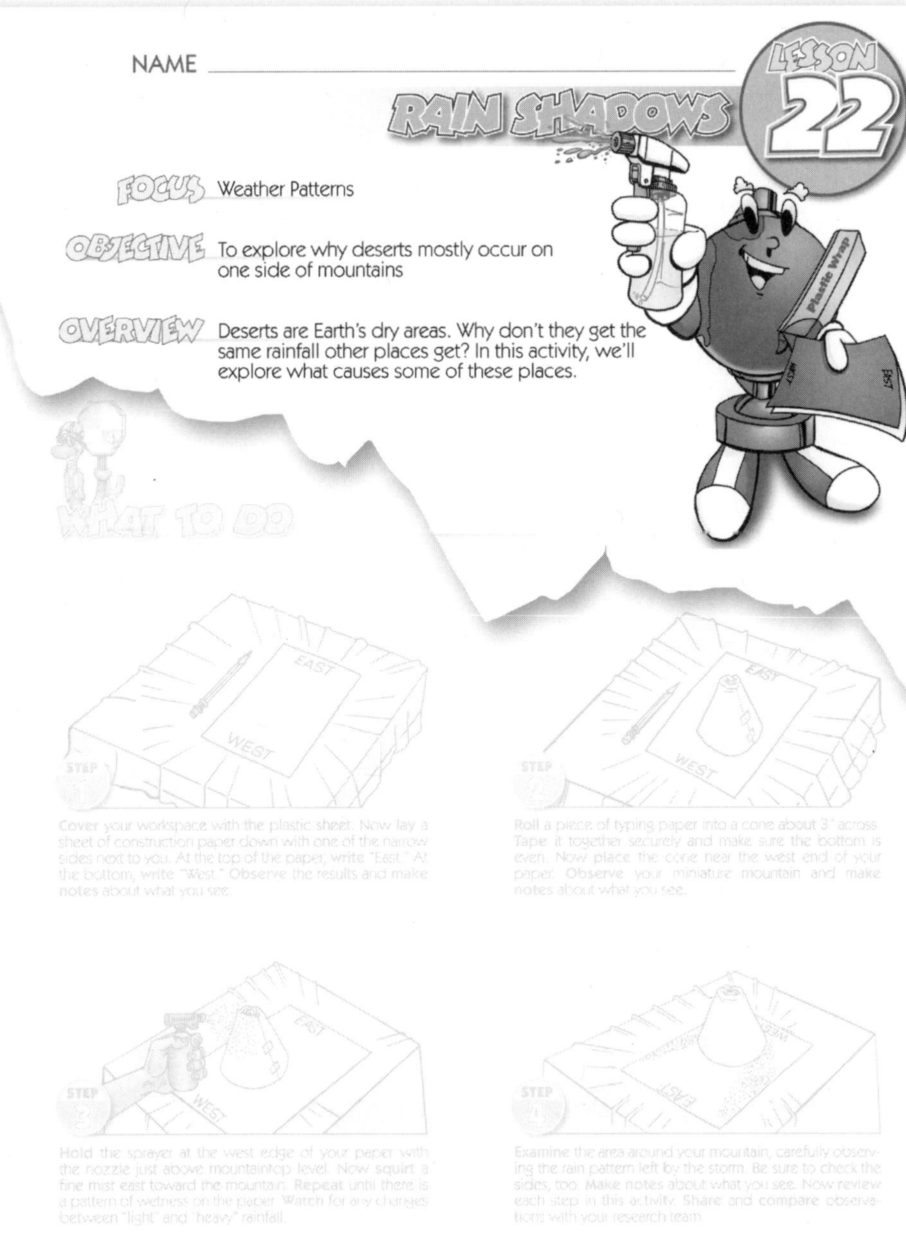
NAME

RAIN SHADOWS

LESSON 22

FOCUS Weather Patterns

OBJECTIVE To explore why deserts mostly occur on one side of mountains

OVERVIEW Deserts are Earth's dry areas. Why don't they get the same rainfall other places get? In this activity, we'll explore what causes some of these places.

WHAT TO DO

STEP 1 Cover your workspace with the plastic sheet. Now lay a sheet of construction paper down with one of the narrow sides next to you. At the top of the paper, write "East." At the bottom, write "West." Observe the results and make notes about what you see.

STEP 2 Roll a piece of typing paper into a cone about 3" across. Tape it together securely and make sure the bottom is even. Now place the cone near the west end of your paper. Observe your miniature mountain and make notes about what you see.

STEP 3 Hold the sprayer at the west edge of your paper with the nozzle just above mountaintop level. Now squirt a fine mist east toward the mountain. Repeat until there is a pattern of wetness on the paper. Watch for any changes between "light" and "heavy" rainfall.

STEP 4 Examine the area around your mountain, carefully observing the rain pattern left by the storm. Be sure to check the sides, too. Make notes about what you see. Now review each step in this activity. Share and compare observations with your research team.

EARTH

Category

Earth Science

Focus

Weather Patterns

Objective

To explore why deserts mostly occur on one side of mountains

National Standards

A1, A2, B1, B2, B3, C1, C4, D1, G1, G2

Materials Needed

plastic sheet
construction paper
typing paper
tape
spray bottle
water

Safety Concerns

4. Slipping
There is a potential for spills with this activity. Remind students to exercise caution.

Additional Comments

Monitor to make sure teams do not use too much water. Once a clear pattern emerges, they should stop using the spray bottle.

Overview

Read the overview aloud to your students. The goal is to create an atmosphere of curiosity and inquiry.

WHAT TO DO

Monitor student research teams as they complete each step.

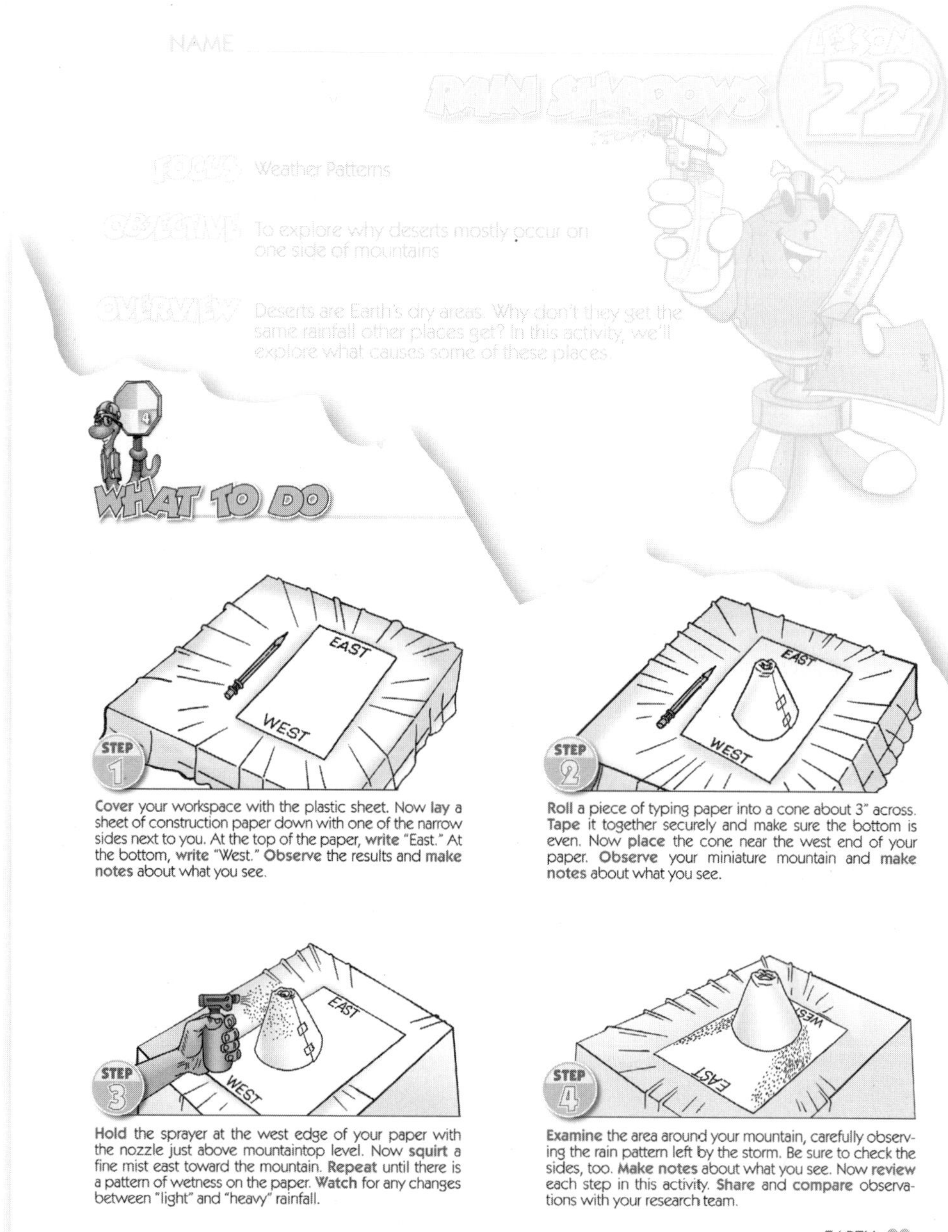

Teacher to Teacher

A desert is defined as an area with less than 10 inches of annual precipitation, which can be rain, dew, fog, snow, or any other moisture form. It's important to note that temperature is not a factor! Many parts of the arctic circle are considered desert because they get little snow. Deserts are such unique habitats that they're classified as a "biome" — an area that has its own specific climate, plants, and animals.

The paper cone represents the **mountains**, and the sprayer represents **moisture-laden winds.** Moist, warm air traveling east hits mountains, is **pushed** up the slopes, and then runs into cold air at the higher elevations. The cold air causes **condensation** (see Lesson 20) resulting in **precipitation** in the form of rain or snow.

Notice that most of the moisture ended up on the west side of the mountains. The dry area you observed on the east side reflects the **rain shadow** created by the Rockies and similar mountains.

Weather patterns in the U.S. (including most storm systems) move primarily from the west to the east. Using a map, locate the **deserts** of the United States. Notice that they are all east of the Rocky Mountains and other western **mountain ranges.**

1. **What did the paper cone represent? What did the sprayer represent? Why were the direction labels important?**

a) a mountain

b) moisture-laden winds

c) to show the direction the winds were blowing

2. **Describe the movement of most U.S. weather systems. What effect does this have on the climate near mountains?**

a) from west to east

b) wet on the west, dry on the east

3. **What is the dry area on the leeward side of a mountain called? Name two such areas. (Use a map if needed.)**

a) a rain shadow

b) answers will vary (ie: Death Valley, Palm Springs, Mojave, etc.)

4. **If the prevailing winds were from the east (as in Maui, Hawaii) which side of the island would have the most rain? Why?**

a) the east

b) because that's the way the moisture is coming from

5. **If you were going to open a ski resort in Colorado, which side of the mountain might be the best place to build? Why?**

a) high on the western slopes

b) high for cold air, west for most moisture

What Happened

Review the section with students. Emphasize bold-face words that identify key concepts and introduce new vocabulary.

*The paper cone represents the **mountains**, and the sprayer represents **moisture-laden winds**. Moist, warm air traveling east hits mountains, is **pushed** up the slopes, and then runs into cold air at the higher elevations. The cold air causes **condensation** (see Lesson 20) resulting in **precipitation** in the form of rain or snow.*

*Notice that most of the moisture ended up on the west side of the mountains. The dry area you observed on the east side reflects the **rain shadow** created by the Rockies and similar mountains.*

***Weather patterns** in the U.S. (including most storm systems) move primarily from the west to the east. Using a map, locate the **deserts** of the United States. Notice that they are all east of the Rocky Mountains and other western **mountain ranges**.*

What We Learned

Answers will vary. Suggested responses are shown at left.

Conclusion

Read this section aloud to the class to summarize the concepts learned in this activity.

Food for Thought

Read the Scripture aloud to the class. Talk about how our lives can be dry and barren without God. Discuss ways we can keep this from happening.

Journal

If time permits, have a general class discussion about notes and drawings various students added to their journal pages. Discuss correct and incorrect predictions, and remind students that this "trial and error" process is part of the scientific process.

Deserts are formed in the rain shadow of mountains. As moisture-laden air comes from the ocean, the cold mountain air acts as a barrier. Most of the moisture gets dumped on the mountain side that faces the prevailing wind.

James 5:17-18 Rain shadows are desert-like areas where little rain falls. Without rain, few plants grow. Without plants, animals can't survive. Without plants or animals, people perish! This Scripture talks of a time when Elijah created an unusual kind of rain shadow. He asked God to stop the rain, making the land into a desert. Then a few years later, Elijah asked God to let the rain return, and the land flourished.

Sometimes our lives are dry and barren. We don't spend time with God, and our souls dry up from the lack of living water. When we allow Jesus back into our lives, our lives can once again grow strong!

JOURNAL **My Science Notes**

102 EARTH

Extended Teaching

1. Invite a meteorologist to visit your classroom. Discuss rain shadows and how they affect regional weather. Find out if there are any similar weather patterns in your area. Have students write a paragraph about one thing they learn.

2. Have teams research areas of the U.S. that rely on irrigation. How do these relate to the location of mountains? Challenge each team to create a poster with a map and descriptions of one such area.

3. Using newspapers or the Internet, follow a weather system across the U.S. Focus on a system that has storms or significant moisture. Plot the amounts and locations of rainfall, especially on both sides of the Rockies.

4. Visit a large agricultural operation (farm, greenhouse, vegetable grower, etc.). Find out how water plays a role in this operation. Have students write a paragraph about one thing they learn.

5. Have teams research water conservation. Challenge each team to make a presentation to the class about something they learn.

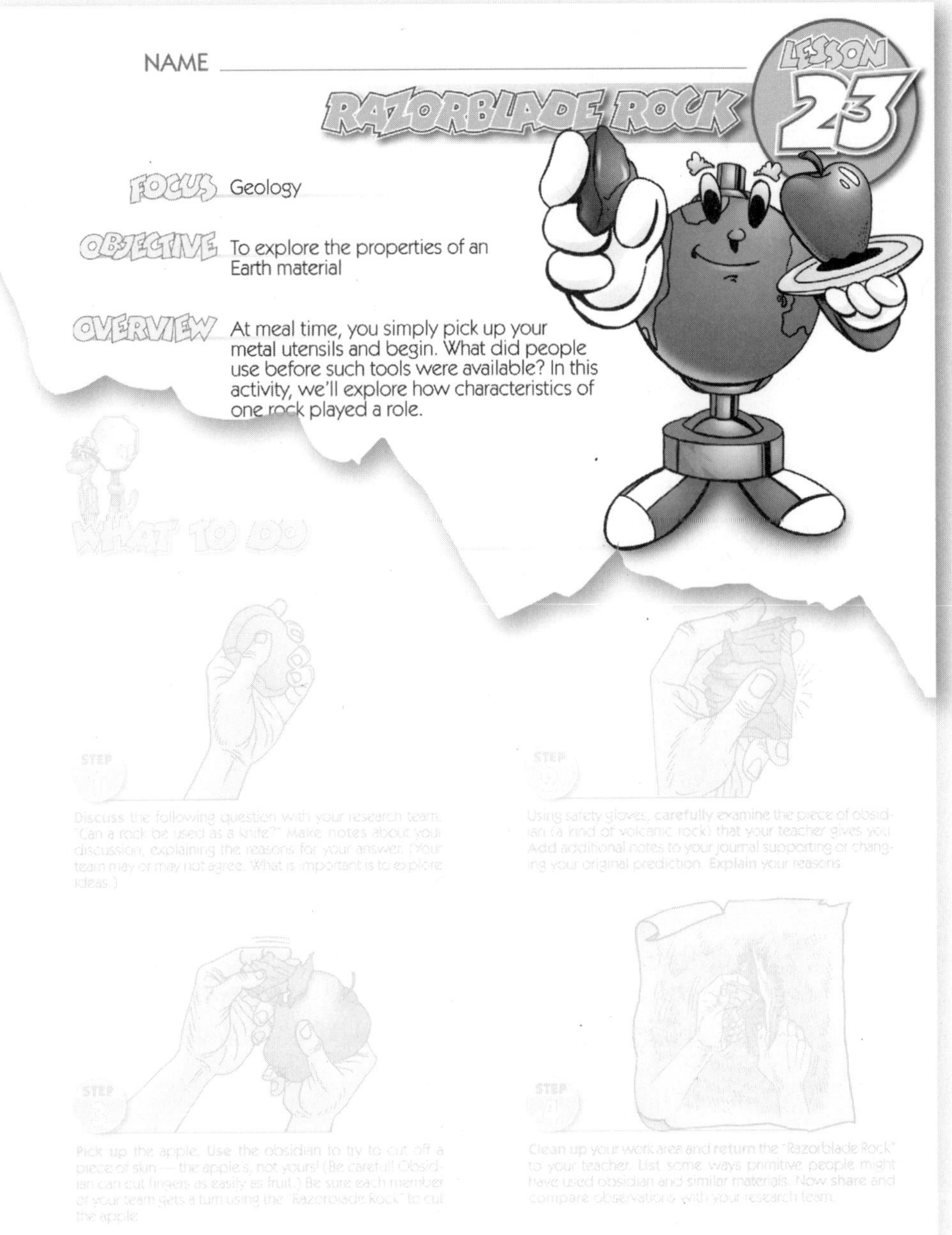

NAME ______________________

LESSON 23

RAZORBLADE ROCK

FOCUS Geology

OBJECTIVE To explore the properties of an Earth material

OVERVIEW At meal time, you simply pick up your metal utensils and begin. What did people use before such tools were available? In this activity, we'll explore how characteristics of one rock played a role.

WHAT TO DO

STEP 1
Discuss the following question with your research team: "Can a rock be used as a knife?" Make notes about your discussion, explaining the reasons for your answer. (Your team may or may not agree. What is important is to explore ideas.)

STEP 2
Using safety gloves, carefully examine the piece of obsidian (a kind of volcanic rock) that your teacher gives you. Add additional notes to your journal supporting or changing your original prediction. Explain your reasons.

STEP 3
Pick up the apple. Use the obsidian to try to cut off a piece of skin — the apple's, not yours! (Be careful! Obsidian can cut fingers as easily as fruit.) Be sure each member of your team gets a turn using the "Razorblade Rock" to cut the apple.

STEP 4
Clean up your work area and return the "Razorblade Rock" to your teacher. List some ways primitive people might have used obsidian and similar materials. Now share and compare observations with your research team.

EARTH

Category
Earth Science

Focus
Geology

Objective
To explore the properties of an Earth material

National Standards
A1, A2, B1, B2, D1, D2, E1, G1, G2

Materials Needed
obsidian
gloves
apple

Safety Concerns
4. Sharp Objects
Obsidian can be as sharp as a knife. Remind students to exercise caution.

Additional Comments
Obsidian is much sharper than it appears! Historically it has been used for spears, arrow points, and knives. Even today, some forms are used for specialized scalpels. Monitor students carefully throughout this activity.

Overview
Read the overview aloud to your students. The goal is to create an atmosphere of curiosity and inquiry.

WHAT TO DO

Monitor student research teams as they complete each step.

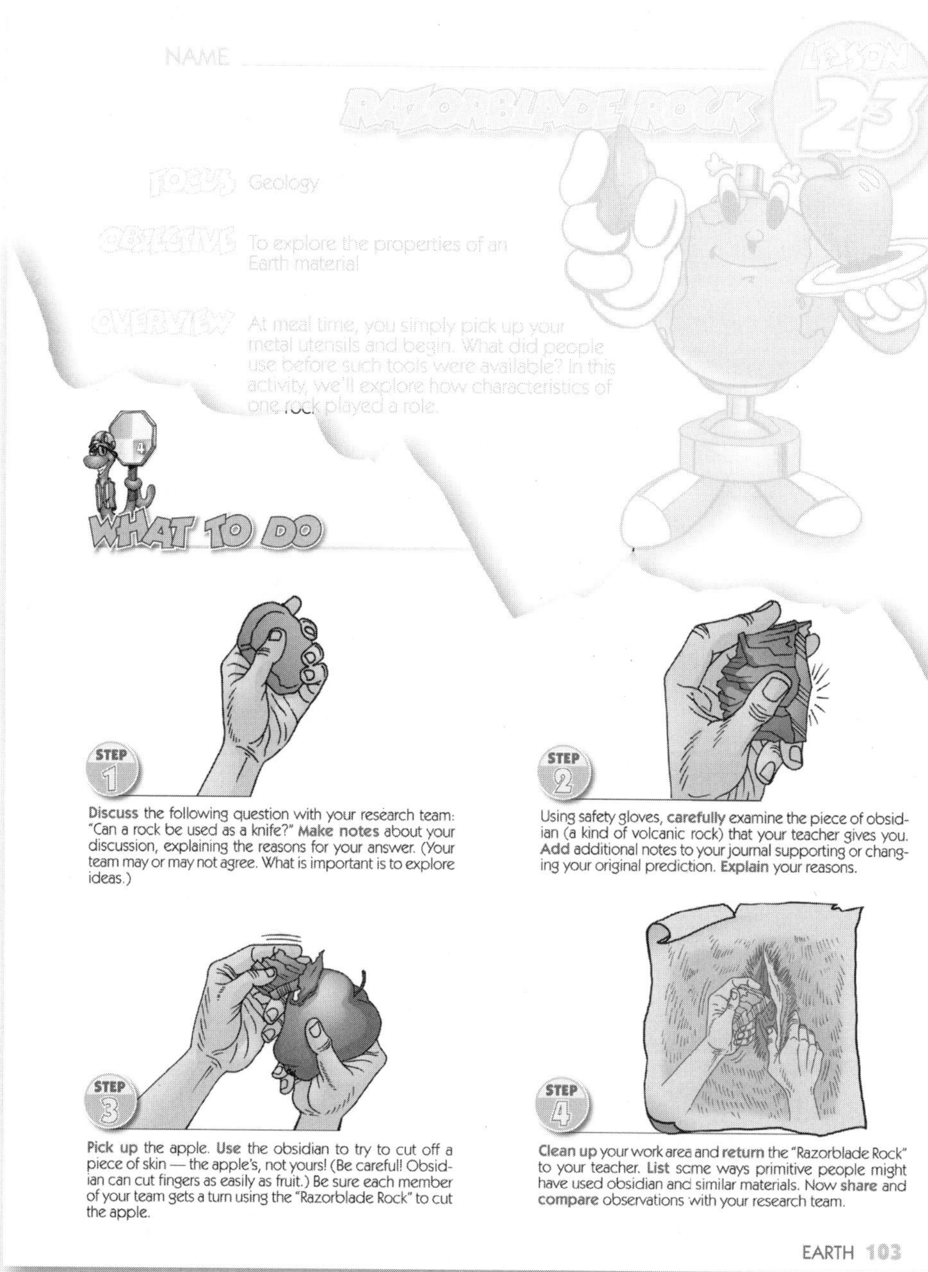

NAME

LESSON 23

RAZORBLADE ROCK

FOCUS Geology

OBJECTIVE To explore the properties of an Earth material

OVERVIEW At meal time, you simply pick up your metal utensils and begin. What did people use before such tools were available? In this activity, we'll explore how characteristics of one rock played a role.

WHAT TO DO

STEP 1

Discuss the following question with your research team: "Can a rock be used as a knife?" **Make notes** about your discussion, explaining the reasons for your answer. (Your team may or may not agree. What is important is to explore ideas.)

STEP 2

Using safety gloves, **carefully** examine the piece of obsidian (a kind of volcanic rock) that your teacher gives you. **Add** additional notes to your journal supporting or changing your original prediction. **Explain** your reasons.

STEP 3

Pick up the apple. **Use** the obsidian to try to cut off a piece of skin — the apple's, not yours! (Be careful! Obsidian can cut fingers as easily as fruit.) Be sure each member of your team gets a turn using the "Razorblade Rock" to cut the apple.

STEP 4

Clean up your work area and **return** the "Razorblade Rock" to your teacher. **List** some ways primitive people might have used obsidian and similar materials. Now **share** and **compare** observations with your research team.

EARTH 103

Teacher to Teacher

Generally the faster a rock cools, the smaller the crystals that form the rock. In obsidian's case the crystals are extremely small, forming a kind of volcanic glass. If you look closely at the broken edge of a chunk of obsidian, you'll see that it looks more like a piece of glass than a rock!

Obsidian is an **igneous rock**, a material formed from the rapid cooling of rock that was once molten. Obsidian cools so quickly that it takes on the glass-like structure you see. In fact, another name for obsidian is **volcanic glass**. The most common source of molten rock is lava from **volcanoes**. (When it's underground, lava is referred to as **magma** — but it's the same stuff.)

In the ancient world, obsidian was sometimes prized as a valuable jewel! The Egyptians considered it valuable because it was so rare. Many ancient peoples used obsidian for knives, arrow heads, and spear points because of its ability to **cleave**, forming very sharp edges. Today, surgeons actually use some scalpels made of obsidian for very fine surgery. Because obsidian is so sharp, it leaves flat-cut edges that heal more easily, leading to less scar tissue, and less infection.

1. **What was your prediction in Step 1? Did it change in Step 2? Explain the basis for your predictions.**

   Answers will vary, but should reflect logical comparisons.

2. **Describe the obsidian from Step 2. What were some of its major features?**

   a) dark color, slick surface, hard, etc.

   b) answers will vary

104 EARTH

3. **Describe how obsidian is formed. What is another name for obsidian?**

   a) formed from rapidly cooling rock that was molten, often in a volcano

   b) volcanic glass

4. **List some ways primitive people might have used obsidian.**

   as jewelry, for knives, arrowheads, spear points, scrapers, etc.

5. **What properties of obsidian make it useful as a tool? Name at least one way obsidian is used today.**

   a) is it extremely sharp and hard

   b) to make special scalpels

EARTH 105

What Happened

Review the section with students. Emphasize bold-face words that identify key concepts and introduce new vocabulary.

***Obsidian** is an **igneous rock**, a material formed from the rapid cooling of rock that was once molten. Obsidian cools so quickly that it takes on the glass-like structure you see. In fact, another name for obsidian is **volcanic glass**. The most common source of molten rock is **lava** from **volcanoes**. (When it's underground, lava is referred to as **magma** – but it's the same stuff.)*

*In the ancient world, obsidian was sometimes prized as a valuable jewel! The Egyptians considered it valuable because it was so rare. Many ancient peoples used obsidian for knives, arrow heads, and spear points because of its ability to **cleave**, forming very sharp edges. Today, surgeons actually use some scalpels made of obsidian for very fine surgery. Because obsidian is so sharp, it leaves flat-cut edges that heal more easily, leading to less scar tissue, and less infection.*

What We Learned

Answers will vary. Suggested responses are shown at left.

Conclusion

Read this section aloud to the class to summarize the concepts learned in this activity.

Food for Thought

Read the Scripture aloud to the class. Talk about how God's word can protect, guide, comfort, and support us.

Journal

If time permits, have a general class discussion about notes and drawings various students added to their journal pages. Discuss correct and incorrect predictions, and remind students that this "trial and error" process is part of the scientific process.

The materials (rocks, minerals) that geologists study have many uses. Before the age of metal tools, many of these earth materials played a useful role. The specific properties of an Earth material determine how it is used.

Hebrews 4:12 The obsidian was able to slice the skin off the apple with its razor sharp edge. It made a surprisingly good knife.

God's Word is sharper than the sharpest knife ever made! Like a mighty sword, it can cut right through the deceptions of this world. It also protects us, guides us, comforts us, and supports us.

You wouldn't think of cutting meat without a knife. Why try to cut through the evil that surrounds you without the sharp sword of Scripture?

JOURNAL **My Science Notes**

106 EARTH

Extended Teaching

1. Repeat this activity using other fruits, vegetables, and even meats. Have teams compare the results with the original activity. Be sure students wash their hands and work surfaces thoroughly after finishing.

2. Invite a "Rock Hound" to visit your classroom. Ask him/her to bring samples of igneous rocks. Compare these with your obsidian samples. Have students write a paragraph about one thing they learn.

3. Using the Internet, have teams research the "Ring of Fire" that circles most of the Pacfic Ocean. Challenge each team to create a poster showing some aspect of this geological phenomenon.

4. Take a field trip to a geological or mining museum. Have teams list the types of rocks on display, draw pictures, and write descriptions. Have a class discussion about their findings.

5. Have teams research active and inactive volcanoes in the U.S. (including Hawaii and Alaska). Make a bulletin board showing the results.

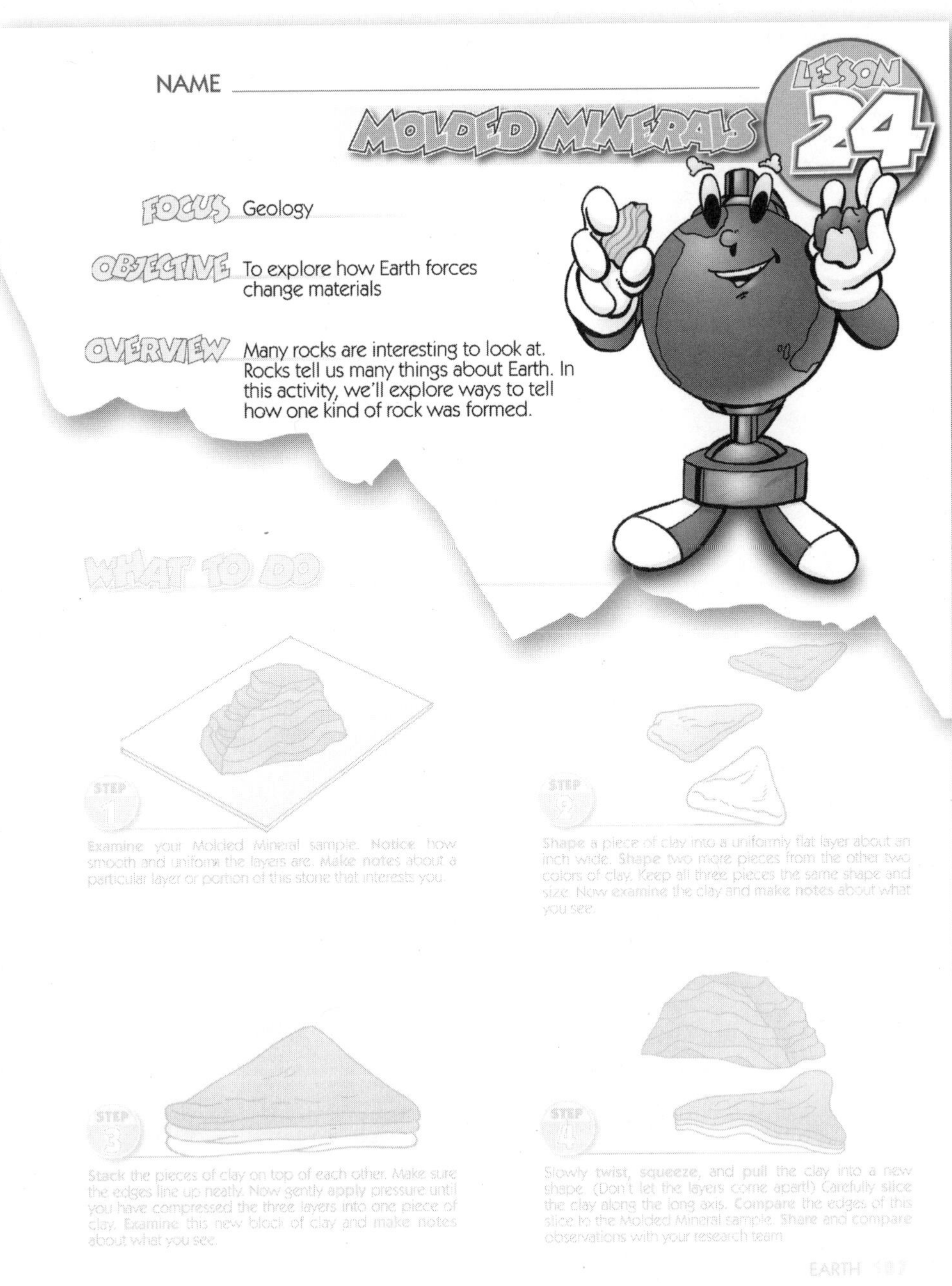

NAME ______________________________

LESSON 24

MOLDED MINERALS

FOCUS Geology

OBJECTIVE To explore how Earth forces change materials

OVERVIEW Many rocks are interesting to look at. Rocks tell us many things about Earth. In this activity, we'll explore ways to tell how one kind of rock was formed.

WHAT TO DO

STEP 1

Examine your Molded Mineral sample. Notice how smooth and uniform the layers are. Make notes about a particular layer or portion of this stone that interests you.

STEP 2

Shape a piece of clay into a uniformly flat layer about an inch wide. Shape two more pieces from the other two colors of clay. Keep all three pieces the same shape and size. Now examine the clay and make notes about what you see.

STEP 3

Stack the pieces of clay on top of each other. Make sure the edges line up neatly. Now gently apply pressure until you have compressed the three layers into one piece of clay. Examine this new block of clay and make notes about what you see.

STEP 4

Slowly twist, squeeze, and pull the clay into a new shape. (Don't let the layers come apart!) Carefully slice the clay along the long axis. Compare the edges of this slice to the Molded Mineral sample. Share and compare observations with your research team.

EARTH 187

Category

Earth Science

Focus

Geology

Objective

To explore how Earth forces change materials

National Standards

A1, A2, B1, B2, D1, D2, G1, G2

Materials Needed

wonderstone
clay - 3 colors
plastic knife

Safety Concerns

none

Additional Comments

Wonderstone is composed of volcanic glass particles welded together by intense heat and compacted by the weight of overlying material. The colorful layering is caused by various minerals in the surrounding ground water. Since wonderstones vary so widely, encourage teams to compare their samples.

Overview

Read the overview aloud to your students. The goal is to create an atmosphere of curiosity and inquiry.

WHAT TO DO

Monitor student research teams as they complete each step.

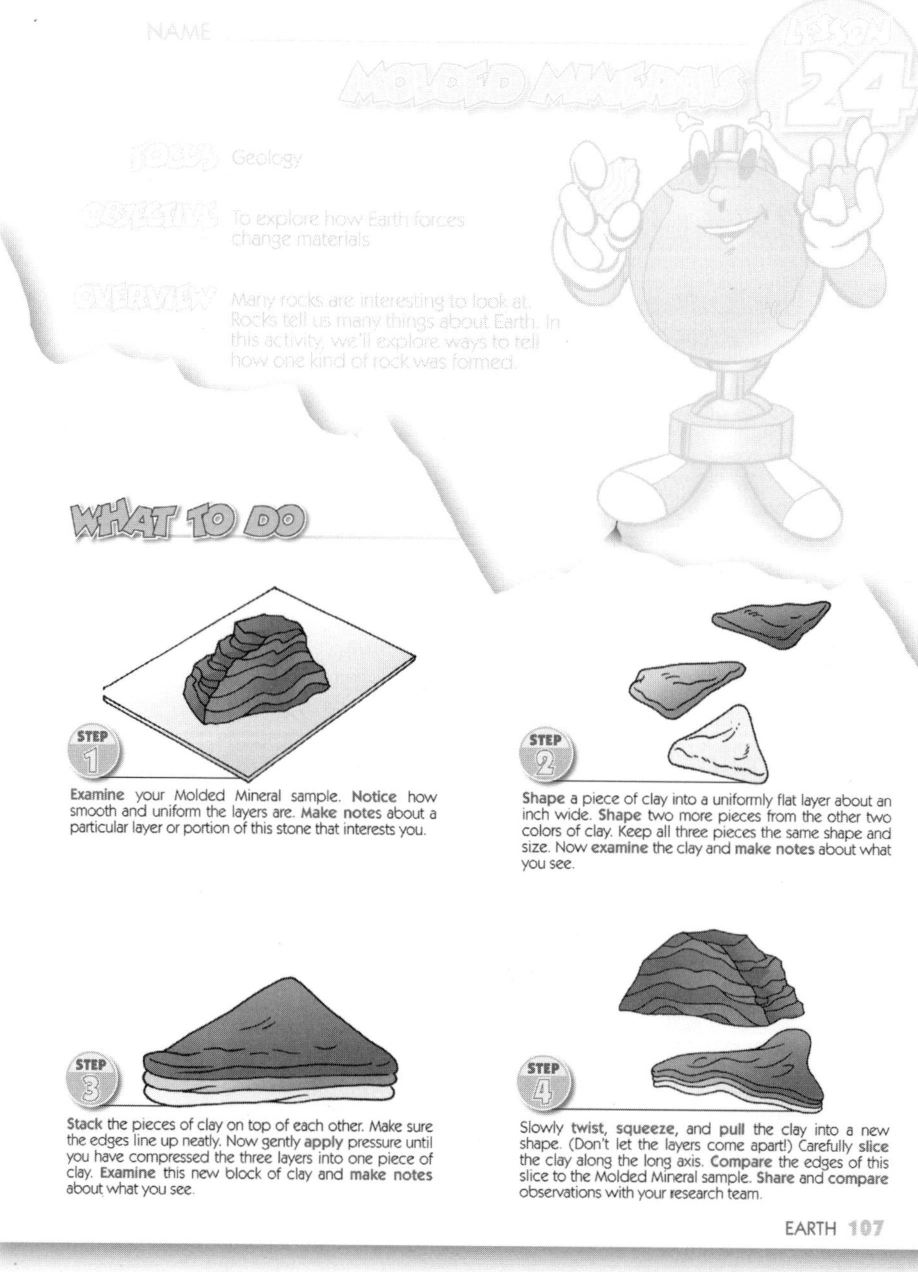

NAME

MOLDED MINERALS

LESSON 24

FOCUS Geology

OBJECTIVE To explore how Earth forces change materials

OVERVIEW Many rocks are interesting to look at. Rocks tell us many things about Earth. In this activity, we'll explore ways to tell how one kind of rock was formed.

WHAT TO DO

STEP 1

Examine your Molded Mineral sample. **Notice** how smooth and uniform the layers are. **Make notes** about a particular layer or portion of this stone that interests you.

STEP 2

Shape a piece of clay into a uniformly flat layer about an inch wide. **Shape** two more pieces from the other two colors of clay. Keep all three pieces the same shape and size. Now **examine** the clay and **make notes** about what you see.

STEP 3

Stack the pieces of clay on top of each other. Make sure the edges line up neatly. Now gently **apply** pressure until you have compressed the three layers into one piece of clay. **Examine** this new block of clay and **make notes** about what you see.

STEP 4

Slowly **twist, squeeze,** and **pull** the clay into a new shape. (Don't let the layers come apart!) Carefully **slice** the clay along the long axis. **Compare** the edges of this slice to the Molded Mineral sample. **Share** and **compare** observations with your research team.

EARTH 107

Teacher to Teacher

The Earth's surface is broken into a series of tectonic plates which float on a thin, semi-molten layer of the mantle. Where these plates move apart (divergent plate boundary) or shove together (convergent plate boundary), earthquakes and volcanoes can occur. As molten rock oozes up to the surface, igneous rocks, like obsidian and wonderstone are created.

Like the **obsidian** we studied in Lesson 23, the Molded Mineral (known as Wonderstone) is another **igneous rock**. Igneous rocks that harden on the surface of the earth are called **extrusive**. Igneous rocks that harden inside the earth are called **intrusive**.

When you squeeze a tube of striped toothpaste, different materials ooze out and blend together in layers. Something similar happens with this rock, only the "toothpaste" is super hot lava called **rhyolite**. Beautiful swirls and shapes come from **mineral impurities**, and the unique markings reflect the squeezing of molten rock layers.

The clay model you made is also a reflection of the process — only the clay is a lot cooler than lava! The layers are blended, twisted, and squeezed under pressure to imitate the look of molten stone.

1. **Describe in detail the layer you chose in Step 1. Also describe the rest of the Molded Mineral.**

   Answers will vary, but should reflect logical comparisons.

2. **What is another igneous rock we have studied? How is it similar to this one? How is it different?**

   a) obsidian

   b) answers will vary, but should reflect logical comparison

3. **What are two kinds of igneous rocks? Describe the formation of each.**

   a) extrusive and intrusive

   b) extrusive rocks harden on the surface; intrusive rocks harden underground

4. **What gives the Molded Mineral its beautiful swirls and shapes? How does this compare to the clay model you made?**

   a) various minerals in the rock plus twisting and pressure

   b) colorful clay was squeezed and twisted, too

5. **Your muscles provided the force to squeeze and blend the clay. What is one force that squeezes and blends Earth materials?**

   volcanoes, earthquakes, the weight of Earth, shifting plates, etc.

What Happened

Review the section with students. Emphasize bold-face words that identify key concepts and introduce new vocabulary.

Like the ***obsidian*** *we studied in Lesson 23, the Molded Mineral (known as Wonderstone) is another* ***igneous rock****. Igneous rocks that harden on the surface of the earth are called* ***extrusive****. Igneous rocks that harden inside the earth are called* ***intrusive****.*

When you squeeze a tube of striped toothpaste, different materials ooze out and blend together in layers. Something similar happens with this rock, only the "toothpaste" is super hot lava called ***rhyolite****. Beautiful swirls and shapes come from* ***mineral impurities****, and the unique markings reflect the squeezing of molten rock layers.*

The clay model you made is also a reflection of the process — only the clay is a lot cooler than lava! The layers are blended, twisted, and squeezed under pressure to imitate the look of molten stone.

What We Learned

Answers will vary. Suggested responses are shown at left.

Conclusion

Read this section aloud to the class to summarize the concepts learned in this activity.

Food for Thought

Read the Scripture aloud to the class. Talk about how the various parts of God's church (its people) can fit together to create a beautiful whole. Discuss ways we can help this process.

Journal

If time permits, have a general class discussion about notes and drawings various students added to their journal pages. Discuss correct and incorrect predictions, and remind students that this "trial and error" process is part of the scientific process.

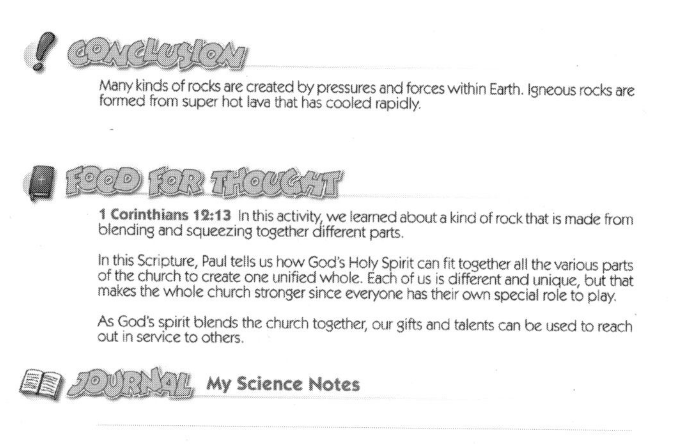
CONCLUSION

Many kinds of rocks are created by pressures and forces within Earth. Igneous rocks are formed from super hot lava that has cooled rapidly.

FOOD FOR THOUGHT

1 Corinthians 12:13 In this activity, we learned about a kind of rock that is made from blending and squeezing together different parts.

In this Scripture, Paul tells us how God's Holy Spirit can fit together all the various parts of the church to create one unified whole. Each of us is different and unique, but that makes the whole church stronger since everyone has their own special role to play.

As God's spirit blends the church together, our gifts and talents can be used to reach out in service to others.

JOURNAL My Science Notes

110 EARTH

Extended Teaching

1. Invite a stone mason to visit your class. Ask him/her to bring samples of various stones. Find out the characteristics of the stones. Have students write a paragraph about one thing they learn.

2. Using the Internet, have teams research mining sites. What kinds of materials are removed and processed in this country. Challenge each team to create a poster depicting something they learn about mining.

3. Take a field trip to a redi-mix plant. Discover how concrete is made. Have each team make a list of several things made from concrete (floors, picnic tables, ornaments, etc.) Have teams share their lists.

4. Using pictures from magazines, photographs, etc., make a "Rare Rocks" bulletin board. Feature rocks that are not found in your area. Divide the board into three sections: igneous, sedimentary, and metamorphic.

5. Challenge teams to find places in your area where earth materials are being used. (Hint: road work, construction sites, beach renovation, etc.) Have each team report its findings to the class.

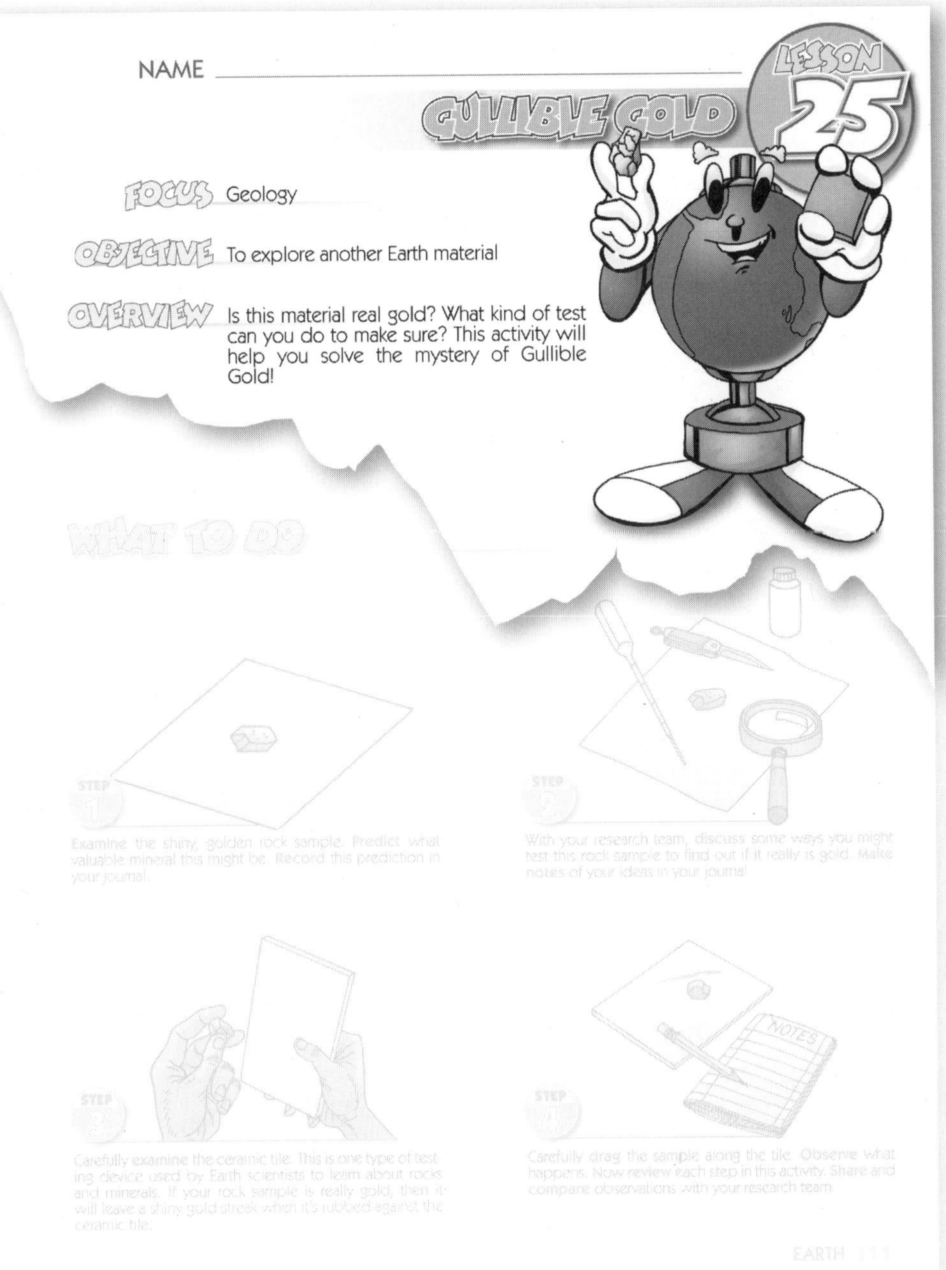

NAME ______________________

LESSON 25

GULLIBLE GOLD

FOCUS Geology

OBJECTIVE To explore another Earth material

OVERVIEW Is this material real gold? What kind of test can you do to make sure? This activity will help you solve the mystery of Gullible Gold!

WHAT TO DO

STEP 1 Examine the shiny, golden rock sample. Predict what valuable mineral this might be. Record this prediction in your journal.

STEP 2 With your research team, discuss some ways you might test this rock sample to find out if it really is gold. Make notes of your ideas in your journal.

STEP 3 Carefully examine the ceramic tile. This is one type of testing device used by Earth scientists to learn about rocks and minerals. If your rock sample is really gold, then it will leave a shiny gold streak when it's rubbed against the ceramic tile.

STEP 4 Carefully drag the sample along the tile. Observe what happens. Now review each step in this activity. Share and compare observations with your research team.

EARTH 111

Category

Earth Science

Focus

Geology

Objective

To explore another Earth material

National Standards

A1, A2, B1, B2, D1, D2, G1, G2

Materials Needed

iron pyrite
ceramic tile

Safety Concerns

none

Additional Comments

Although this is a simple, straight-forward activity, it's identical to the "streak test" scientists use as one of the primary ways to determine mineral sample types.

Overview

Read the overview aloud to your students. The goal is to create an atmosphere of curiosity and inquiry.

WHAT TO DO

Monitor student research teams as they complete each step.

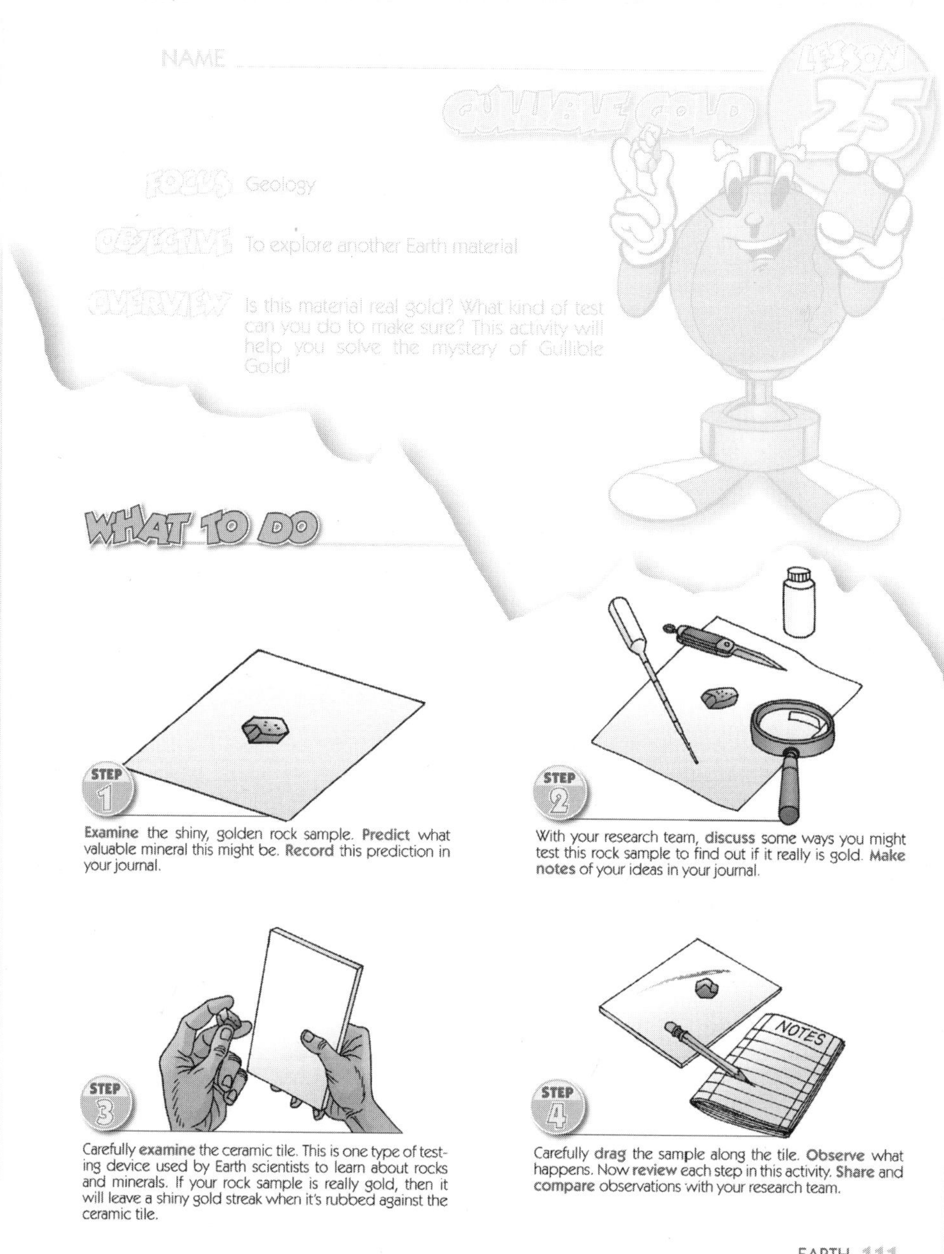

NAME

GULLIBLE GOLD

LESSON 25

FOCUS Geology

OBJECTIVE To explore another Earth material

OVERVIEW Is this material real gold? What kind of test can you do to make sure? This activity will help you solve the mystery of Gullible Gold!

WHAT TO DO

STEP 1
Examine the shiny, golden rock sample. **Predict** what valuable mineral this might be. **Record** this prediction in your journal.

STEP 2
With your research team, **discuss** some ways you might test this rock sample to find out if it really is gold. **Make notes** of your ideas in your journal.

STEP 3
Carefully **examine** the ceramic tile. This is one type of testing device used by Earth scientists to learn about rocks and minerals. If your rock sample is really gold, then it will leave a shiny gold streak when it's rubbed against the ceramic tile.

STEP 4
Carefully **drag** the sample along the tile. **Observe** what happens. Now **review** each step in this activity. **Share** and **compare** observations with your research team.

EARTH 111

Teacher to Teacher

Testing the properties of a material can tell us many things about it. In this case, a simple Streak Test helped us determine that the sample was not gold. Physical properties of minerals include hardness, streak, luster, density, and cleavage (fracture). Optical properties include color and refraction.

Minerals can be **pure** substances; like pure gold. Minerals can also be **compounds**. A compound is two or more **elements** that are **bonded** together by their atoms. A **rock** is usually some combination of minerals in different proportions — a mixture of minerals and other materials.

The test you just did is called a **streak test**. (It's not too hard to figure out why!) Many minerals, once they are powdered by the streak test, show a different color than they do in a big chunk.

Rocks and minerals are some of the most important materials we mine from Earth. We use them in buildings, for fuels, and many other things. The **properties** (or characteristics) of rocks and minerals determine how they can be used.

1 What was your prediction in Step 1? On what did you base your prediction?

Answers will vary, but should reflect logical comparisons.

2 What were your best testing ideas from Step 2? What were your worst ideas?

Answers will vary, but should reflect logical comparisons.

112 EARTH

3 Describe the "streak test" you performed in Step 4? How did the test turn out?

a) rubbed the sample against ceramic tile

b) it didn't leave a gold streak

4 Why is it important to know the properties of Earth materials?

Rocks and minerals are very important; their properties determine how they can be used.

5 Name three common Earth materials. What are these used for?

gravel for road work; sand for concrete; stone for building; iron to make metal; etc.

EARTH 113

What Happened

Review the section with students. Emphasize bold-face words that identify key concepts and introduce new vocabulary.

__Minerals__ can be __pure__ substances—like pure gold. Minerals can also be __compounds__. A compound is two or more __elements__ that are __bonded__ together by their atoms. A __rock__ is usually some combination of minerals in different proportions — a mixture of minerals and other materials.

The test you just did is called a __streak test__. (It's not too hard to figure out why!) Many minerals, once they are powdered by the streak test, show a different color than they do in a big chunk.

Rocks and minerals are some of the most important materials we mine from Earth. We use them in buildings, for fuels, and many other things. The __properties__ (or characteristics) of rocks and minerals determine how they can be used.

What We Learned

Answers will vary. Suggested responses are shown at left.

Conclusion

Read this section aloud to the class to summarize the concepts learned in this activity.

Food for Thought

Read the Scripture aloud to the class. Talk about how we can "store up treasures in heaven." Discuss ways we can learn to trust God more.

Journal

If time permits, have a general class discussion about notes and drawings various students added to their journal pages. Discuss correct and incorrect predictions, and remind students that this "trial and error" process is part of the scientific process.

Earth materials can be identified by their properties. One test of these properties is to check the color of the powdered material (streak) from a streak test.

Matthew 6:19-21 For just a little while, it was fun to imagine that this was a real chunk of gold and that you could buy anything you wanted. Now you can understand why so many people are trapped by the love of money!

This Scripture points out that treasure here on Earth can erode away or be stolen. If we store up "treasure in heaven," then it's safe from all harm. Jesus reminds us that our heart will always be wherever we keep our treasure.

Put your trust in Jesus. That's where the real treasure is!

JOURNAL **My Science Notes**

114 EARTH

Extended Teaching

1. Rocks and minerals have always been important to mankind. Have students research the Stone Age, the Copper Age, the Bronze Age, and the Iron Age — important divisions of history based on minerals!

2. Share the saying, "All is not gold that glitters." Have teams discuss this phrase and what it might mean. Challenge students to write a short story that illustrates this ancient platitude.

3. Let teams repeat this activity using other minerals and rocks. Have them keep a chart describing each sample and the results. Share and compare findings between teams and discuss the results.

4. Ask a rock shop or quarry for scraps of soft sedimentary rocks. Try the streak test on these samples. Discuss the results. Have students write a paragraph summarizing their conclusions.

5. Take a field trip to a rock quarry. Find out how Earth materials are removed and processed. Have students write a paragraph about one thing they learn.

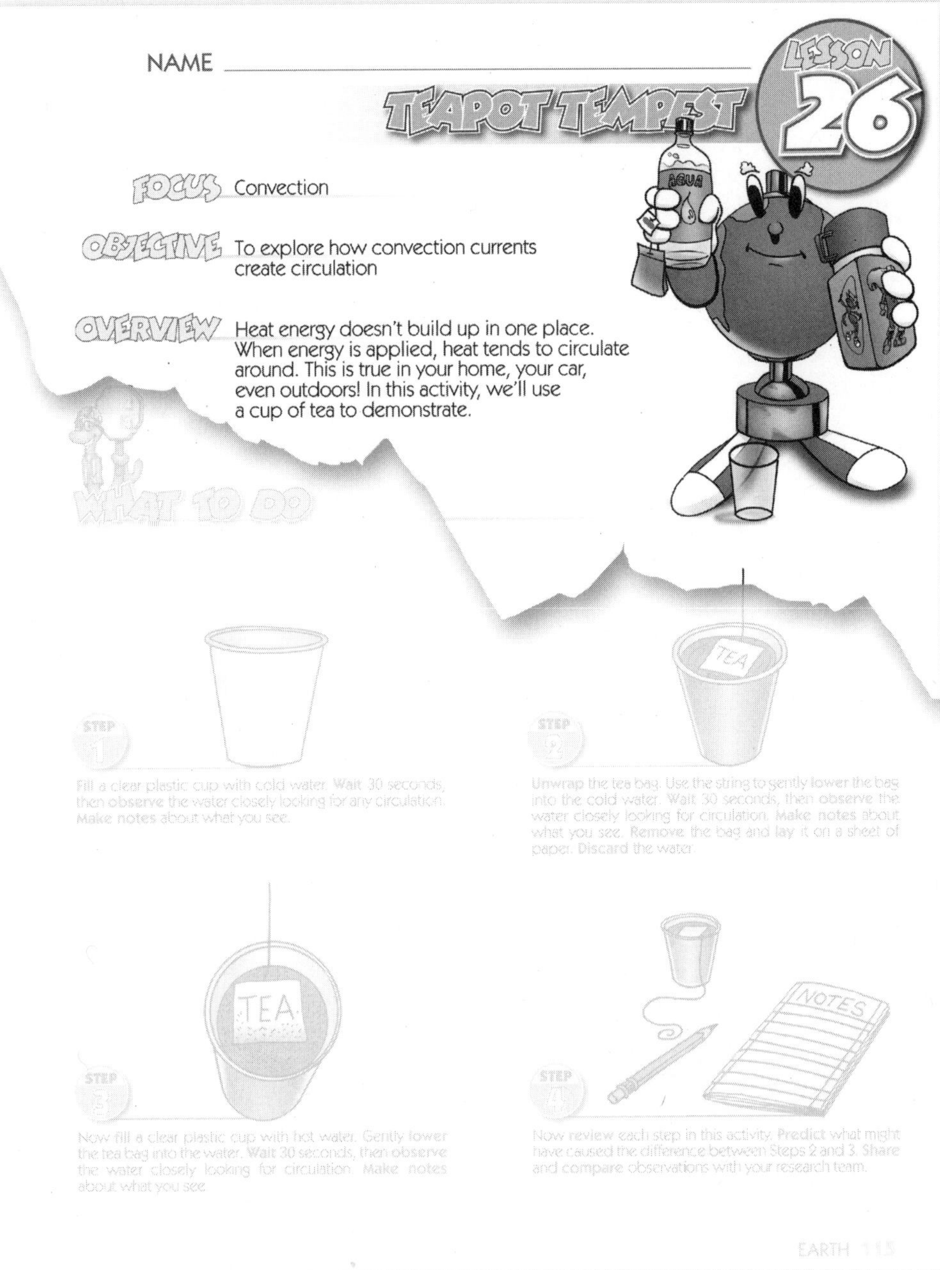

NAME ______________________________

TEAPOT TEMPEST

LESSON 26

FOCUS Convection

OBJECTIVE To explore how convection currents create circulation

OVERVIEW Heat energy doesn't build up in one place. When energy is applied, heat tends to circulate around. This is true in your home, your car, even outdoors! In this activity, we'll use a cup of tea to demonstrate.

WHAT TO DO

STEP 1 Fill a clear plastic cup with cold water. Wait 30 seconds, then observe the water closely looking for any circulation. Make notes about what you see.

STEP 2 Unwrap the tea bag. Use the string to gently lower the bag into the cold water. Wait 30 seconds, then observe the water closely looking for circulation. Make notes about what you see. Remove the bag and lay it on a sheet of paper. Discard the water.

STEP 3 Now fill a clear plastic cup with hot water. Gently lower the tea bag into the water. Wait 30 seconds, then observe the water closely looking for circulation. Make notes about what you see.

STEP 4 Now review each step in this activity. Predict what might have caused the difference between Steps 2 and 3. Share and compare observations with your research team.

EARTH 115

Category

Earth Science

Focus

Convection

Objective

To explore how convection currents create circulation

National Standards

A1, A2, B1, B2, B3, D1, G1, G2

Materials Needed

clear plastic cup
cold water
hot water
tea bag
scrap paper

Safety Concerns

2. Thermal Burn
There is a potential for scalding. Remind students to exercise caution with hot water.

4. Slipping
There is a potential for spills with this activity. Remind students to exercise caution.

Additional Comments

The hot water does not need to be boiling, just very hot. If facilities are limited, you can keep water hot in thermos bottles. Be sure to warn students not to *drink* the tea! Dispose of materials carefully as tea can cause stains.

Overview

Read the overview aloud to your students. The goal is to create an atmosphere of curiosity and inquiry.

WHAT TO DO

Monitor student research teams as they complete each step.

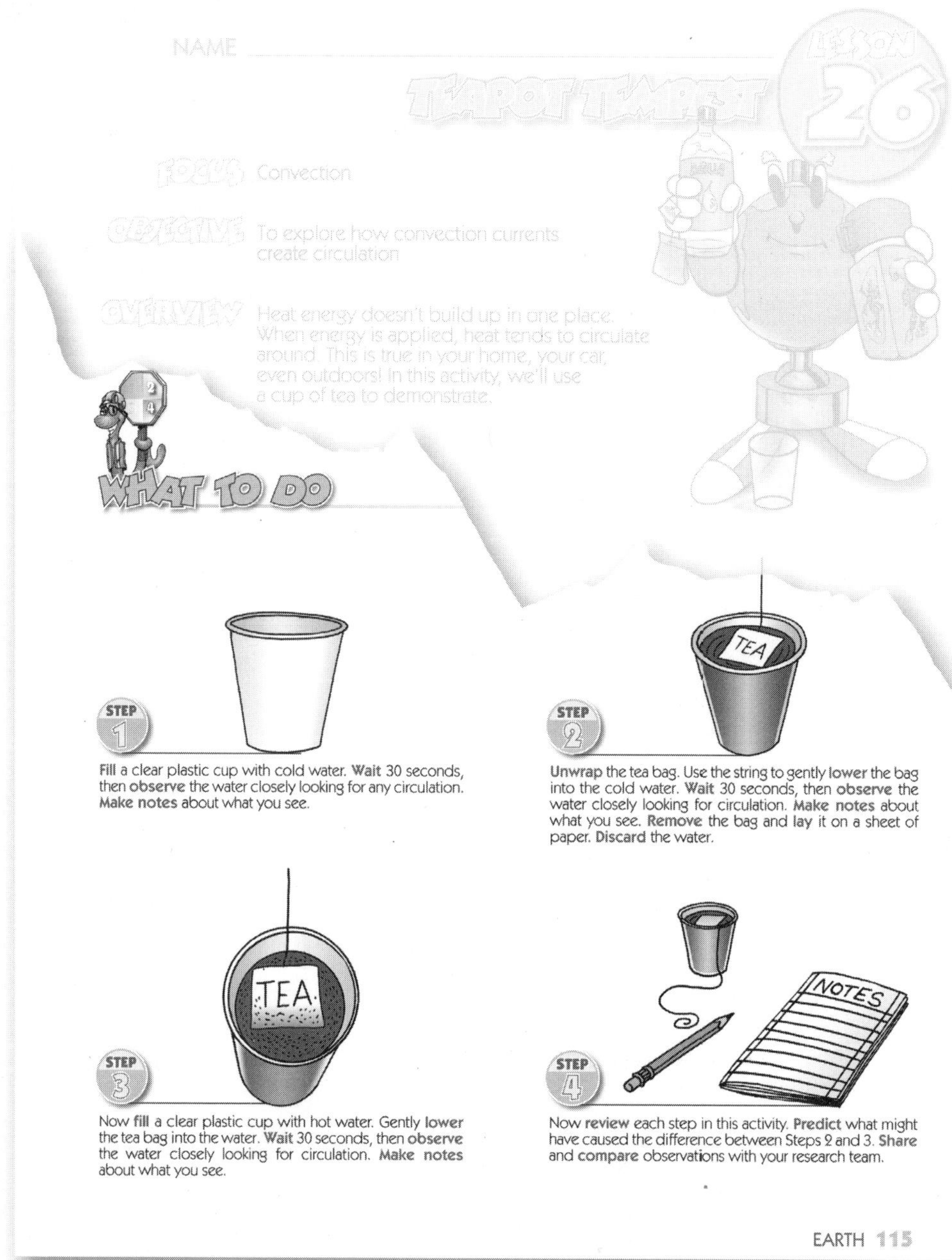

NAME

LESSON 26

TEAPOT TEMPEST

FOCUS Convection

OBJECTIVE To explore how convection currents create circulation

OVERVIEW Heat energy doesn't build up in one place. When energy is applied, heat tends to circulate around. This is true in your home, your car, even outdoors! In this activity, we'll use a cup of tea to demonstrate.

WHAT TO DO

STEP 1

Fill a clear plastic cup with cold water. **Wait** 30 seconds, then **observe** the water closely looking for any circulation. **Make notes** about what you see.

STEP 2

Unwrap the tea bag. Use the string to gently **lower** the bag into the cold water. **Wait** 30 seconds, then **observe** the water closely looking for circulation. **Make notes** about what you see. **Remove** the bag and **lay** it on a sheet of paper. **Discard** the water.

STEP 3

Now **fill** a clear plastic cup with hot water. Gently **lower** the tea bag into the water. **Wait** 30 seconds, then **observe** the water closely looking for circulation. **Make notes** about what you see.

STEP 4

Now **review** each step in this activity. **Predict** what might have caused the difference between Steps 2 and 3. **Share** and **compare** observations with your research team.

EARTH 115

Teacher to Teacher

Earth is a giant example of convection at work. Air and water near the equator absorb great heat from the direct rays of the sun — but at the poles the sun's rays yield little solar energy. These massive temperature differences create convection currents. Without these external convection currents to help create a balance, much of the globe would be uninhabitable — the frozen poles would be huge and the tropics a seething mass of constant hurricanes!

It's important to note that convection currents also occur *within* the Earth's mantle in the flow of magma of different temperatures. These internal convection currents are one of the causes of movement in the Earth's plates.

WHAT HAPPENED?

The hot water **dissolved** part of the tea inside the bag. This made a **solution**. The water at the top of the solution was steaming, changing from a **liquid** state into a **gas**. The rising steam removed **energy**, causing the top water to cool slightly. Cooler water is more **dense** (thicker), so it sank. The less-dense, warmer water underneath rose to replace it. It's hard to see this in clear water, but the tea made it easy to see!

This movement of liquids and gasses caused by **heating** and **cooling** is called a **convection current**. Although you can't see it, your school has heated or cooled air swirling around you in convection currents.

The **ocean** (water) and **atmosphere** (air) are large examples of **fluids** that use convection currents to move heat energy around.

WHAT WE LEARNED

1. **What did you observe in Step 1? Why didn't the water circulate? What was missing?**

a) clear cup, water

b) movement requires energy

c) a form of energy

2. **What did you observe in Step 2? Why didn't the water circulate? What was still missing?**

a) clear cup, water, tea bag

b) movement requires energy

c) a form of energy

116 EARTH

3. **What did you observe in Step 3? What made the water circulate? Why was this circulation easy to see?**

a) clear cup, water, tea bag

b) heat added energy

c) because of the tea

4. **What is the name for the movement of liquids/gasses caused by heating or cooling? Name two places we might see or feel this.**

a) convection

b) examples: anywhere air or water moves because of heat or cooling

5. **Convection currents were very easy to see in Step 3. Explain how they worked, describing each part of the process in detail.**

Answers should be similar to the first paragraph under "What Happened".

EARTH 117

What Happened

Review the section with students. Emphasize bold-face words that identify key concepts and introduce new vocabulary.

*The hot water **dissolved** part of the tea inside the bag. This made a **solution**. The water at the top of the solution was steaming, changing from a **liquid** state into a **gas**. The rising steam removed **energy**, causing the top water to cool slightly. Cooler water is more **dense** (thicker), so it sank. The less-dense, warmer water underneath rose to replace it. It's hard to see this in clear water, but the tea made it easy to see!*

*This movement of liquids and gasses caused by **heating** and **cooling** is called a **convection current**. Although you can't see it, your school has heated or cooled air swirling around you in convection currents.*

*The **ocean** (water) and **atmosphere** (air) are large examples of **fluids** that use convection currents to move heat energy around.*

What We Learned

Answers will vary. Suggested responses are shown at left.

Conclusion

Read this section aloud to the class to summarize the concepts learned in this activity.

Food for Thought

Read the Scripture aloud to the class. Talk about the "storms of life" and how God helps us through difficult times. Discuss how deepening our relationship with God *now* can help us *then*.

Journal

If time permits, have a general class discussion about notes and drawings various students added to their journal pages. Discuss correct and incorrect predictions, and remind students that this "trial and error" process is part of the scientific process.

Moving anything requires energy! There are no exceptions, but sometimes movement is hard to see. The movement of liquids or gasses caused by heat or cold is called a convection current. These currents are present in large oceans as well as tiny cups.

Mark 4:35-41 Heat energy in the atmosphere can create an awesome kind of convection current that we call a storm. Although most storms are harmless, some can be enormously powerful and pretty frightening!

You may live in a place that has few atmospheric storms, but sooner or later everyone will have a "storm" in their life. It may be a frustrating problem or a major tragedy. But no matter what the difficulty, we can rely on the one who can calm any storm!

Let God's power keep you safe from the storms of life!

JOURNAL **My Science Notes**

118 EARTH

Extended Teaching

1. Scatter students around the room. Spray a tiny amount of perfume in front of a vent. Tell students to hold up their hands when they smell the fragrance. Discuss the pattern that convection creates.

2. Take a field trip to a store that sells ceiling fans. Find out how these fans help lower energy costs. Why are most such fans "reversible"? Have students write a paragraph about one thing they learn.

3. Invite a heating and air conditioning specialist to visit your classroom. Discuss how central heat works in a home, and why ducts and vents are different sizes. Have students write a paragraph about one thing they learn.

4. Using the Internet, have teams research convection. Challenge each team to create a poster depicting and describing a specific example of convection (ocean currents, weather patterns, hot tea in a glass, etc.).

5. Hot-air balloons rely on convection currents. Have teams research this interesting sport. If possible, take a field trip to a hot-air balloon meet, or invite an enthusiast to visit your classroom.

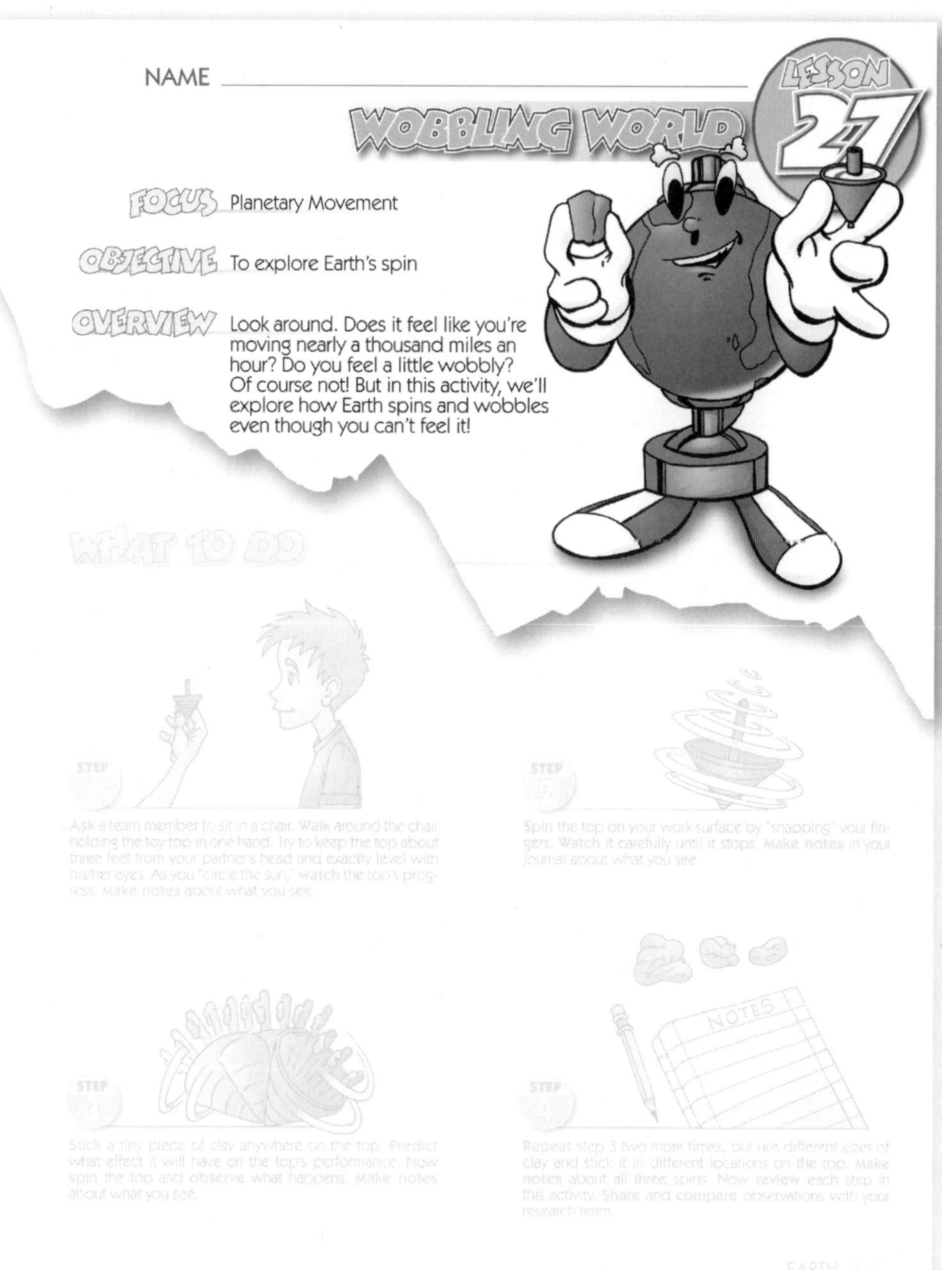

Category

Earth Science

Focus

Planetary Movement

Objective

To explore Earth's spin

National Standards

A1, A2, B1, B2, B3, D1, D2, G1, G2

Materials Needed

toy top
clay

Safety Concerns

none

Additional Comments

Different sizes of clay will create different kinds of wobbling. Make sure students are keeping good notes in their journals about each variation.

Overview

Read the overview aloud to your students. The goal is to create an atmosphere of curiosity and inquiry.

WHAT TO DO

Monitor student research teams as they complete each step.

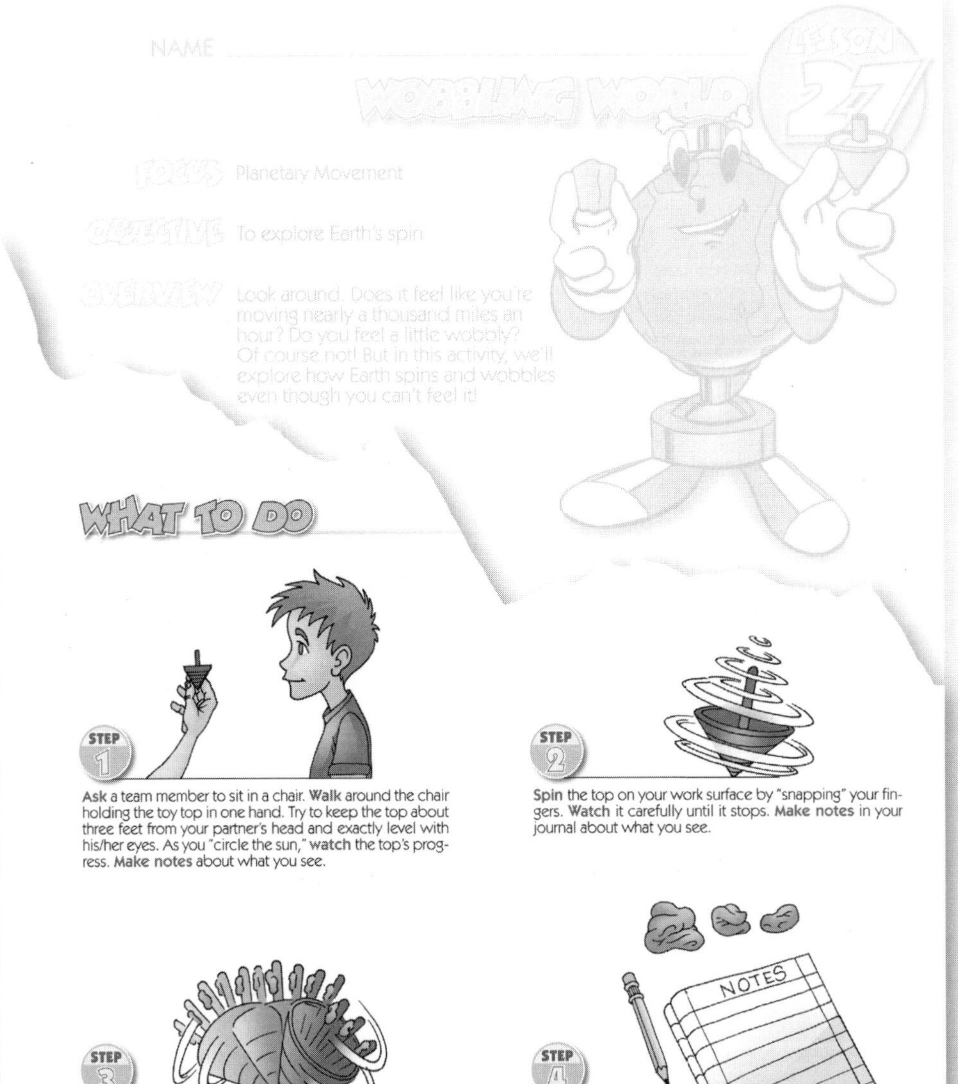

NAME

WOBBLING WORLD

LESSON 27

FOCUS Planetary Movement

OBJECTIVE To explore Earth's spin

OVERVIEW Look around. Does it feel like you're moving nearly a thousand miles an hour? Do you feel a little wobbly? Of course not! But in this activity, we'll explore how Earth spins and wobbles even though you can't feel it!

WHAT TO DO

STEP 1

Ask a team member to sit in a chair. **Walk** around the chair holding the toy top in one hand. Try to keep the top about three feet from your partner's head and exactly level with his/her eyes. As you "circle the sun," **watch** the top's progress. **Make notes** about what you see.

STEP 2

Spin the top on your work surface by "snapping" your fingers. **Watch** it carefully until it stops. **Make notes** in your journal about what you see.

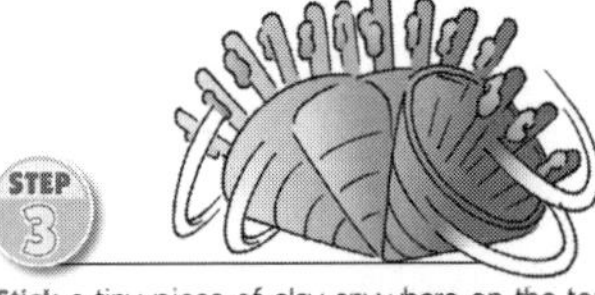

STEP 3

Stick a tiny piece of clay anywhere on the top. **Predict** what effect it will have on the top's performance. Now **spin** the top and **observe** what happens. **Make notes** about what you see.

STEP 4

Repeat step 3 two more times, but use different sizes of clay and stick it in different locations on the top. **Make notes** about all three spins. Now **review** each step in this activity. **Share** and **compare** observations with your research team.

EARTH 119

Teacher to Teacher

Scientists have observed Chandler's wobble for over a century. Common theories have to do with the Earth's shape and structure, although more recent theories blame the fluctuation of pressure on the ocean bottom (caused by temperature and salinity shifts), and wind-driven changes in the ocean's circulation. Chandler's wobble is about 20 feet every 443 days.

What Happened?

Our spinning Earth has two cycles that affect us greatly. The first is **rotation**, turning on an **axis** like a top. We call the time it takes for one full rotation a **day**. The second cycle is **revolution**, circling the sun. We call the time it takes for one full revolution a **year**.

So where does the wobble come in? Earth spins at about a thousand miles an hour. Since Earth's **core** is **liquid** (molten rock), and since it's not perfectly round, it wobbles a little! You saw an example of what scientists call **Chandler's Wobble** with the out-of-balance top. The real Chandler's Wobble isn't noticable — unless you're an astronaut in space trying to get precise measurements!

That's one of the reasons scientists study Earth's wobble. It affects navigation and communication in space. Geologists also use it to learn more about the Earth's core.

What We Learned

1. **Which Earth movement does the top represent in Step 1? Describe this process and tell how long one cycle takes.**

a) revolution

b) Earth revolves around the sun. One full cycle is called a year

2. **Which Earth movement does the top represent in Step 2? Describe this process and tell how long one cycle takes.**

a) rotation

b) Earth turns on its axis. One full rotation is called a day

3. **What was your prediction in Step 3? How did it reflect what actually happened?**

Answers will vary, but should reflect logical comparisons.

4. **Describe "Chandler's Wobble." Explain what causes it and why scientists study it.**

a) answers will vary

b) Earth not being perfectly round. It affects navigation and communication in space.

5. **Earth spins amazingly fast. It's also rushing around the sun. Why don't we feel these motions? Discuss this with your team. Record your ideas.**

Because gravity "attaches" us to Earth, because Earth is so large, and because everything else is moving, too.

What Happened

Review the section with students. Emphasize bold-face words that identify key concepts and introduce new vocabulary.

*Our spinning Earth has two cycles that affect us greatly. The first is **rotation**, turning on an **axis** like a top. We call the time it takes for one full rotation a **day**. The second cycle is **revolution**, circling the sun. We call the time it takes for one full revolution a **year**.*

*So where does the wobble come in? Earth spins at about a thousand miles an hour. Since Earth's **core** is **liquid** (molten rock), and since it's not perfectly round, it wobbles a little! You saw an example of what scientists call **Chandler's Wobble** with the out-of-balance top. The real Chandler's Wobble isn't noticeable – unless you're an astronaut in space trying to get precise measurements!*

That's one of the reasons scientists study Earth's wobble. It affects navigation and communication in space. Geologists also use it to learn more about the Earth's core.

What We Learned

Answers will vary. Suggested responses are shown at left.

Conclusion

Read this section aloud to the class to summarize the concepts learned in this activity.

Food for Thought

Read the Scripture aloud to the class. Talk about the importance of performing "random acts of kindness." Discuss things we can do to make someone's day brighter!

Journal

If time permits, have a general class discussion about notes and drawings various students added to their journal pages. Discuss correct and incorrect predictions, and remind students that this "trial and error" process is part of the scientific process.

Although you don't feel it, Earth constantly moves in many ways. These movements include rotation, revolution, and Chandler's Wobble.

Psalm 103:14-18 In this activity, we looked at some of the Earth's movements. The time and distances involved are huge, and to truly understand every aspect of it all would take more than one lifetime.

The Psalmist reminds us that compared to God's great universe, our time on Earth is brief. So isn't it even more important to make every moment count? Use some of your time to do something nice for someone today!

Remember to trust in God, whose Kingdom will endure forever!

JOURNAL **My Science Notes**

122 EARTH

Extended Teaching

1. Repeat this activity with a much larger top and bigger chunks of clay. Have students compare the results with the original activity. How were they similar? How were they different?

2. Have teams list other things that revolve or rotate. Challenge each team to create a poster to explain the difference between rotation and revolution. They must use pictures of common items for illustrations.

3. Take a field trip to a tire shop. Have a technician demonstrate how tires are balanced. Find out why this is important on a spinning tire. Have students write a paragraph about one thing they learn.

4. Have teams research how the Earth's rotation affects time keeping. Using the Internet, check out the U.S. Naval Observatory and the official USNO Clock. Have students write a paragraph about one thing they learn.

5. Invite a machinist to visit your classroom. Talk about the precision needed to balance rotating parts. Ask him/her to bring some samples of machined parts. Have a class discussion about balance and rotation.

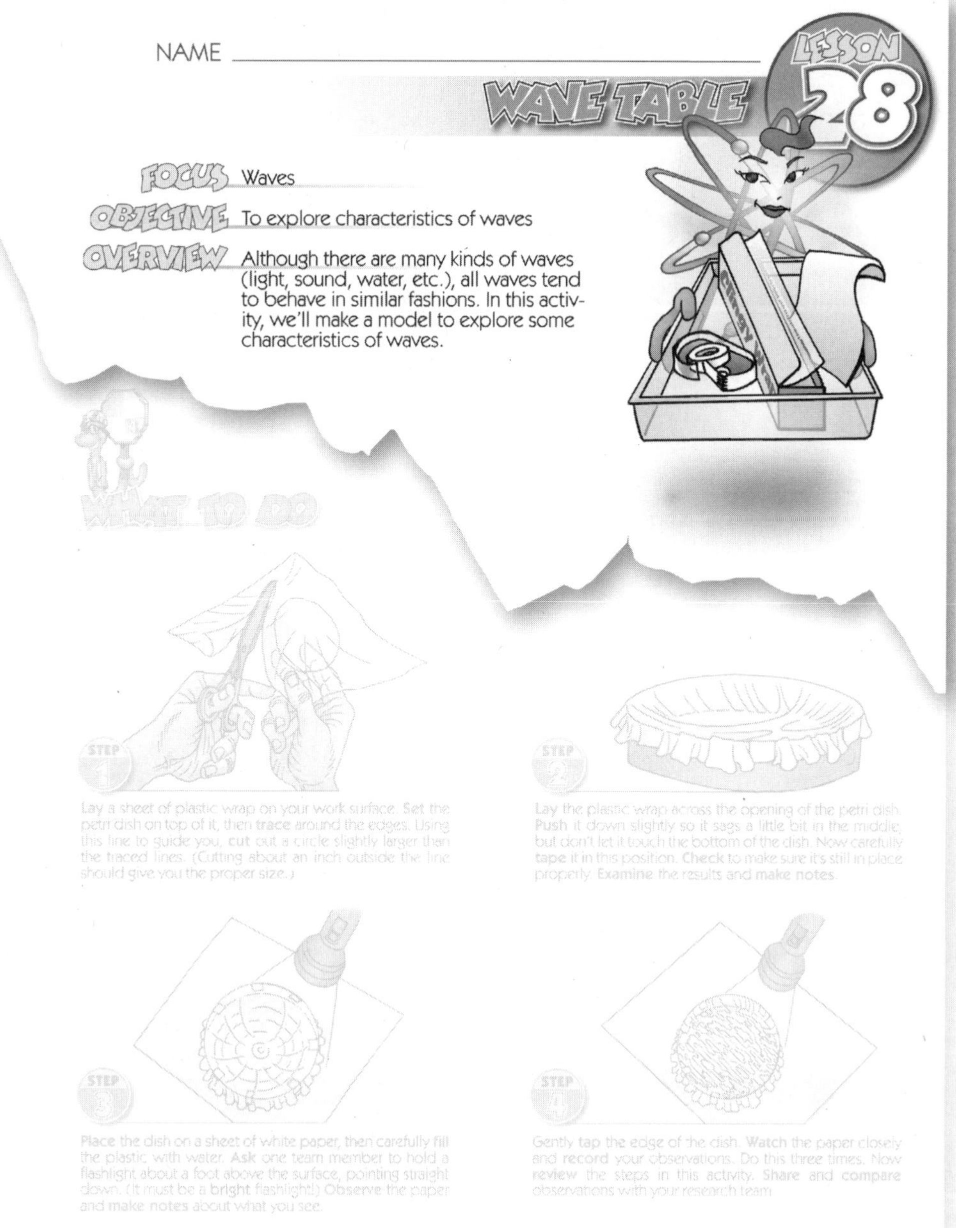
NAME ______________________________

LESSON 28

WAVE TABLE

FOCUS Waves

OBJECTIVE To explore characteristics of waves

OVERVIEW Although there are many kinds of waves (light, sound, water, etc.), all waves tend to behave in similar fashions. In this activity, we'll make a model to explore some characteristics of waves.

WHAT TO DO

STEP 1
Lay a sheet of plastic wrap on your work surface. Set the petri dish on top of it, then trace around the edges. Using this line to guide you, cut out a circle slightly larger than the traced lines. (Cutting about an inch outside the line should give you the proper size.)

STEP 2
Lay the plastic wrap across the opening of the petri dish. Push it down slightly so it sags a little bit in the middle, but don't let it touch the bottom of the dish. Now carefully tape it in this position. Check to make sure it's still in place properly. Examine the results and make notes.

STEP 3
Place the dish on a sheet of white paper, then carefully fill the plastic with water. Ask one team member to hold a flashlight about a foot above the surface, pointing straight down. (It must be a bright flashlight!) Observe the paper and make notes about what you see.

STEP 4
Gently tap the edge of the dish. Watch the paper closely and record your observations. Do this three times. Now review the steps in this activity. Share and compare observations with your research team.

ENERGY · MATTER 125

Category

Physical Science
Energy/Matter

Focus

Waves

Objective

To explore the characteristics of waves

National Standards

A1, A2, B1, B2, B3, E1, E2, F5, G1, G2

Materials Needed

petri dish
plastic wrap
scissors
tape
white paper
water
flashlight

Safety Concerns

4. Slipping
There is a potential for spills with this activity. Remind students to exercise caution.

Additional Comments

Teams may need assistance with Step 2. The plastic wrap needs to be loose enough to hold plenty of water, yet tight enough it doesn't touch the bottom of the petri dish. Encourage students to take turns taping and observing the petri dish in Step 4.

Overview

Read the overview aloud to your students. The goal is to create an atmosphere of curiosity and inquiry.

WHAT TO DO

Monitor student research teams as they complete each step.

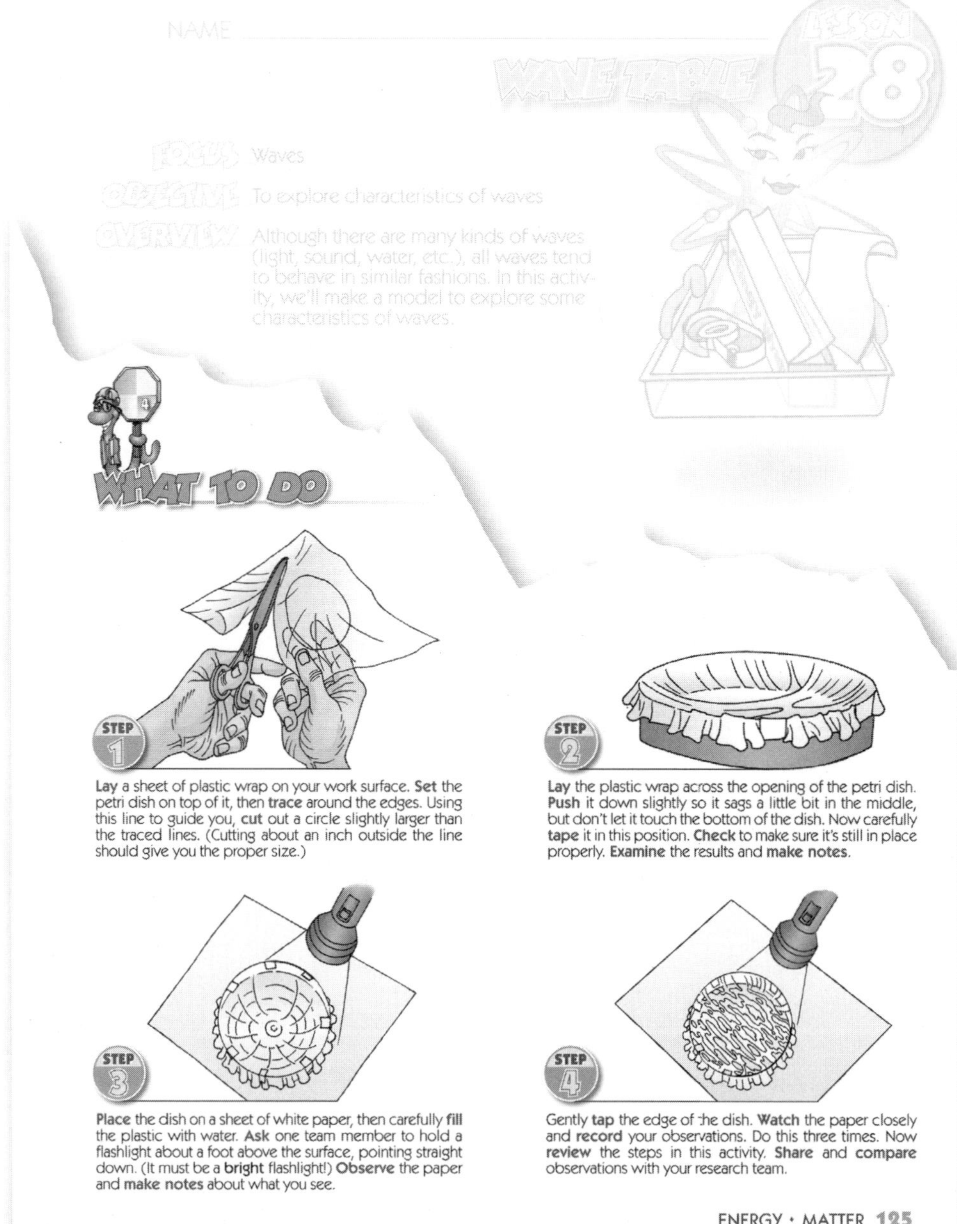

Teacher to Teacher

As you saw in this activity, waves grow weaker as they spread out. This is true for radio, television, heat, light, and other waves. It's important to note, however, that the total amount of energy stays the same. The farther you get from your favorite radio station, for instance, the harder it is to receive the signal — but the station is still putting out the same amount of power.

WHAT HAPPENED?

The pattern on the paper was created by a bright **light** shining on the two primary parts of a **wave** — the **crest** (top) and the **trough** (bottom). When the light hits a crest, the light is **concentrated** (squeezed together) making a bright line in the pattern. When the light hits a trough, the light is **diffused** (spread apart) making a darker line in the pattern.

Notice that when you touched the water, the **energy** you supplied moved outward from the point of contact. That's the most important aspect of waves — they carry energy from one place to another.

The operation of a television, a radio, a cell phone, (even a surfboard) depends on this ability of waves to **transfer** energy.

WHAT WE LEARNED

1. What is a crest? What is a trough? How are they similar? How are they different?

a) the top of a wave

b) the low point between waves

c) they're the opposite extremes of a wave

2. What effect did the crest of the wave have on the light? Why?

a) made the light brighter

b) it concentrated the light

3. What effect did the trough of the wave have on the light? Why?

a) made the light dimmer

b) it diffused the light

4. Where did the energy come from to make the waves for this activity. Where did the energy go?

a) from a student tapping the petri dish

b) into the water to make waves

5. Give three examples of waves and tell how they transfer energy.

radio, from station to receiver; surfboard, from ocean to shore; cell phone, from mouth to ear; etc.

What Happened

Review the section with students. Emphasize bold-face words that identify key concepts and introduce new vocabulary.

The pattern on the paper was created by a bright ***light*** *shining on the two primary parts of a* ***wave*** *— the* ***crest*** *(top) and the* ***trough*** *(bottom). When the light hits a crest, the light is* ***concentrated*** *(squeezed together) making a bright line in the pattern. When the light hits a trough, the light is* ***diffused*** *(spread apart), making a darker line in the pattern.*

Notice that when you touched the water, the ***energy*** *you supplied moved outward from the point of contact. That's the most important aspect of waves — they carry energy from one place to another.*

The operation of a television, a radio, a cell phone, (even a surfboard) depends on this ability of waves to ***transfer*** *energy.*

What We Learned

Answers will vary. Suggested responses are shown at left.

Conclusion

Read this section aloud to the class to summarize the concepts learned in this activity.

Food for Thought

Read the Scripture aloud to the class. Talk about Jesus calming the sea. Discuss ways we can learn to trust God's awesome power, and let it work in our lives.

Journal

If time permits, have a general class discussion about notes and drawings various students added to their journal pages. Discuss correct and incorrect predictions, and remind students that this "trial and error" process is part of the scientific process.

Conclusion

Although there are many kinds of waves, all waves have common characteristics (like crests and troughs). Waves transfer energy from one place to another.

Food for Thought

Matthew 8:23-27 As we discovered, waves carry energy. The energy can be productive (like radio waves), or it can be destructive (like storm waves).

Scripture describes a time of angry, destructive waves. A powerful storm frightened the disciples, threatening to sink their boat. In their despair, they suddenly remembered that Jesus was near! With just a word, Jesus calmed the angry sea.

Remember that no matter what the situation, no matter how frightened you are, the master of the waves is always near.

Journal **My Science Notes**

128 ENERGY • MATTER

Extended Teaching

1. Repeat this activity using a child's wading pool and a flood lamp. (Keep electricity away from water!) Have students compare the results with the original activity. How were they similar? How were they different?

2. Have teams list different kinds of waves and the energy they carry. Challenge each team to create a poster depicting and describing a specific kind of wave.

3. Invite an electric company representative to visit your classroom. Talk about challenges in providing electricity and about energy conservation. Have students write a paragraph about one thing they learn.

4. Take a field trip to a power plant to find out how electricity is generated. Discuss how it is transferred from the power plant to homes and businesses. Have students write a paragraph about one thing they learn.

5. Darken the classroom and shine a flashlight at the ceiling in one corner. Ask students to compare the brightness there with the opposite corner of the room. Share the energy comparison from "Teacher to Teacher."

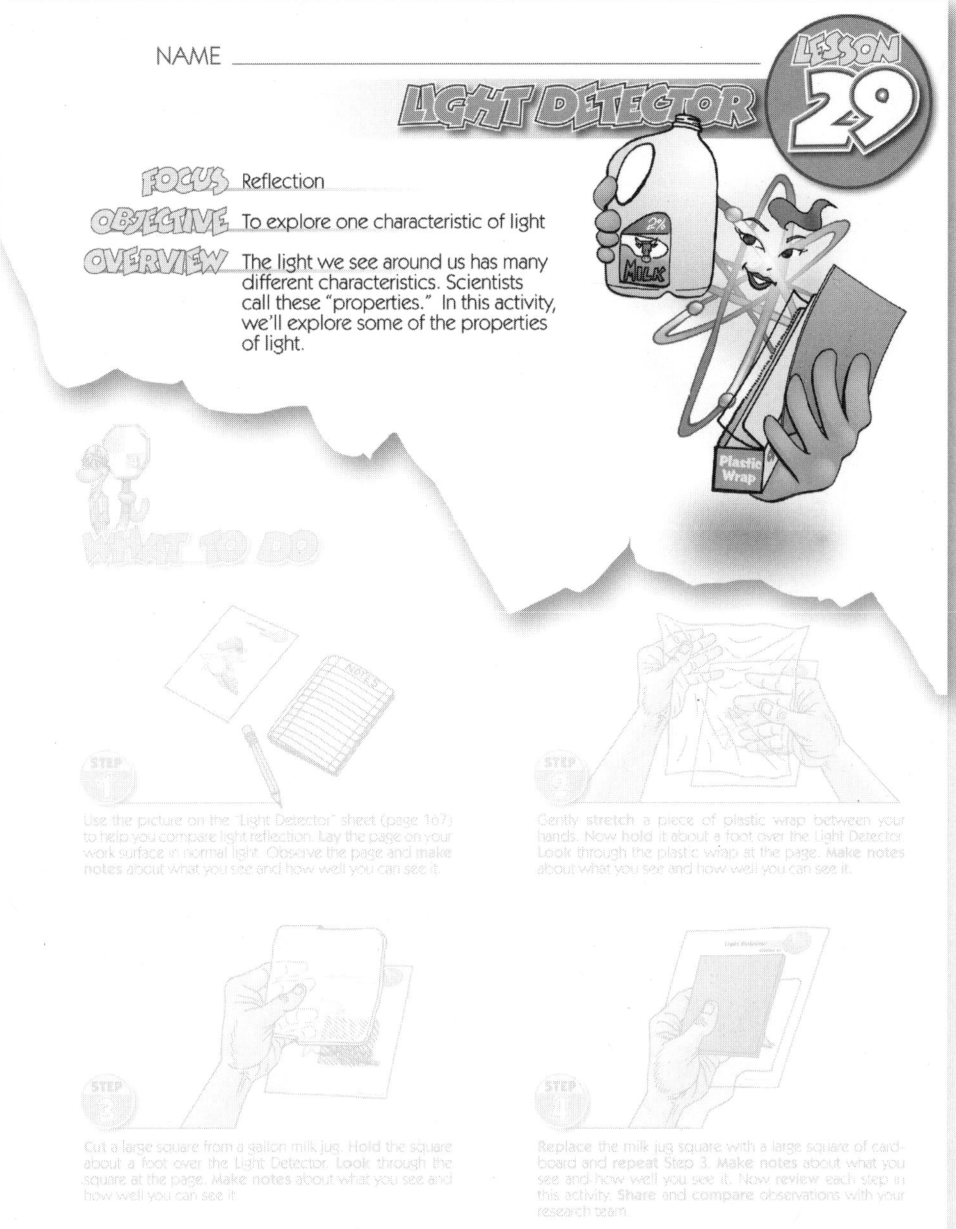

NAME ____________________

LIGHT DETECTOR

LESSON 29

FOCUS Reflection

OBJECTIVE To explore one characteristic of light

OVERVIEW The light we see around us has many different characteristics. Scientists call these "properties." In this activity, we'll explore some of the properties of light.

WHAT TO DO

STEP 1 Use the picture on the "Light Detector" sheet (page 167) to help you compare light reflection. Lay the page on your work surface in normal light. Observe the page and make notes about what you see and how well you can see it.

STEP 2 Gently stretch a piece of plastic wrap between your hands. Now hold it about a foot over the Light Detector. Look through the plastic wrap at the page. Make notes about what you see and how well you can see it.

STEP 3 Cut a large square from a gallon milk jug. Hold the square about a foot over the Light Detector. Look through the square at the page. Make notes about what you see and how well you can see it.

STEP 4 Replace the milk jug square with a large square of cardboard and repeat Step 3. Make notes about what you see and how well you see it. Now review each step in this activity. Share and compare observations with your research team.

ENERGY • MATTER 129

Category

Physical Science
Energy/Matter

Focus

Reflection

Objective

To explore one characteristic of light

National Standards

A1, A2, B1, B2, B3, E1, E2, F5, G1, G2

Materials Needed

Light Detector worksheet *(student worktext, p. 169)*
plastic wrap
milk jug (transparent)
scissors
cardboard

Safety Concerns

4. Sharp Objects
Remind students to exercise caution when using scissors.

Additional Comments

To avoid students using scissors on tough material, you may wish to cut the material in advance. Each piece should be about six inches square. Remind students that materials should only be tested by looking through them at the page — never directly at a light source (especially not the sun!).

Overview

Read the overview aloud to your students. The goal is to create an atmosphere of curiosity and inquiry.

WHAT TO DO

Monitor student research teams as they complete each step.

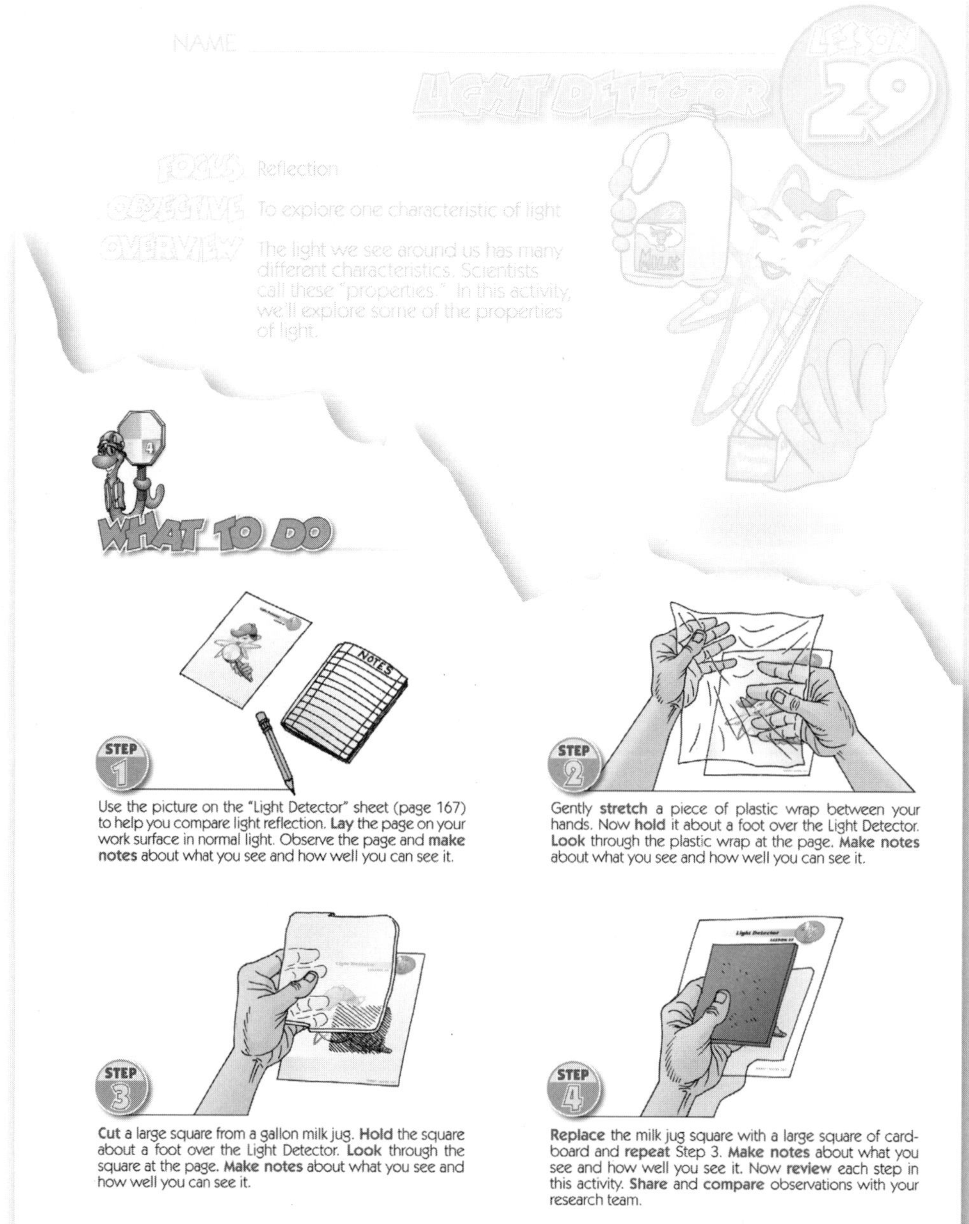

NAME

LESSON 29

LIGHT DETECTOR

FOCUS Reflection

OBJECTIVE To explore one characteristic of light

OVERVIEW The light we see around us has many different characteristics. Scientists call these "properties." In this activity, we'll explore some of the properties of light.

WHAT TO DO

STEP 1 Use the picture on the "Light Detector" sheet (page 167) to help you compare light reflection. **Lay** the page on your work surface in normal light. Observe the page and **make notes** about what you see and how well you can see it.

STEP 2 Gently **stretch** a piece of plastic wrap between your hands. Now **hold** it about a foot over the Light Detector. **Look** through the plastic wrap at the page. **Make notes** about what you see and how well you can see it.

STEP 3 **Cut** a large square from a gallon milk jug. **Hold** the square about a foot over the Light Detector. **Look** through the square at the page. **Make notes** about what you see and how well you can see it.

STEP 4 **Replace** the milk jug square with a large square of cardboard and **repeat** Step 3. **Make notes** about what you see and how well you see it. Now **review** each step in this activity. **Share** and **compare** observations with your research team.

ENERGY • MATTER 129

Teacher to Teacher

It's important to note that this activity only tests visible light. Different wave forms can behave quite differently with the same materials. For instance, your body is opaque to visible light, but it's transparent to x-rays! This is because different forms of light have different wavelengths and frequencies, and the amount of energy they carry can vary greatly. (Radio waves won't hurt you, but gamma rays can kill you!)

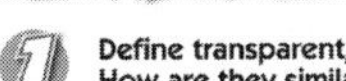

Light is a form of **energy** that travels in **waves**. **Light waves** travel through space, eventually hitting objects, then bouncing off. Scientists call this ability of light to "bounce off" objects **reflection**.

In Step 1, reflection bounced light from the page toward your eyes. You had no trouble at all seeing the page. In the other steps, however, something was between your eyes and the page.

When most of the light gets through a material (like plastic wrap), scientists call it **transparent**. When only some of the light gets through (like the milk jug), the material is called **translucent**. When no light gets through (like the cardboard), the material is called **opaque**.

WHAT WE LEARNED

1. **Define transparent, translucent, and opaque. How are they similar? How are they different?**

   transparent: most light gets through
   translucent: some light gets through
   opaque: no light gets through

2. **Describe what you saw through the transparent material in Step 2. Compare this to Step 1.**

   a) relatively clear image

   b) answers should reflect logical comparisons

3. **Describe what you saw through the translucent material in Step 3. Compare this to Step 1.**

   a) fuzzy, blurred image

   b) answers should reflect logical comparisons

4. **Describe what you saw through the opaque material in Step 4. Compare this to Step 1.**

   a) could not see through opaque material

   b) answers should reflect logical comparisons

5. **Name a transparent material. Describe how it's used. Do the same for a translucent and an opaque material.**

   examples: transparent, glass, windows; translucent, covers for lights; opaque, blinds, to block light; etc.

What Happened

Review the section with students. Emphasize bold-face words that identify key concepts and introduce new vocabulary.

***Light** is a form of **energy** that travels in **waves**. **Light waves** travel through space, eventually hitting objects, then bouncing off. Scientists call this ability of light to "bounce off" objects, **reflection**.*

In Step 1, reflection bounced light from the page toward your eyes. You had no trouble at all seeing the page. In the other steps, however, something was between your eyes and the page.

*When most of the light gets through a material (like plastic wrap), scientists call it **transparent**. When only some of the light gets through (like the milk jug), the material is called **translucent**. When no light gets through (like the cardboard), the material is called **opaque**.*

What We Learned

Answers will vary. Suggested responses are shown at left.

Conclusion

Read this section aloud to the class to summarize the concepts learned in this activity.

Food for Thought

Read the Scripture aloud to the class. Talk about the "light" that comes from God. Discuss how we can share this with others.

Journal

If time permits, have a general class discussion about notes and drawings various students added to their journal pages. Discuss correct and incorrect predictions, and remind students that this "trial and error" process is part of the scientific process.

When light bounces off an object, scientists call it "reflection." In relation to visible light, materials may be transparent, translucent, or opaque.

FOOD FOR THOUGHT

Matthew 5:14-16 Imagine a world of darkness with very little light visible anywhere. Imagine how hard it would be to survive, how difficult to see, how sad and lonely you would be. Now imagine how you would feel if someone came along and offered you a light!

This Scripture talks about a world living in spiritual darkness, a world trying to survive without God. But you have a light — the power of God's love! Jesus tells us to share that light, to reach out to others with love, caring, and compassion. By letting this light shine, you can bring hope and gladness to a dark and lonely world.

JOURNAL **My Science Notes**

132 ENERGY · MATTER

Extended Teaching

1. Have teams list transparent, translucent, and opaque materials. Compare these lists and discuss how each item is used. Challenge each team to make a three-column poster with samples of each kind of material.

2. Invite a photographer to visit your class. Ask them to demonstrate a light meter and how it works. Test it with transparent, translucent, and opaque materials. Have students write a paragraph about one thing they learn.

3. Discuss natural materials that filter light (clouds, leaves, etc.) How are these helpful? Have students write a short story about what the world might be like if there were no way to escape direct sunlight.

4. Take a field trip to a plant where milk is processed. Find out why translucent or opaque materials are used to make milk containers (photosensitivity). Have students write a paragraph about one thing they learn.

5. Invite a health care professional to visit your class. Discuss the importance of using sunscreen and sunblock. Find out what sunscreen ratings mean. Have students write a paragraph about one thing they learn.

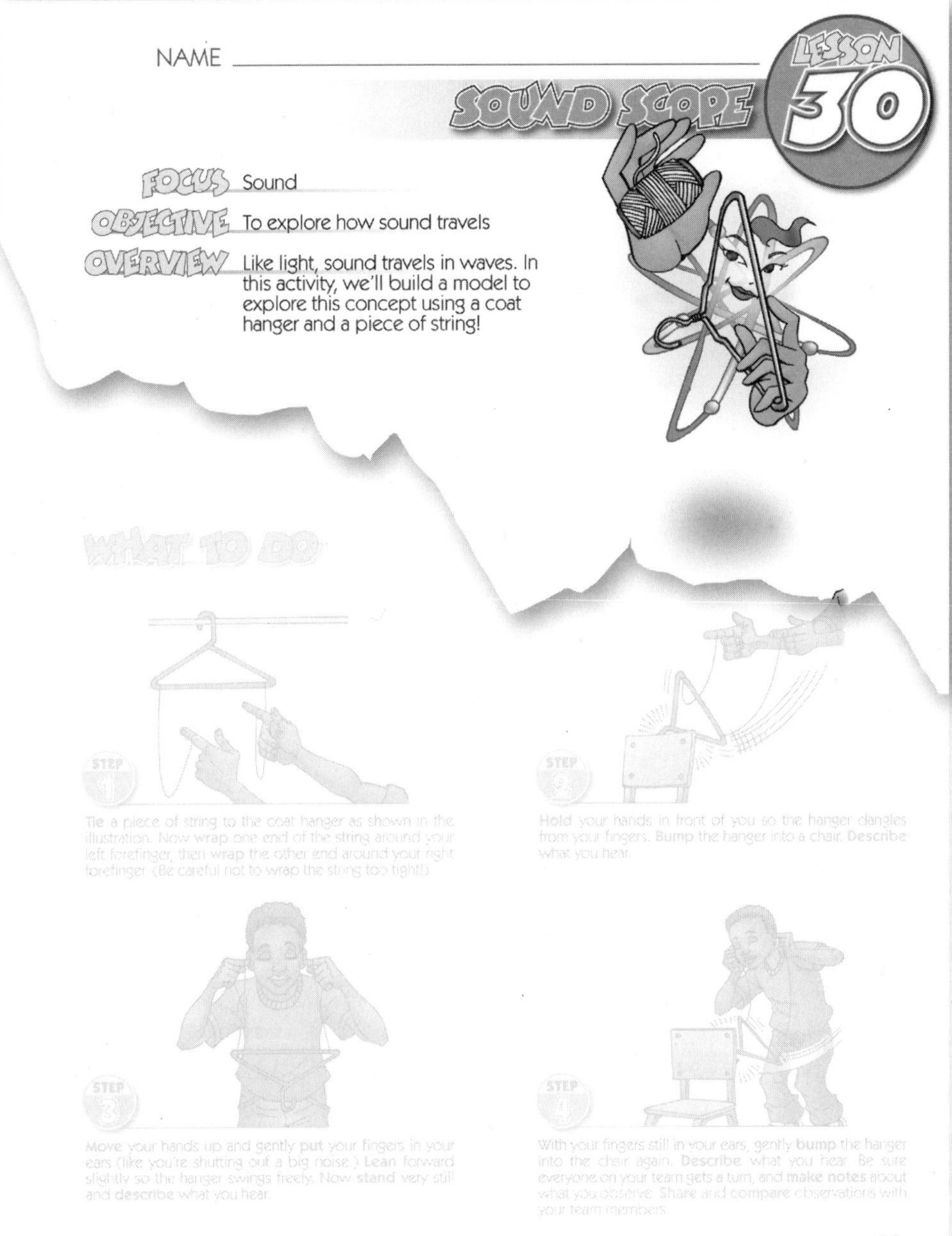
NAME ______________________________

LESSON 30

SOUND SCOPE

FOCUS Sound

OBJECTIVE To explore how sound travels

OVERVIEW Like light, sound travels in waves. In this activity, we'll build a model to explore this concept using a coat hanger and a piece of string!

WHAT TO DO

STEP 1

Tie a piece of string to the coat hanger as shown in the illustration. Now **wrap** one end of the string around your left forefinger, then wrap the other end around your right forefinger. (Be careful not to wrap the string too tight!)

STEP 2

Hold your hands in front of you so the hanger dangles from your fingers. **Bump** the hanger into a chair. **Describe** what you hear.

STEP 3

Move your hands up and gently **put** your fingers in your ears (like you're shutting out a big noise.) **Lean** forward slightly so the hanger swings freely. Now **stand** very still and **describe** what you hear.

STEP 4

With your fingers still in your ears, gently **bump** the hanger into the chair again. **Describe** what you hear. Be sure everyone on your team gets a turn, and **make notes** about what you observe. Share and compare observations with your team members.

ENERGY • MATTER 133

Category

Physical Science
Energy/Matter

Focus

Sound

Objective

To explore how sound travels

National Standards

A1, A2, B1, B2, B3, E1, E2, F5, G1, G2

Materials Needed

string
coat hanger

Safety Concerns

none

Additional Comments

A four-foot piece of string works well for this activity. You can have students either wrap the string around the hanger and tie at the corners, or cut the string in two and tie at the corners. Remind students to exercise caution as they move around with this device.

Overview

Read the overview aloud to your students. The goal is to create an atmosphere of curiosity and inquiry.

WHAT TO DO

Monitor student research teams as they complete each step.

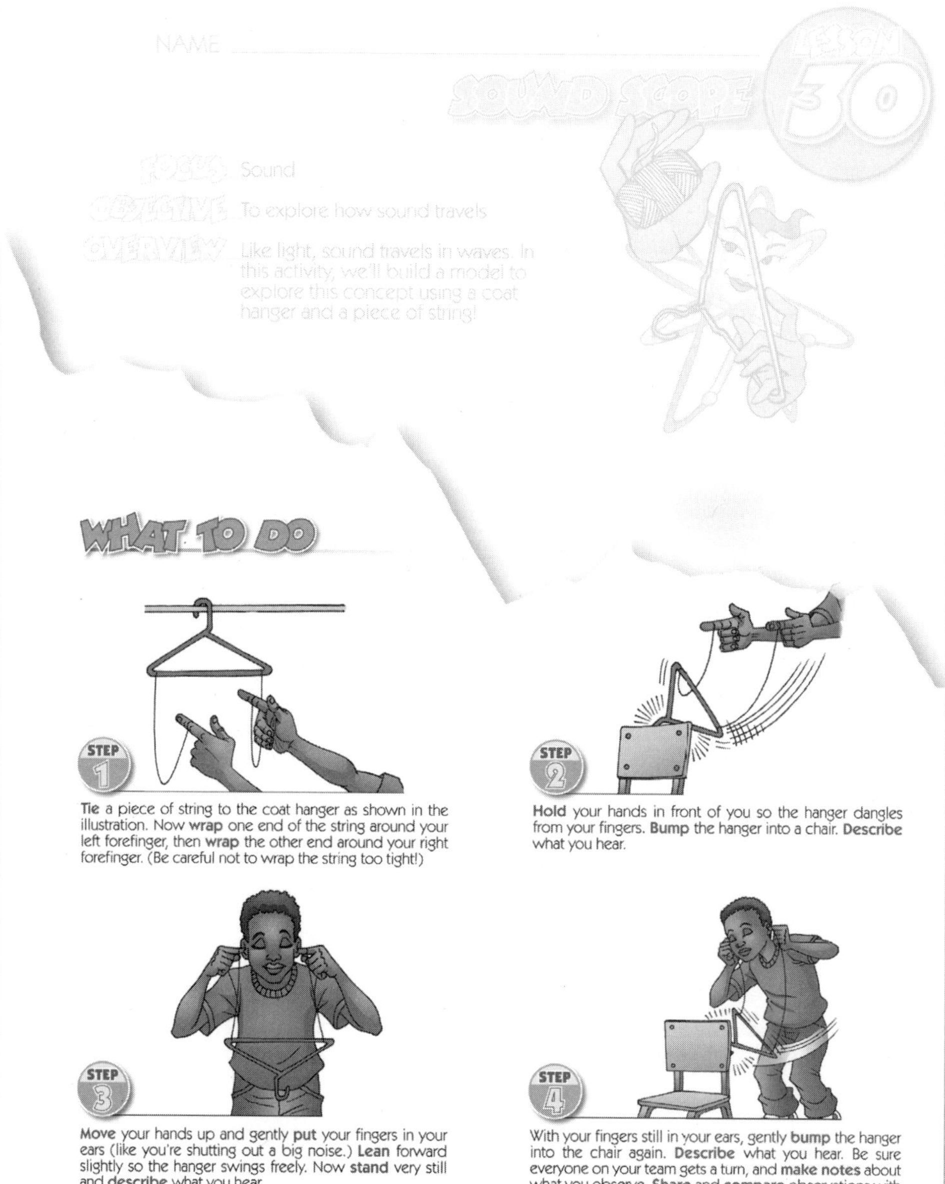

NAME

SOUND SCOPE

LESSON 30

FOCUS Sound

OBJECTIVE To explore how sound travels

OVERVIEW Like light, sound travels in waves. In this activity, we'll build a model to explore this concept using a coat hanger and a piece of string!

WHAT TO DO

STEP 1

Tie a piece of string to the coat hanger as shown in the illustration. Now **wrap** one end of the string around your left forefinger, then **wrap** the other end around your right forefinger. (Be careful not to wrap the string too tight!)

STEP 2

Hold your hands in front of you so the hanger dangles from your fingers. **Bump** the hanger into a chair. **Describe** what you hear.

STEP 3

Move your hands up and gently **put** your fingers in your ears (like you're shutting out a big noise.) **Lean** forward slightly so the hanger swings freely. Now **stand** very still and **describe** what you hear.

STEP 4

With your fingers still in your ears, gently **bump** the hanger into the chair again. **Describe** what you hear. Be sure everyone on your team gets a turn, and **make notes** about what you observe. **Share** and **compare** observations with your team members.

ENERGY • MATTER 133

Teacher to Teacher

Sound is measured in decibels. A decibel (written dB) is actually 1/10 of a "bel" — a unit of measurement named after Alexander Graham Bell! Continuous sound at 85 dB or above can begin to damage hearing. Sounds over 120 dB can cause immediate damage.

According to some sources (see http://www.abelard.org/hear/hear.htm), listening to amplified music in the 110 and 130 dB range for as little as 30 minutes per day can lead to permanent hearing damage.

Sound waves are created by the **vibration** of **molecules** (little particles of **matter**). These can be molecules of almost anything — air, concrete, paper, metal, or even a piece of string! Each time a molecule vibrates, it passes some of its **energy** on to the molecule next to it.

In Step 2 you bumped the wire hanger into a chair. This made the wire vibrate hard enough to make the surrounding air molecules vibrate, too. That vibration traveled through the air molecules to your ear. You heard this vibration as sound.

In Step 3 you bumped the chair again. But this time the vibration traveled from the wire through the string to your ear. Since string molecules are much more closely packed than air molecules, the sound traveled much better!

WHAT WE LEARNED

1. **Describe one way that sound waves are created. What role do molecules play?**

a) answers will vary

b) sound waves are created by the vibration of molecules

2. **Why might some sounds travel better through concrete than air? Describe what you heard in Step 2.**

a) the molecules are closer

b) a faint buzzing noise, etc.

134 ENERGY • MATTER

3. **Describe what you heard in Step 3. How was it similar to Step 2? How was it different?**

a) a loud buzzing

b) similar: same noise

c) different: much louder

4. **In general, would sound travel faster though the air or under the water? Would sound travel in space (no air)? Why or why not?**

a) under water because molecules are closer

b) no

c) no air molecules to transfer sound

5. **Based on what you've learned, why might foam rubber be a good sound barrier? What other materials might be good sound barriers?**

a) isolated air spaces, molecules spread apart

b) fiberglass, foam core, blankets, rubber, etc.

ENERGY • MATTER 135

What Happened

Review the section with students. Emphasize bold-face words that identify key concepts and introduce new vocabulary.

***Sound waves** are created by the **vibration** of **molecules** (little particles of **matter**). These can be molecules of almost anything — air, concrete, paper, metal, or even a piece of string! Each time a molecule vibrates, it passes some of its **energy** on to the molecule next to it.*

In Step 2, you bumped the wire hanger into a chair. This made the wire vibrate hard enough to make the surrounding air molecules vibrate, too. That vibration traveled through the air molecules to your ear. You heard this vibration as sound.

In Step 3, you bumped the chair again. But this time the vibration traveled from the wire through the string to your ear. Since string molecules are much more closely packed than air molecules, the sound traveled much better!

What We Learned

Answers will vary. Suggested responses are shown at left.

Conclusion

Read this section aloud to the class to summarize the concepts learned in this activity.

Food for Thought

Read the Scripture aloud to the class. Talk about the difference between just hearing and really listening. Discuss ways we can "listen" to God.

Journal

If time permits, have a general class discussion about notes and drawings various students added to their journal pages. Discuss correct and incorrect predictions, and remind students that this "trial and error" process is part of the scientific process.

Sound waves are created by the vibration of molecules. The more compact the molecules, the easier the sound can travel. In other words, the more dense the material, the better sound travels through it.

Mark 4:9,23 In Step 3, you heard every little bump to the coat hanger — loud and clear! The combination of metal and string worked together to transfer the sound directly to your ears.

This Scripture is a reminder that your ears and mind must work together to transfer meaning to your soul. In other words, really listening means more than just hearing! As Jesus shared parables with the crowd, he would occasionally say something like, "If you have ears, then listen!" He wanted people to hear more than just mere words. He wanted to touch their hearts — just as he wants to touch yours!

JOURNAL **My Science Notes**

136 ENERGY · MATTER

Extended Teaching

1. Give each team the cardboard tube from a roll of paper towels. Have them take turns listening to someone across the table whispering. Discuss how using the tube changed what they heard.

2. Invite a nurse to visit your classroom. Ask him/her to demonstrate the correct use of a stethoscope, then let students listen through the stethoscope. Have students write a paragraph about one thing they learn.

3. Wait for a stormy day. Have students watch for lightning strikes, then count the delay until they hear the thunder to estimate distance. (A five second delay in sound equals about one mile of distance.)

4. Have teams research how dolphins, bats, and other creatures use sound waves. Challenge each team to create a poster illustrating a specific activity that uses sound waves (finding food, dodging objects, etc.).

5. Invite a state trooper to visit your classroom. Ask him/her to demonstrate a radar gun and explain how it works. Have students write a paragraph about one thing they learn.

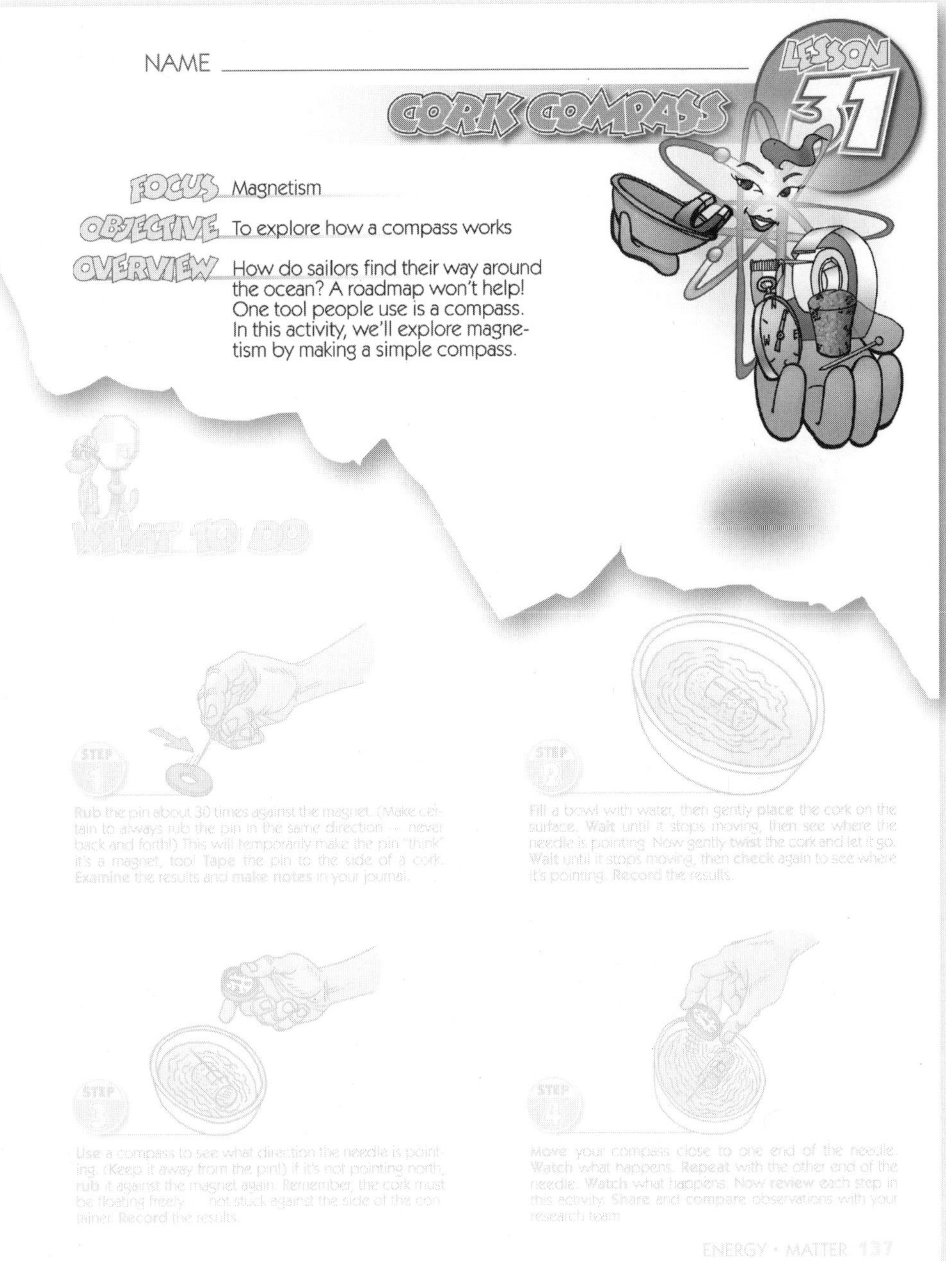
NAME ____________________

LESSON 31

CORK COMPASS

FOCUS Magnetism

OBJECTIVE To explore how a compass works

OVERVIEW How do sailors find their way around the ocean? A roadmap won't help! One tool people use is a compass. In this activity, we'll explore magnetism by making a simple compass.

WHAT TO DO

STEP 1 Rub the pin about 30 times against the magnet. (Make certain to always rub the pin in the same direction — never back and forth!) This will temporarily make the pin "think" it's a magnet, too! Tape the pin to the side of a cork. Examine the results and make notes in your journal.

STEP 2 Fill a bowl with water, then gently place the cork on the surface. Wait until it stops moving, then see where the needle is pointing. Now gently twist the cork and let it go. Wait until it stops moving, then check again to see where it's pointing. Record the results.

STEP 3 Use a compass to see what direction the needle is pointing. (Keep it away from the pin!) If it's not pointing north, rub it against the magnet again. Remember, the cork must be floating freely — not stuck against the side of the container. Record the results.

STEP 4 Move your compass close to one end of the needle. Watch what happens. Repeat with the other end of the needle. Watch what happens. Now review each step in this activity. Share and compare observations with your research team.

ENERGY • MATTER 137

Category

Physical Science
Energy/Matter

Focus

Magnetism

Objective

To explore how a compass works

National Standards

A1, A2, B1, B2, D1, E1, E2, F5, G1, G2, G3

Materials Needed

straight pin
magnet
cork
tape
bowl (non-metallic)
water
compass

Safety Concerns

4. Sharp Objects
Remind students to exercise caution with the needle.

4. Slipping
There is also a potential for spills with this activity. Remind students to exercise caution.

Additional Comments

Remind students to be patient. Sometimes it takes a lot of rubbing to convince a needle that it's a magnet! Monitor to make sure students are rubbing it the same direction, not back-and-forth. Also, keep water well below the rim of the bowls, or corks will be drawn to the edge.

Overview

Read the overview aloud to your students. The goal is to create an atmosphere of curiosity and inquiry.

WHAT TO DO

Monitor student research teams as they complete each step.

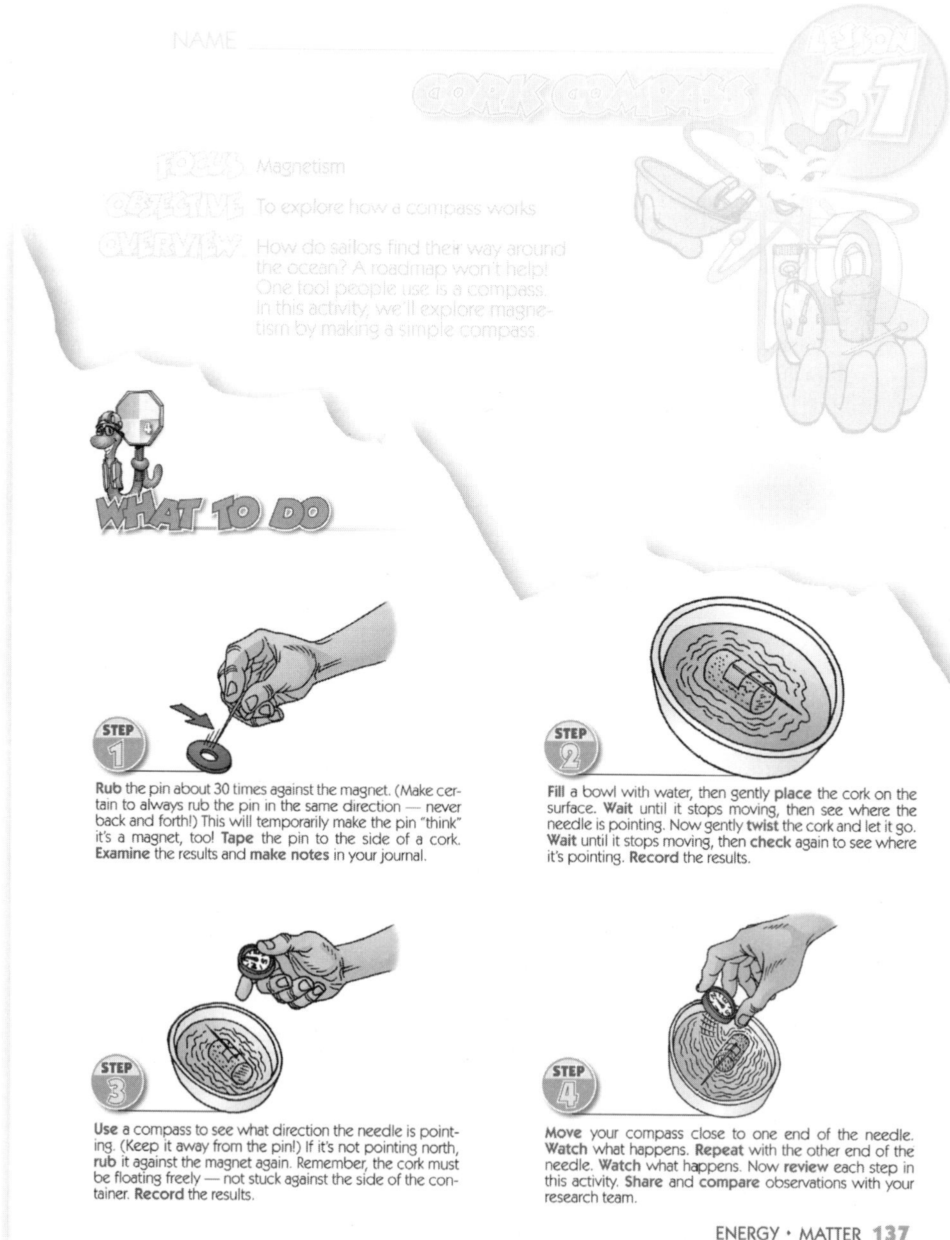

NAME

CORK COMPASS

LESSON 31

TOPIC Magnetism

OBJECTIVE To explore how a compass works

OVERVIEW How do sailors find their way around the ocean? A roadmap won't help! One tool people use is a compass. In this activity, we'll explore magnetism by making a simple compass.

WHAT TO DO

STEP 1

Rub the pin about 30 times against the magnet. (Make certain to always rub the pin in the same direction — never back and forth!) This will temporarily make the pin "think" it's a magnet, too! **Tape** the pin to the side of a cork. **Examine** the results and **make notes** in your journal.

STEP 2

Fill a bowl with water, then gently **place** the cork on the surface. **Wait** until it stops moving, then see where the needle is pointing. Now gently **twist** the cork and let it go. **Wait** until it stops moving, then **check** again to see where it's pointing. **Record** the results.

STEP 3

Use a compass to see what direction the needle is pointing. (Keep it away from the pin!) If it's not pointing north, **rub** it against the magnet again. Remember, the cork must be floating freely — not stuck against the side of the container. **Record** the results.

STEP 4

Move your compass close to one end of the needle. **Watch** what happens. **Repeat** with the other end of the needle. **Watch** what happens. Now **review** each step in this activity. **Share** and **compare** observations with your research team.

ENERGY • MATTER 137

Teacher to Teacher

For centuries, navigators relied on the compass to help them find their way across vast, trackless seas. Early compasses were made from magnetite, a magnetic iron ore. Because of its unique properties, magnetite was also known as lodestone, which means "leading stone." Today's navigators rely on GPS (global positioning satellites) systems. These devices are extremely accurate, often to within a few feet!

Magnetism is a special property found only in a few materials. **Iron** and **steel** are two materials affected by magnetism. If you place a magnet near these metals, they are **attracted** (pulled) by the magnetism. If you rub a small piece of metal (like the pin) with a magnet, you make the iron or steel particles line up. This temporarily turns the metal into a magnet too!

The needle of a **compass** is a small magnet used for a specific purpose. Since it always lines itself up with the **magnetic field** of the Earth, it always points in a certain direction. (A magnetic field is the area where a magnet can **pull** or **push** on magnetic material.) In this activity, you magnetized the pin, then set it on the cork making a simple compass. Just like a real compass, the Earth's magnetic field made your pin into a pointer.

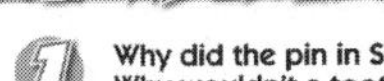

1. Why did the pin in Step 1 have to be iron or steel? Why wouldn't a toothpick work?

   Iron or steel are affected by magnetism; a toothpick (wood) is not.

2. What happened when you twisted the cork and released it in Step 2? Why?

   a) it moved around, but then pointed in one way

   b) it was lining up with Earth's magnetic field

3. What did you observe when you compared the compass to the needle in Step 3?

   The needle was lined up north/south; the needle pointed north; etc.

4. Describe what happened when you brought the compass near the needle in Step 4. Why did this happen?

   a) the compass tried to point to the needle

   b) the needle was the closest source of magnetism

5. How can a compass help hikers in the wilderness? What might happen if a large iron deposit were near?

   a) it helps them know which way is north

   b) the compass would not work properly

What Happened

Review the section with students. Emphasize bold-face words that identify key concepts and introduce new vocabulary.

***Magnetism** is a special property found only in a few materials. **Iron** and **steel** are two materials affected by magnetism. If you place a magnet near these metals, they are **attracted** (pulled) by the magnetism. If you rub a small piece of metal (like the pin) with a magnet, you make the iron or steel particles line up. This temporarily turns the metal into a magnet!*

*The needle of a **compass** is a small magnet used for a specific purpose. Since it always lines itself up with the **magnetic field** of the Earth, it always points in a certain direction. (A magnetic field is the area where a magnet can **pull** or **push** on magnetic material.) In this activity, you magnetized the pin, then set it on the cork, making a simple compass. Just like a real compass, the Earth's magnetic field made your pin into a pointer.*

What We Learned

Answers will vary. Suggested responses are shown at left.

Conclusion

Read this section aloud to the class to summarize the concepts learned in this activity.

Food for Thought

Read the Scripture aloud to the class. Talk about how God's word provides guidance for our lives. Discuss ways we can get closer to God.

Journal

If time permits, have a general class discussion about notes and drawings various students added to their journal pages. Discuss correct and incorrect predictions, and remind students that this "trial and error" process is part of the scientific process.

Magnetism is a property of some materials. Some metals can be made magnetic by rubbing them with a magnet. The needle of a compass is a magnetized piece of metal used for a specific purpose.

Psalm 25:4-5 Although today most professionals rely on GPS (global positioning system) units to determine where they are, a compass is still a handy reference tool for pointing the way.

Just as these tools provide physical guidance, God's Word provides spiritual guidance. It's all too easy to get lost in this world of sin. Temptations surround us, and we often get distracted and confused. But Scripture tells us that God is always there to show us the way. If you spend time learning to trust him, then he will direct your path!

JOURNAL **My Science Notes**

Extended Teaching

1. Using the Internet, have students research magnetism. Challenge each team to create a poster illustrating one aspect of magnetism.

2. Find someone whose hobby is orienteering. Invite him/her to visit your classroom. Discuss orienteering and have him/her demonstrate compass skills. Have students write a paragraph about one thing they learn.

3. Take a field trip to a sporting good store. Ask for a demonstration of various GPS devices. Find out how they are used in surveying, navigation, and rescue. Have students write a paragraph about one thing they learn.

4. Learn more about the longitude and latitude lines on maps. Locate the equator, prime meridian, and the international date line. See if students can find the Tropic of Capricorn and the Tropic of Cancer, too!

5. Have students discover the exact longitude and latitude of your school! (Rely on advanced map skills, not a GPS device.) Challenge teams to find towns with the same latitude as yours, but a different longitude.

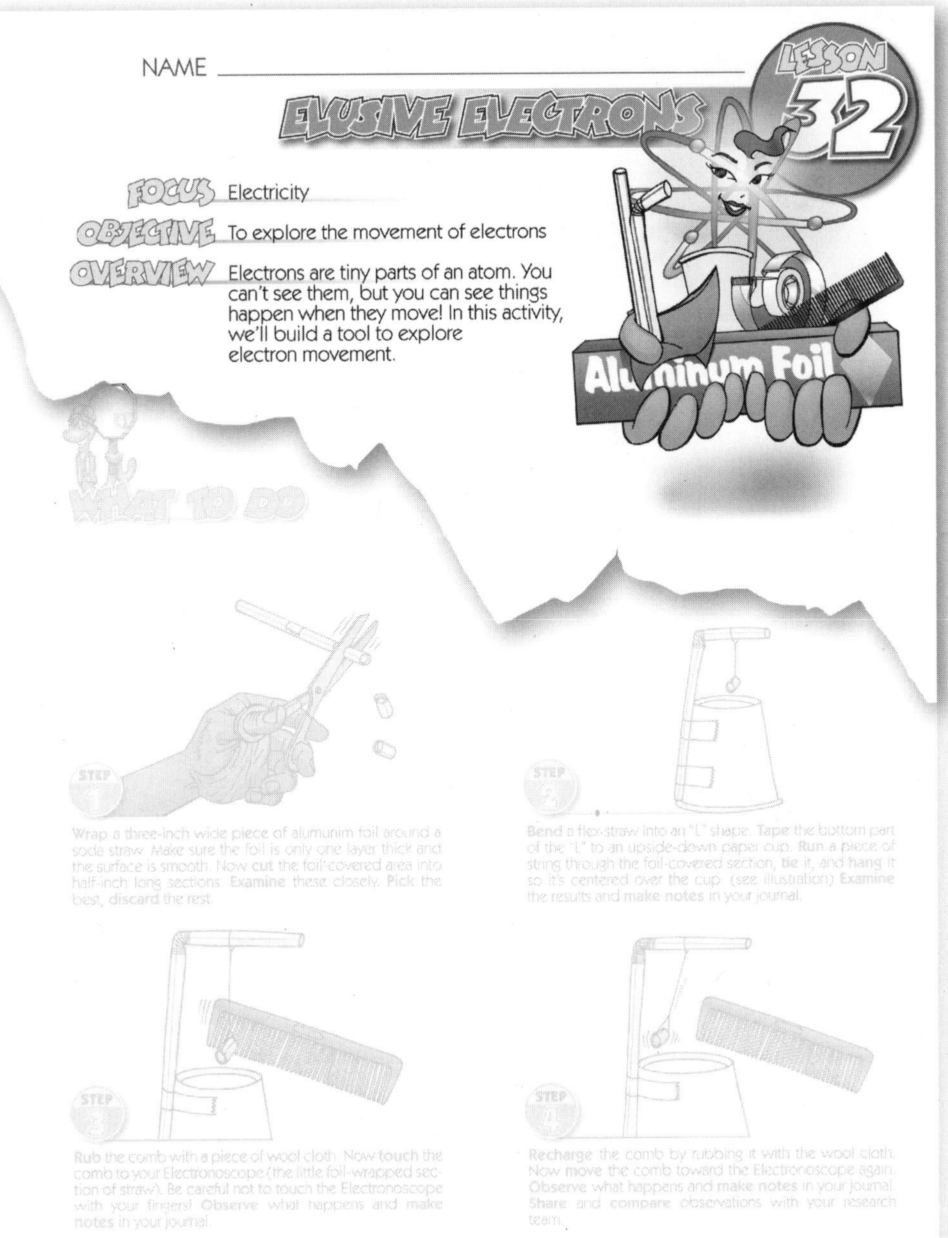

NAME ______________________

ELUSIVE ELECTRONS

LESSON 32

FOCUS Electricity

OBJECTIVE To explore the movement of electrons

OVERVIEW Electrons are tiny parts of an atom. You can't see them, but you can see things happen when they move! In this activity, we'll build a tool to explore electron movement.

WHAT TO DO

STEP 1 Wrap a three-inch wide piece of alumunim foil around a soda straw. Make sure the foil is only one layer thick and the surface is smooth. Now **cut** the foil-covered area into half-inch long sections. **Examine** these closely. **Pick** the best, **discard** the rest.

STEP 2 Bend a flex-straw into an "L" shape. Tape the bottom part of the "L" to an upside-down paper cup. **Run** a piece of string through the foil-covered section, **tie** it, and **hang** it so it's centered over the cup (see illustration) **Examine** the results and **make notes** in your journal.

STEP 3 Rub the comb with a piece of wool cloth. Now **touch** the comb to your Electronoscope (the little foil-wrapped section of straw). Be careful not to touch the Electronoscope with your fingers! **Observe** what happens and **make notes** in your journal.

STEP 4 **Recharge** the comb by rubbing it with the wool cloth. Now **move** the comb toward the Electronoscope again. **Observe** what happens and **make notes** in your journal. **Share** and **compare** observations with your research team.

ENERGY • MATTER 141

Category

Physical Science
Energy/Matter

Focus

Electricity

Objective

To explore the movement of electrons

National Standards

A1, A2, B1, B2, B3, E1, E2, F5, G1, G2

Materials Needed

soda straw - 1
flex straw - 1
paper cup
string
comb
wool
aluminum foil
scissors
tape

Safety Concerns

4. Sharp Objects
Remind students to exercise caution with the needle.

Additional Comments

Ask students if they know the names of the three main parts of an atom. Briefly discuss protons, neutrons, and electrons. Tell students they'll be making a special device to show the presence of invisible electrons! The device they create is a simple version of an "electronoscope."

Overview

Read the overview aloud to your students. The goal is to create an atmosphere of curiosity and inquiry.

WHAT TO DO

Monitor student research teams as they complete each step.

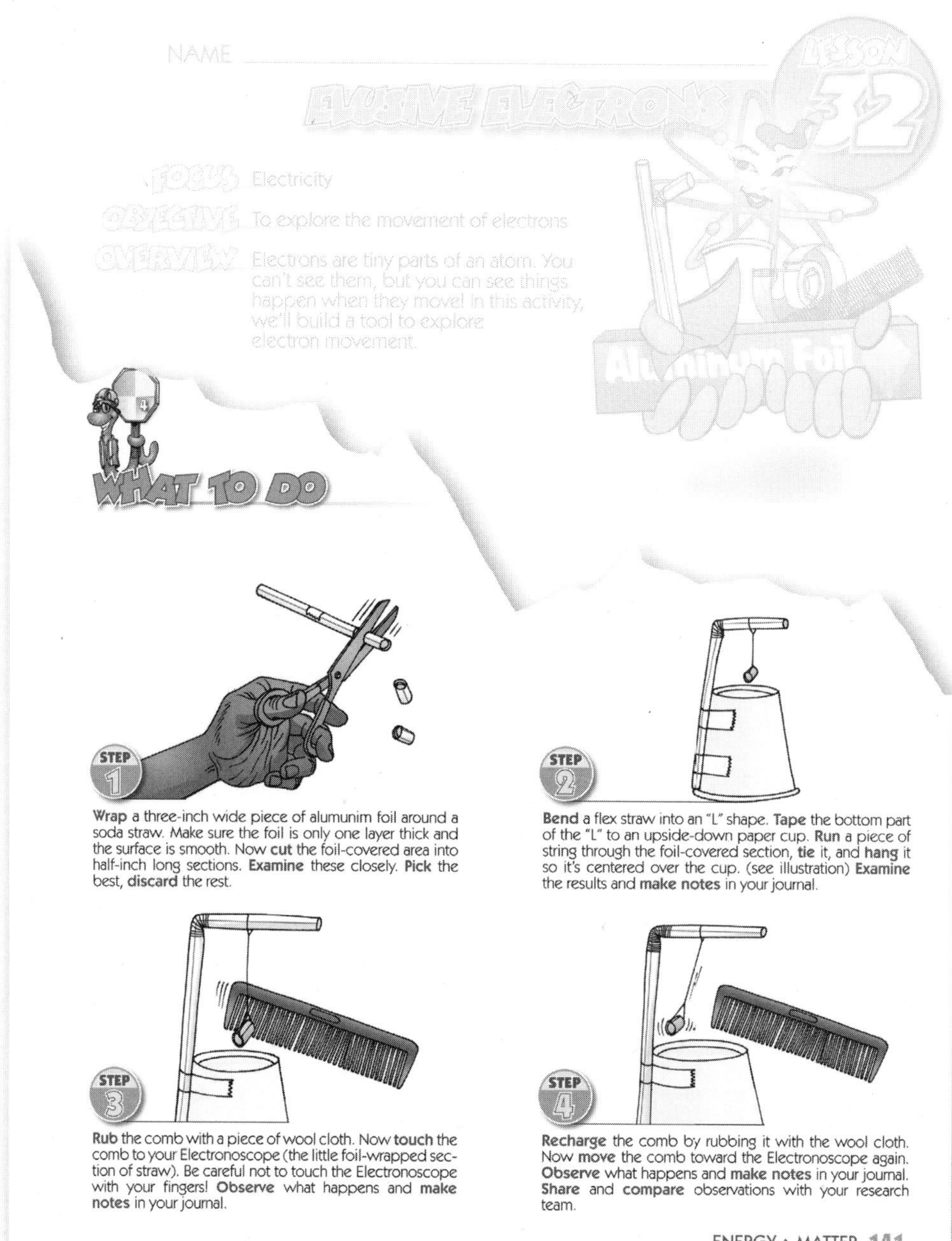

NAME

LESSON 32

ELUSIVE ELECTRONS

FOCUS Electricity

OBJECTIVE To explore the movement of electrons

OVERVIEW Electrons are tiny parts of an atom. You can't see them, but you can see things happen when they move! In this activity, we'll build a tool to explore electron movement.

WHAT TO DO

STEP 1

Wrap a three-inch wide piece of alumunim foil around a soda straw. Make sure the foil is only one layer thick and the surface is smooth. Now **cut** the foil-covered area into half-inch long sections. **Examine** these closely. **Pick** the best, **discard** the rest.

STEP 2

Bend a flex straw into an "L" shape. **Tape** the bottom part of the "L" to an upside-down paper cup. **Run** a piece of string through the foil-covered section, **tie** it, and **hang** it so it's centered over the cup. (see illustration) **Examine** the results and **make notes** in your journal.

STEP 3

Rub the comb with a piece of wool cloth. Now **touch** the comb to your Electronoscope (the little foil-wrapped section of straw). Be careful not to touch the Electronoscope with your fingers! **Observe** what happens and **make notes** in your journal.

STEP 4

Recharge the comb by rubbing it with the wool cloth. Now **move** the comb toward the Electronoscope again. **Observe** what happens and **make notes** in your journal. **Share** and **compare** observations with your research team.

ENERGY • MATTER 141

Teacher to Teacher

The three particles discussed in this lesson (protons, neutrons, electrons) are only a few of many subatomic particles found in the atom. While electrons flow freely from atom to atom (and through electric wires), the proton and neutron are bound within the nucleus. To get them moving requires a nuclear reaction!

Atoms are made of tiny particles: **protons, neutrons,** and **electrons**. We can't make the first two do much, but we can really get those electrons moving! In fact, that's just what **electricity** is — the process of electrons moving around or being stored. (The electricity in this activity was **static electricity**.)

So what happened? The rubbing comb pulled electrons off the wool. Then when you touched the comb to your home-made **electronoscope**, a few electrons jumped off and got stuck there.

But when you re-charged the comb and moved it toward the aluminum, the straw tried to move away. This happened because every electron has a negative charge, and charges that are alike repel (push away from) each other!

WHAT WE LEARNED

1. **In Step 1, why did we use a plastic straw? Why wouldn't a piece of wire work?**

a) plastic is an insulator, won't let electrons flow

b) wire is made of metal, no insulation value

2. **Name the three main parts of an atom. Which part can we make move?**

a) proton, neutron, electron

b) the electrons

3. **Describe what happened in Step 3. What kind of electricity was produced?**

a) answers will vary

b) static or stationary electricity

4. **Describe what happened in Step 4. How was this similar to Step 3? How was it different?**

a) answers will vary

b) same materials, but in Step 4 it moved away

5. **What is the common name for moving electrons? Name three things that use moving electrons to do work.**

a) electricity

b) examples: blender, clock, computer, toaster, etc.

What Happened

Review the section with students. Emphasize bold-face words that identify key concepts and introduce new vocabulary.

***Atoms** are made of tiny particles: **protons**, **neutrons**, and **electrons**. We can't make the first two do much, but we can really get those electrons moving! In fact, that's just what **electricity** is — the process of electrons moving around or being stored. (The electricity in this activity was **static electricity**.)*

*So what happened? The rubbing comb pulled electrons off the wool. Then when you touched the comb to your home-made **electronoscope**, a few electrons jumped off and got stuck there.*

But when you recharged the comb and moved it toward the aluminum, the straw tried to move away. This happened because every electron has a negative charge, and charges that are alike repel (push away from) each other!

What We Learned

Answers will vary. Suggested responses are shown at left.

Conclusion

Read this section aloud to the class to summarize the concepts learned in this activity.

Food for Thought

Read the Scripture aloud to the class. Talk about God's awesome power. Discuss how we can tap into God's power by learning to trust him.

Journal

If time permits, have a general class discussion about notes and drawings various students added to their journal pages. Discuss correct and incorrect predictions, and remind students that this "trial and error" process is part of the scientific process.

Atoms are composed of protons, neutrons, and electrons. Electrons are always negatively charged. Particles with the same charge repel each other. The movement of electrons is called electricity.

Mark 16:3-4 Even though you can't see it, there's power all around you. This activity demonstrated the presence of one kind of unseen power (electrons) and even used the power to do a little work (moving the straw). Imagine the tremendous power available if you could harness millions of these electrons!

But God's power is infinitely greater! The women who went to Jesus' tomb caught a glimpse of God's power. They were concerend about moving the massive stone that blocked the entrance — only to find it was already rolled away, and Jesus was raised from the dead! Even though you can't see it, God's tremendous power is everywhere. To tap into this power, learn to trust in God.

JOURNAL My Science Notes

144 ENERGY • MATTER

Extended Teaching

1. Repeat this activity using a glass rod rubbed with silk. (Hint: it takes a LOT of rubbing!) Have students compare the results with the original activity. How were they similar? How were they different?

2. Invite someone from the electric company to visit your classroom. Discuss how electricity is made and learn about electrical safety rules. Have students write a paragraph about one thing they learn.

3. Using the Internet, have teams research other ways to make electricity (wind power, solar energy, etc.). Challenge each team to create a poster illustrating one kind of alternate power generation.

4. According to NOAA, nearly 100 people are killed (and roughly 250 injured) by lightning strikes each year. Have teams research this topic, then create a bulletin board about lightning safety.

5. Take a field trip to a hydroelectric, coal, or nuclear generating plant. Find out how electricity is generated and transferred. Have students write a paragraph about one thing they learn.

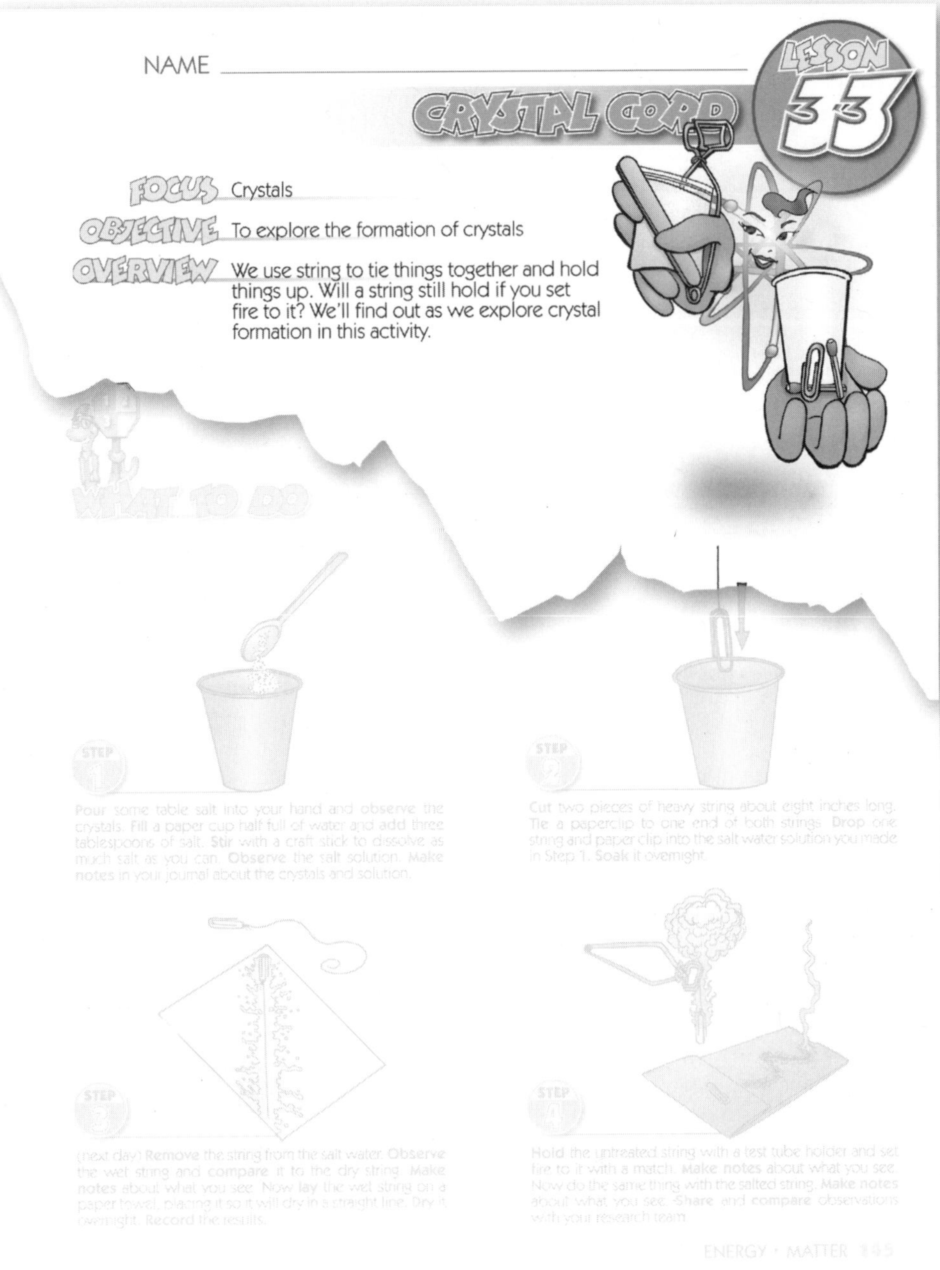

NAME ______________________________

CRYSTAL CORD

LESSON 33

FOCUS Crystals

OBJECTIVE To explore the formation of crystals

OVERVIEW We use string to tie things together and hold things up. Will a string still hold if you set fire to it? We'll find out as we explore crystal formation in this activity.

WHAT TO DO

STEP 1

Pour some table salt into your hand and observe the crystals. Fill a paper cup half full of water and add three tablespoons of salt. Stir with a craft stick to dissolve as much salt as you can. Observe the salt solution. Make notes in your journal about the crystals and solution.

STEP 2

Cut two pieces of heavy string about eight inches long. Tie a paperclip to one end of both strings. Drop one string and paper clip into the salt water solution you made in Step 1. Soak it overnight.

STEP 3

(next day) Remove the string from the salt water. Observe the wet string and compare it to the dry string. Make notes about what you see. Now lay the wet string on a paper towel, placing it so it will dry in a straight line. Dry it overnight. Record the results.

STEP 4

Hold the untreated string with a test tube holder and set fire to it with a match. Make notes about what you see. Now do the same thing with the salted string. Make notes about what you see. Share and compare observations with your research team.

ENERGY · MATTER 145

Category

Physical Science
Energy/Matter

Focus

Crystals

Objective

To explore the formation of crystals

National Standards

A1, A2, B1, B2, G1, G2

Materials Needed

salt
paper cup
spoon
craft stick
heavy string-2
paperclips-2
test tube holder
water
paper towel
match

Safety Concerns

1. Goggles/Gloves
Take precautions to protect students' eyes and hands.

2. Thermal Burn
Remind students to exercise caution around open flame.

3. Slipping
There is a potential for spills with this activity. Remind students to exercise caution.

Additional Comments

Use heavy string to soak up plenty of salt. Have extra "salted" strings on hand in case some break. To avoid students handling matches, light the strings yourself. Burning strings must be held over a sink or non-flammable surface. Always hold burning strings with a test tube holder! If this activity seems too advanced for your students, use it as a demonstration only.

Overview

Read the overview aloud to your students. The goal is to create an atmosphere of curiosity and inquiry.

WHAT TO DO

Monitor student research teams as they complete each step.

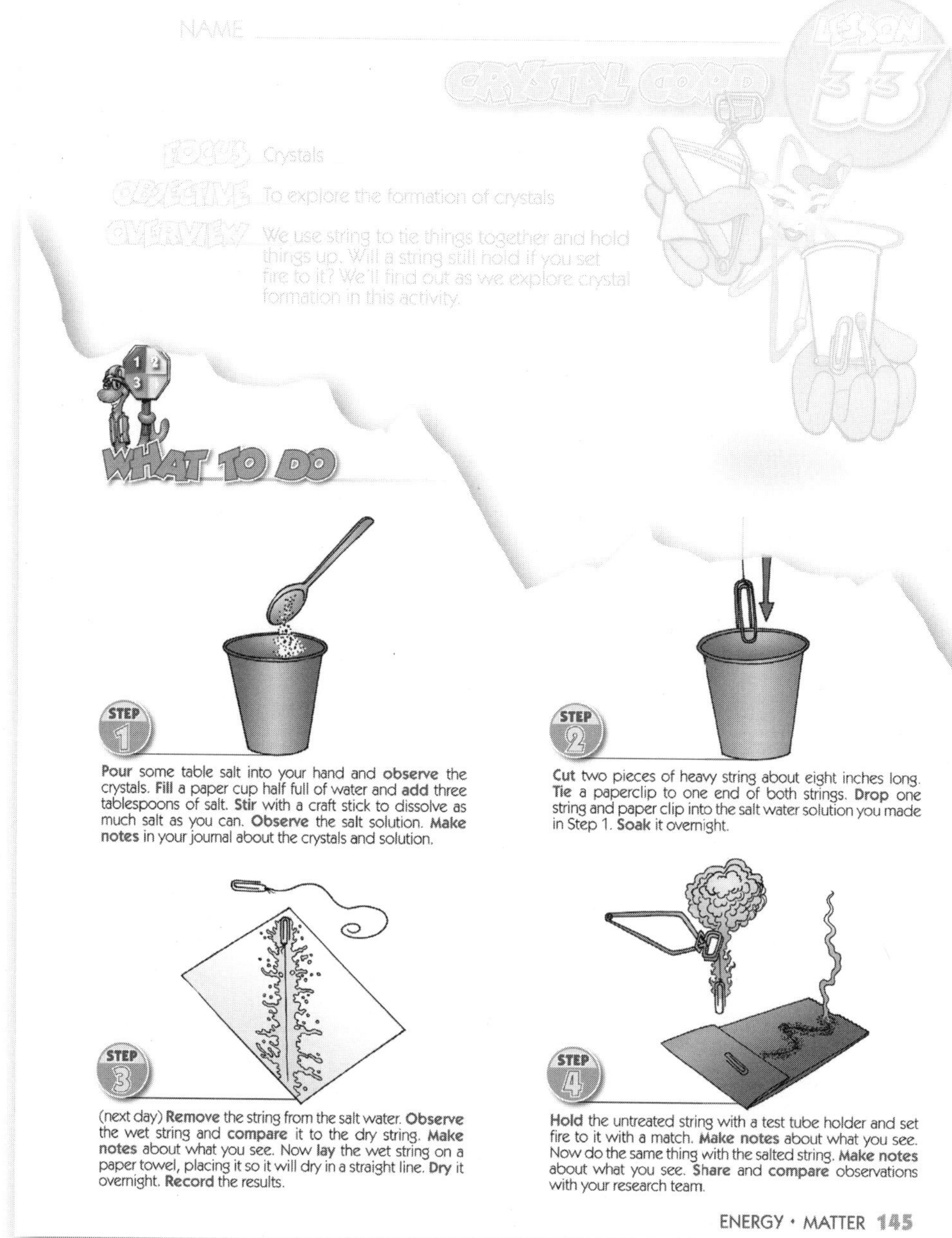

Teacher to Teacher

Crystals form in different ways and under different conditions. Generally the slower a crystal forms, the larger it is. Depending on heat, pressure, and other factors, the same element can form different kinds of crystals. For instance, diamonds and graphite are both forms of carbon. The carbon that creates diamonds, however, has been subjected to huge pressures and much higher temperatures.

WHAT HAPPENED?

Gravity is the **force** that pulled the paperclip down. Your arm (holding the string) provided the **opposing force.** When the string burned, the paperclip wasn't connected to you anymore. This let the force of gravity win.

But when you soaked the string in the salt water, the **solution** entered the string's **fibers**. As the string dried, the water **evaporated**, and **crystals** of salt were left behind. (A crystal is a **solid** whose tiny particles are arranged in a specific pattern.)

When you set fire to the string whose fibers were permeated with salt crystals, the fire burned the string fibers up, just like before. Since salt doesn't burn easily, the **bond** of the salt crystals held them together, making a Crystal String that supported the paperclip — beating the **pull** of gravity!

WHAT WE LEARNED

1 Describe the salt crystals in Step 1? What happened to the crystals when you added them to water?

a) answers should reflect color, hardness, shape, etc.

b) they dissolved

2 Compare the two strings in Step 3. How were they similar? How were they different?

a) similar: both tied to paperclip, same material

b) different: one soaked with salt water.

146 ENERGY • MATTER

3 What happened to the paperclip when you burned the unsalted string in Step 4?

The string burned up and the paper clip fell.

4 What happened to the paperclip when you burned the salted string in Step 4?

The string burned up, but the salt crystals made a "rope" that kept the paperclip from falling.

5 Define "solution," "fiber," and "crystal." What role did these play in Step 4?

a) solution: a mixture (liquid + dissolved solid); fiber: the strands of string; crystal: a solid whose particles are arranged in a specific pattern

b) answers will vary

ENERGY • MATTER 147

What Happened

Review the section with students. Emphasize bold-face words that identify key concepts and introduce new vocabulary.

***Gravity** is the **force** that pulled the paperclip down. Your arm (holding the string) provided the **opposing force**. When the string burned, the paperclip wasn't connected to you anymore. This let the force of gravity win.*

*But when you soaked the string in the salt water, the **solution** entered the string's **fibers**. As the string dried, the water **evaporated**, and **crystals** of salt were left behind. (A crystal is a **solid** whose tiny particles are arranged in a specific pattern.)*

*When you set fire to the string whose fibers were permeated with salt crystals, the fire burned the string fibers up, just like before. Since salt doesn't burn easily, the **bond** of the salt crystals held them together, making a "Crystal String" that supported the paperclip – beating the **pull** of gravity!*

What We Learned

Answers will vary. Suggested responses are shown at left.

Conclusion

Read this section aloud to the class to summarize the concepts learned in this activity.

Food for Thought

Read the Scripture aloud to the class. Talk about what learning to trust God really means. Discuss ways we can create time to be alone with God.

Journal

If time permits, have a general class discussion about notes and drawings various students added to their journal pages. Discuss correct and incorrect predictions, and remind students that this "trial and error" process is part of the scientific process.

A crystal is a solid whose tiny particles are arranged in a specific pattern. Crystals are held together by forces called bonds.

FOOD FOR THOUGHT

Matthew 21:21-22 Setting fire to the string supporting the paperclip didn't seem to make much sense. But you trusted that your teacher knew more than you did, so you gave it a try. And look at how much you learned!

God wants us to learn to trust him, too. Sometimes we think that we know what's best for our lives, but God knows infinitely more than we do. When we trust him, we find there are so many exciting new things to learn! Spend time with God, and let your faith grow strong.

JOURNAL **My Science Notes**

148 ENERGY · MATTER

Extended Teaching

1. Repeat this activity using Epsom salts. Be sure to use heavy string. Have students compare the results with the original activity. How are they similar? How are they different?

2. Using the Internet, have teams research crystals. Challenge teams to create posters illustrating at least one unusual kind of crystal, and describing its use. Download pictures or use photos from magazines.

3. Invite a spelunker (caving enthusiast) to visit your classroom. Ask him/her to bring photos or samples. Find out how crystalline structures like stalactites form. Have students write a paragraph about one thing they learn.

4. Using the Internet, have teams research "crystalline" and "amorphous" solids. Most metals, rocks, and powders are crystalline. Most woods, plastics, and glass are not. Challenge teams to explain the difference.

5. Take a field trip to a machine shop. Find out about alloys (mixture of metals). What are some common alloys and what are they used for? Have students write a paragraph about one thing they learn.

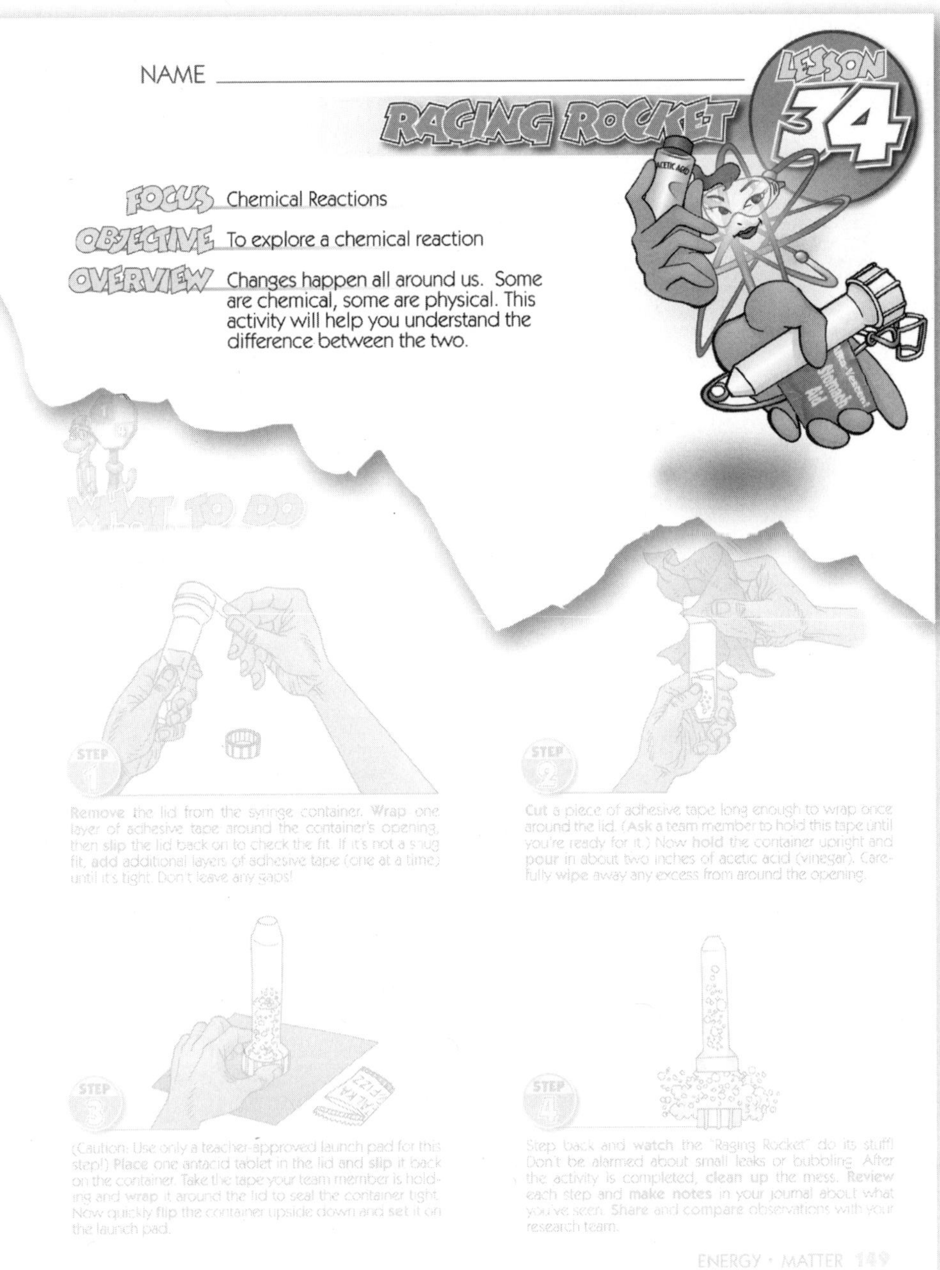

NAME ______________________________

LESSON 34

RAGING ROCKET

FOCUS Chemical Reactions

OBJECTIVE To explore a chemical reaction

OVERVIEW Changes happen all around us. Some are chemical, some are physical. This activity will help you understand the difference between the two.

WHAT TO DO

STEP 1 Remove the lid from the syringe container. Wrap one layer of adhesive tape around the container's opening, then slip the lid back on to check the fit. If it's not a snug fit, add additional layers of adhesive tape (one at a time) until it's tight. Don't leave any gaps!

STEP 2 Cut a piece of adhesive tape long enough to wrap once around the lid. (Ask a team member to hold this tape until you're ready for it.) Now hold the container upright and pour in about two inches of acetic acid (vinegar). Carefully wipe away any excess from around the opening.

STEP 3 (Caution: Use only a teacher-approved launch pad for this step!) Place one antacid tablet in the lid and slip it back on the container. Take the tape your team member is holding and wrap it around the lid to seal the container tight. Now quickly flip the container upside down and set it on the launch pad.

STEP 4 Step back and watch the "Raging Rocket" do its stuff! Don't be alarmed about small leaks or bubbling. After the activity is completed, clean up the mess. Review each step and make notes in your journal about what you've seen. Share and compare observations with your research team.

ENERGY • MATTER 149

Category

Physical Science
Energy/Matter

Focus

Chemical Reactions

Objective

To explore a chemical reaction

National Standards

A1, A2, B1, B2, B3, E1, E2, F5, G1, G2

Materials Needed

syringe container
acetic acid
antacid tablet
tape
paper towel

Safety Concerns

1. Goggles/Gloves
Take precautions to protect students' eyes and hands.

4. Slipping
This is definitely a messy activity! Remind students to exercise caution.

Additional Comments

Due to the mess, this activity works best outdoors. Goggles, gloves, and aprons help keep the mess off the students. Monitor to make certain no one is in a rocket's path! To increase speed, distance, or explosive force, retape for a tighter fit and repeat.

Overview

Read the overview aloud to your students. The goal is to create an atmosphere of curiosity and inquiry.

WHAT TO DO

Monitor student research teams as they complete each step.

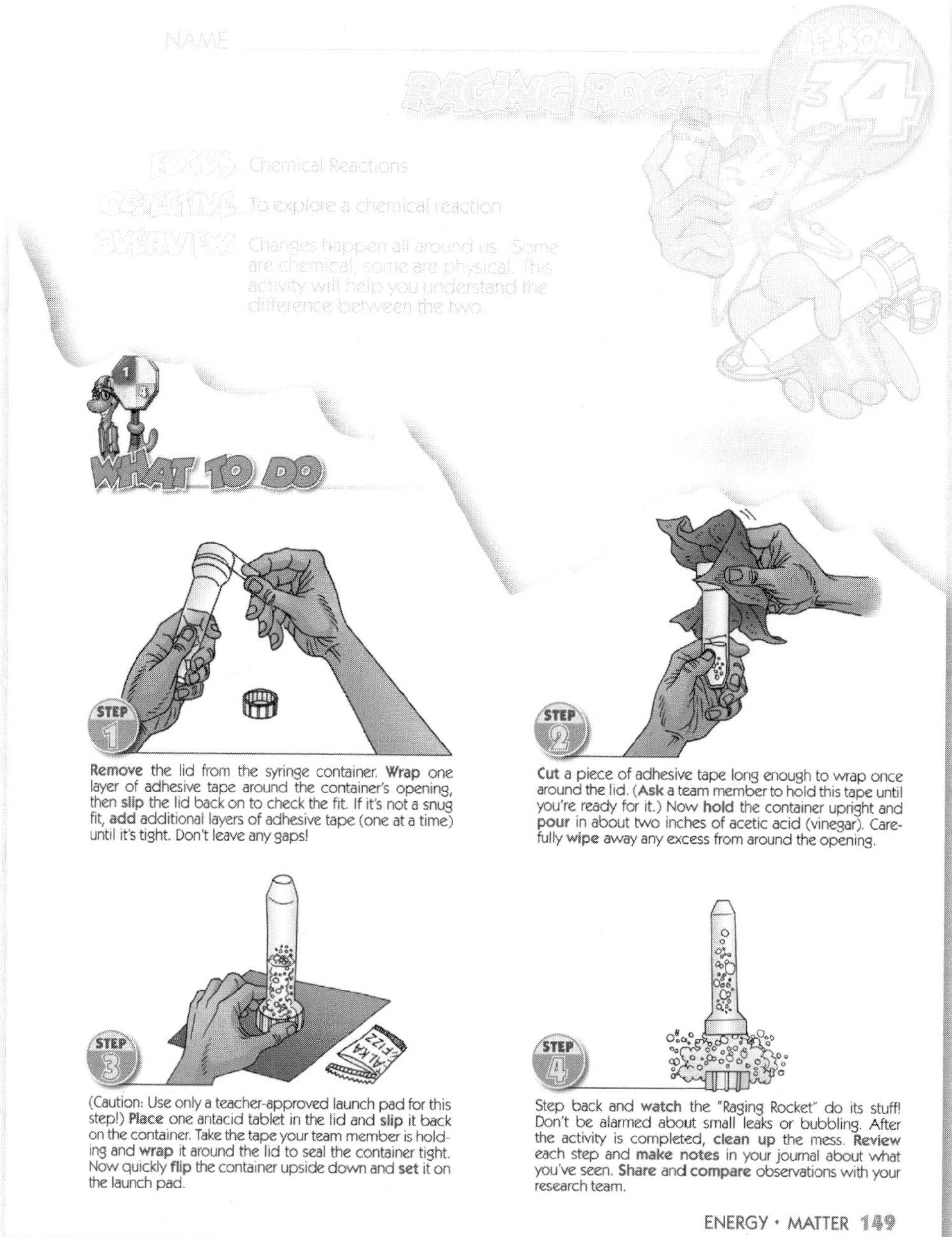

NAME

RAGING ROCKET

LESSON 34

FOCUS Chemical Reactions

OBJECTIVE To explore a chemical reaction

OVERVIEW Changes happen all around us. Some are chemical, some are physical. This activity will help you understand the difference between the two.

WHAT TO DO

STEP 1

Remove the lid from the syringe container. **Wrap** one layer of adhesive tape around the container's opening, then **slip** the lid back on to check the fit. If it's not a snug fit, **add** additional layers of adhesive tape (one at a time) until it's tight. Don't leave any gaps!

STEP 2

Cut a piece of adhesive tape long enough to wrap once around the lid. (**Ask** a team member to hold this tape until you're ready for it.) Now **hold** the container upright and **pour** in about two inches of acetic acid (vinegar). Carefully **wipe** away any excess from around the opening.

STEP 3

(Caution: Use only a teacher-approved launch pad for this step!) **Place** one antacid tablet in the lid and **slip** it back on the container. Take the tape your team member is holding and **wrap** it around the lid to seal the container tight. Now quickly **flip** the container upside down and **set** it on the launch pad.

STEP 4

Step back and **watch** the "Raging Rocket" do its stuff! Don't be alarmed about small leaks or bubbling. After the activity is completed, **clean up** the mess. **Review** each step and **make notes** in your journal about what you've seen. **Share** and **compare** observations with your research team.

ENERGY • MATTER 149

Teacher to Teacher

Physical change results in a different form of the same material. By contrast, chemical change creates a different substance entirely. In chemical terms, here's what happened in this activity: $NaHCO_3$ + $HC_2H_3O_2$ resulted in CO_2 + H_20 + $NaC_2H_3O_2$. Or in layman's terms, adding sodium bicarbonate to acetic acid produces carbon dioxide gas — and a LOT of it!

What Happened?

Combining the vinegar with the antacid resulted in a **chemical change**. In any **chemical reaction**, a new substance is created. In this case, it was a kind of **gas**. The tape you used in Step 2 helped trap this gas inside. As more gas was produced and expanded, **pressure** began to build until WHOOSH!

By contrast, a **physical change** makes something look different, but the substance is still the same. A block of ice (frozen water) can be broken into thousands of pieces, but every little piece is still water. When the ice melts, it's still water. Even if water is heated and boils into steam, it's still water! All of these are physical changes.

Remember that with a chemical change, you get a new substance. With a physical change, the substance remains the same.

What We Learned

1. **Why was it so important to make certain the lid fit tightly?**

   The tight lid allowed pressure to build up in the container.

2. **What was the purpose of the second piece of tape (Step 2)?**

   To help seal the edge of the lid against leakage.

3. **Describe the acetic acid. Describe the antacid tablets.**

   Answers will vary, but should reflect logical descriptions.

4. **Describe what happened when the acetic acid and the antacid tablets were combined.**

   Answers will vary, but should reflect a violent reaction.

5. **Describe the difference between a chemical and a physical change. Give one example of each.**

   physical change = same material, different form; chemical change = different substance entirely.

What Happened

Review the section with students. Emphasize bold-face words that identify key concepts and introduce new vocabulary.

*Combining the vinegar with the antacid resulted in a **chemical change**. In any **chemical reaction**, a new substance is created. In this case, it was a kind of **gas**. The tape you used in Step 2 helped trap this gas inside. As more gas was produced and expanded, **pressure** began to build until WHOOSH!*

*By contrast, a **physical change** makes something look different, but the substance is still the same. A block of ice (frozen water) can be broken into thousands of pieces, but every little piece is still water. When the ice melts, it's still water. Even if water is heated and boils into steam, it's still water! All of these are physical changes.*

Remember that with a chemical change, you get a new substance. With a physical change, the substance remains the same.

What We Learned

Answers will vary. Suggested responses are shown at left.

Conclusion

Read this section aloud to the class to summarize the concepts learned in this activity.

Food for Thought

Read the Scripture aloud to the class. Talk about the importance of being patient in God's work. Discuss stories that illustrate how patience eventually pays off.

Journal

If time permits, have a general class discussion about notes and drawings various students added to their journal pages. Discuss correct and incorrect predictions, and remind students that this "trial and error" process is part of the scientific process.

CONCLUSION

After a chemical change, a totally different substance results. After a physical change, a new form appears, but the substance is still the same.

FOOD FOR THOUGHT

2 Timothy 4:1-2 In this activity, you put the ingredients together but nothing happened at first. It wasn't until you turned your Raging Rocket upside down that things suddenly took off. Your patience was rewarded.

Spiritual things can sometimes happen the same way. You may not immediately see the results of your efforts. You may tell others about Jesus without seeing any real changes. But Scripture reminds us to keep on working, regardless of the circumstances. Patient effort in doing God's will is always rewarded.

JOURNAL My Science Notes

152 ENERGY · MATTER

Extended Teaching

1. Sodium bicarbonate is also called baking soda. Have students research the importance of this chemical in baking. Have them write a paragraph about one thing they learn.

2. Using the Internet, have students research rockets and their propulsion systems. Challenge each team to create a poster illustrating a particular rocket and how it works.

3. Invite a pharmacist to visit your classroom. Have him/her describe different types of antacids and how they work. (A model of the stomach would be helpful!) Have students write a paragraph about one thing they learn.

4. Invite someone to demonstrate a model rocket for your class. Ask teams to make a list comparing the model rocket to the Raging Rocket used in this activity. How are they similar? How are they different.

5. Take a field trip to a bakery. Find out how sodium bicarbonate and similar chemicals are used in manufacturing bread. Have students write a paragraph about one thing they learn.

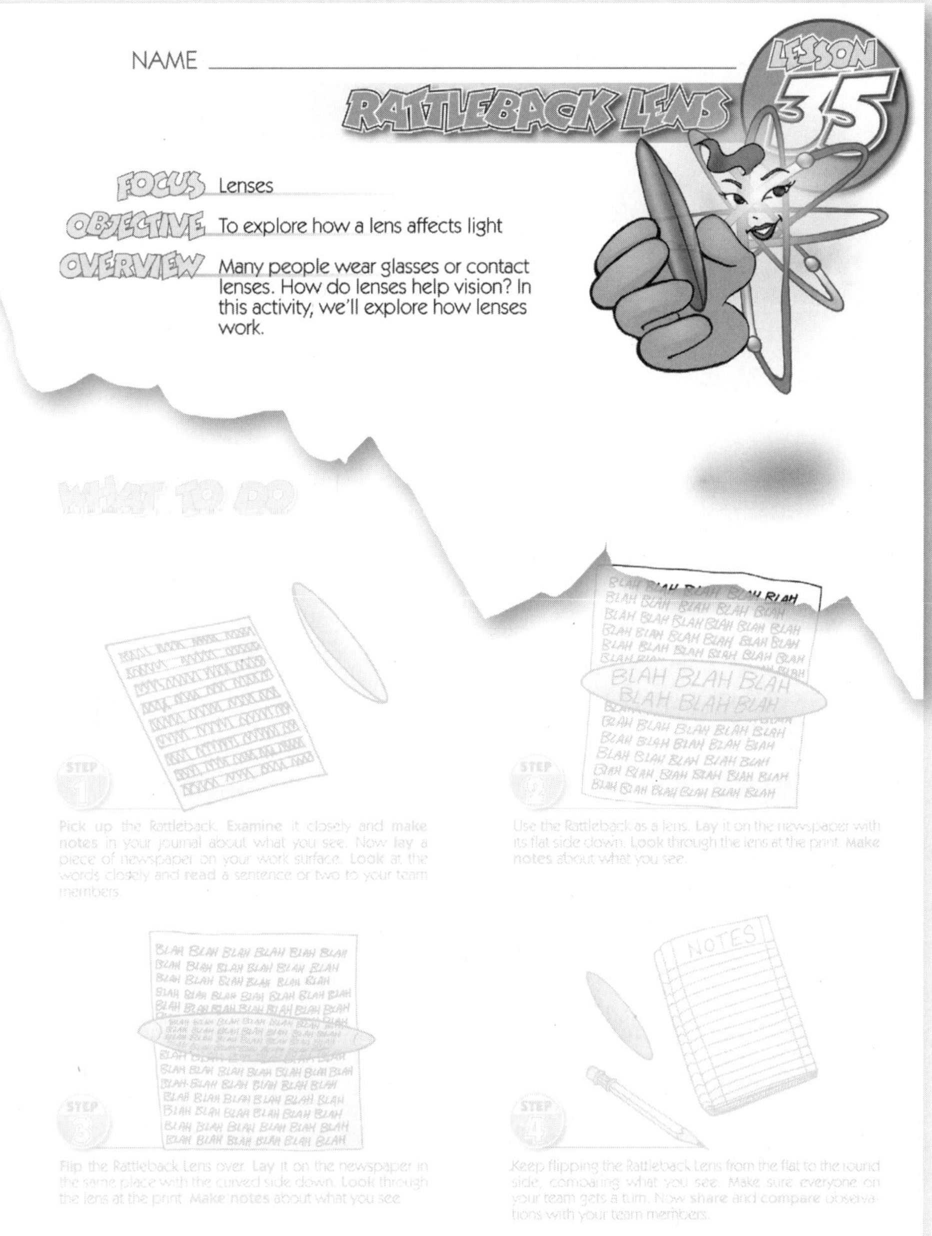
NAME ______________________________

LESSON 35

RATTLEBACK LENS

FOCUS Lenses

OBJECTIVE To explore how a lens affects light

OVERVIEW Many people wear glasses or contact lenses. How do lenses help vision? In this activity, we'll explore how lenses work.

WHAT TO DO

STEP 1 Pick up the Rattleback. Examine it closely and make notes in your journal about what you see. Now lay a piece of newspaper on your work surface. Look at the words closely and read a sentence or two to your team members.

STEP 2 Use the Rattleback as a lens. Lay it on the newspaper with its flat side down. Look through the lens at the print. Make notes about what you see.

STEP 3 Flip the Rattleback Lens over. Lay it on the newspaper in the same place with the curved side down. Look through the lens at the print. Make notes about what you see

STEP 4 Keep flipping the Rattleback Lens from the flat to the round side, comparing what you see. Make sure everyone on your team gets a turn. Now share and compare observations with your team members.

ENERGY · MATTER 153

Category

Physical Science
Energy/Matter

Focus

Lenses

Objective

To explore how a lens affects light

National Standards

A1, A2, B1, B2, B3, E1, E2, F5, G1, G2, G3

Materials Needed

rattleback lens
newspaper

Safety Concerns

none

Additional Comments

The rattleback is very safe and nearly impossible to damage with normal use. Focus on the way its shape causes light to bend, resulting in the image looking different. Compare this with glasses and contacts.

Overview

Read the overview aloud to your students. The goal is to create an atmosphere of curiosity and inquiry.

WHAT TO DO

Monitor student research teams as they complete each step.

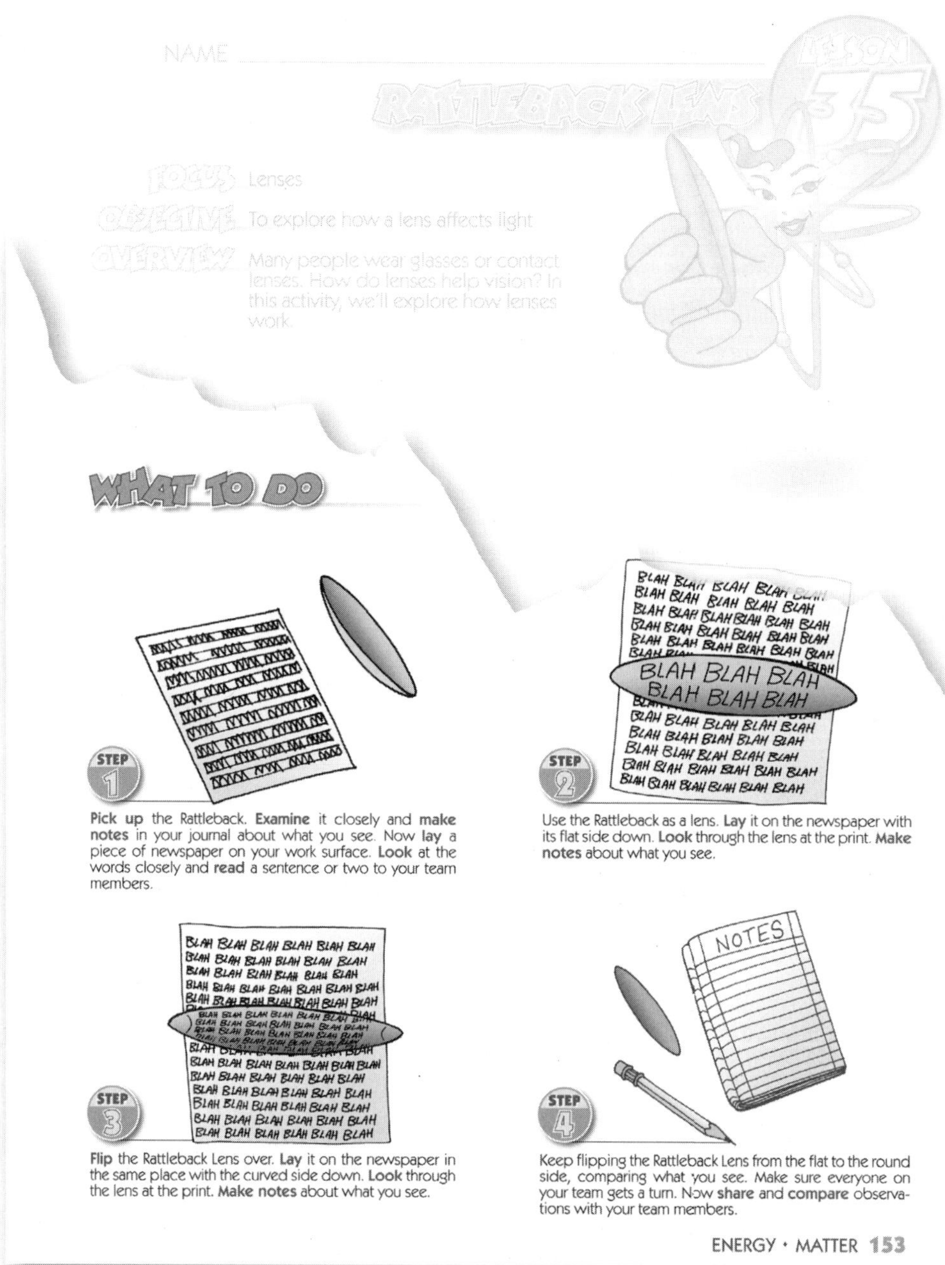

NAME

RATTLEBACK LENS

LESSON 35

FOCUS Lenses

OBJECTIVE To explore how a lens affects light

OVERVIEW Many people wear glasses or contact lenses. How do lenses help vision? In this activity, we'll explore how lenses work.

WHAT TO DO

STEP 1

Pick up the Rattleback. **Examine** it closely and **make notes** in your journal about what you see. Now **lay** a piece of newspaper on your work surface. **Look** at the words closely and **read** a sentence or two to your team members.

STEP 2

Use the Rattleback as a lens. **Lay** it on the newspaper with its flat side down. **Look** through the lens at the print. **Make notes** about what you see.

STEP 3

Flip the Rattleback Lens over. **Lay** it on the newspaper in the same place with the curved side down. **Look** through the lens at the print. **Make notes** about what you see.

STEP 4

Keep flipping the Rattleback Lens from the flat to the round side, comparing what you see. Make sure everyone on your team gets a turn. Now **share** and **compare** observations with your team members.

ENERGY • MATTER 153

Teacher to Teacher

Light is a form of energy that travels in waves. A lens bends these waves to create certain kinds of images. The concave lens is also called a diverging lens because it diverts or spreads out light. The convex lens is also called a converging lens because it converges or brings together light. Lenses are used in thousands of ways, from science and industry to improving human vision.

A **lens** works by bending light. Scientists call this **refraction**.

In general, the result of refraction depends on whether a lens is **convex** (bowed out) or **concave** (dished in).

When you placed the flat side of the Rattleback on the newsprint, light hit the letters and **reflected** (bounced off) toward your eyes. Because the lens was convex, the light spread out, making the letters look bigger. But when you put the round side down, the light was compressed, causing the letters to look smaller.

This is the basic principle on which all lenses operate.

WHAT WE LEARNED

1. **Describe how the newspaper looked in Step 1. How easy was it to read?**

a) answers will vary

b) you could read it normally

2. **Describe how the newspaper looked in Step 2. Was it easier or harder to read?**

a) the print looked bigger

b) it was easier to read

154 ENERGY • MATTER

3. **Describe how the newspaper looked in Step 3. Compare it with Steps 1 and 2.**

a) the print looked smaller

b) answers will vary but should reflect logical comparisons

4. **What is a "bowed out" lens called? What is a "dished in" lens called?**

a) convex

b) concave

5. **List three devices that use a lens. Tell whether each is convex, concave, or maybe either one.**

a) examples: microscope, telescope, glasses, camera, etc.

b) answers will vary

ENERGY • MATTER 155

What Happened

Review the section with students. Emphasize bold-face words that identify key concepts and introduce new vocabulary.

*A **lens** works by bending light. Scientists call this **refraction**.*

*In general, the result of refraction depends on whether a lens is **convex** (bowed out) or **concave** (dished in).*

*When you placed the flat side of the rattleback on the newsprint, light hit the letters and **reflected** (bounced off) toward your eyes. Because the lens was convex, the light spread out, making the letters look bigger. But when you put the round side down, the light was compressed, causing the letters to look smaller.*

This is the basic principle on which all lenses operate.

What We Learned

Answers will vary. Suggested responses are shown at left.

Conclusion

Read this section aloud to the class to summarize the concepts learned in this activity.

Food for Thought

Read the Scripture aloud to the class. Talk about what it means to truly "see" the world around us. Discuss ways we can learn to be more sensitive to the needs of those around us.

Journal

If time permits, have a general class discussion about notes and drawings various students added to their journal pages. Discuss correct and incorrect predictions, and remind students that this "trial and error" process is part of the scientific process.

Conclusion

Lenses work by bending light in a process called refraction. The image a lens produces depends on its shape. In general, convex lenses make things appear bigger and concave lenses make them appear smaller.

Food for Thought

Psalm 66:5 Vision is a precious gift — one we should thank God for every day! Imagine living in a world where you couldn't see a beautiful sunset, a pretty flower, or a twinkling star.

Even with the best eyesight or perfect lenses, we may miss things we really need to see. It may be a classmate who is sad and needs cheering up . . . or a friend who needs help solving a problem . . . or even a parent who could use a little help around the house! Just as listening is more than hearing, truly "seeing" involves more than just sight. Why not ask God to help you develop this special sense?

Journal — My Science Notes

156 ENERGY · MATTER

Extended Teaching

1. Repeat this activity using different kinds of print and various objects. Have teams compare the results with the original activity. How are they similar? How are they different?

2. Invite an optometrist to visit your classroom. Ask him/her to bring samples of lenses. Discuss how lenses can help correct vision problems. Have students write a paragraph about one thing they learn.

3. Using the Internet, have students research various devices that use lenses. Challenge teams to create a poster illustrating one of these devices and how it works.

4. As a class, make a bulletin board depicting various kinds of vision problems and their solutions. Sponsor an "eye awareness" week at school. Create appropriate posters (using safety goggles, proper light for reading, etc.).

5. Have students research Braille. Contact a local organization for the vision impaired and they can bring samples of Braille for your students. Have students write a paragraph about one thing they learn.

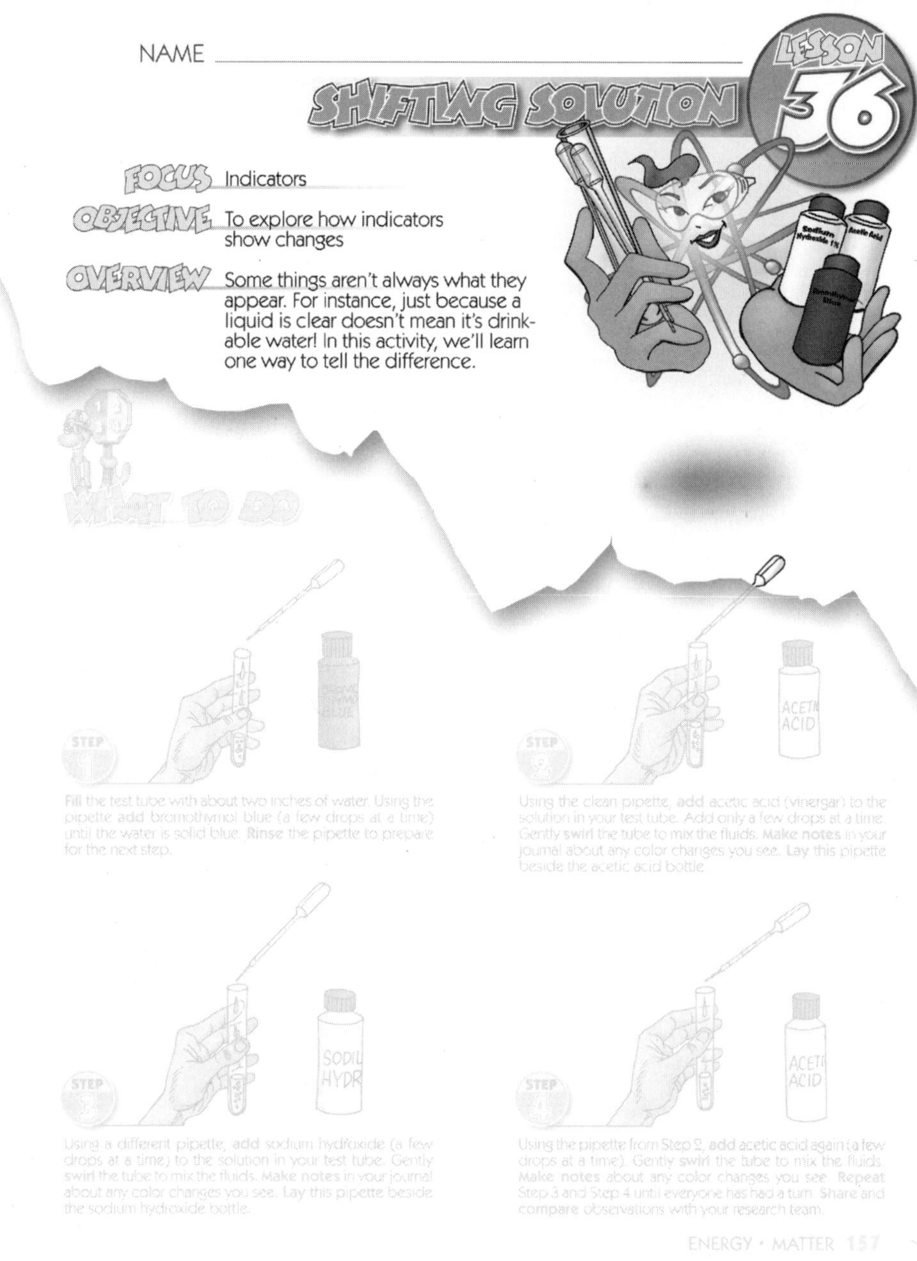

Category

Physical Science
Energy/Matter

Focus

Indicators

Objective

To explore how indicators show changes

National Standards

A1, A2, B1, B2, E1, E2, F5, G1, G2, G3

Materials Needed

test tube
pipettes - 2
bromothymol blue
acetic acid
sodium hydroxide
water

Safety Concerns

1. Goggles/Gloves
Take precautions to protect students' eyes and hands.

2. Corrosion
Use appropriate precautions with all chemicals

3. Vapor
Chemical fumes must not be inhaled.

4. Breakage
Remind students to exercise caution with glass test tube.

Additional Comments

Before beginning this lesson, carefully review all rules for working with chemicals. Remind students to replace and tighten lids when finished. Be sure to use a different pipette for Step 3, or the activity will not work.

Overview

Read the overview aloud to your students. The goal is to create an atmosphere of curiosity and inquiry.

WHAT TO DO

Monitor student research teams as they complete each step.

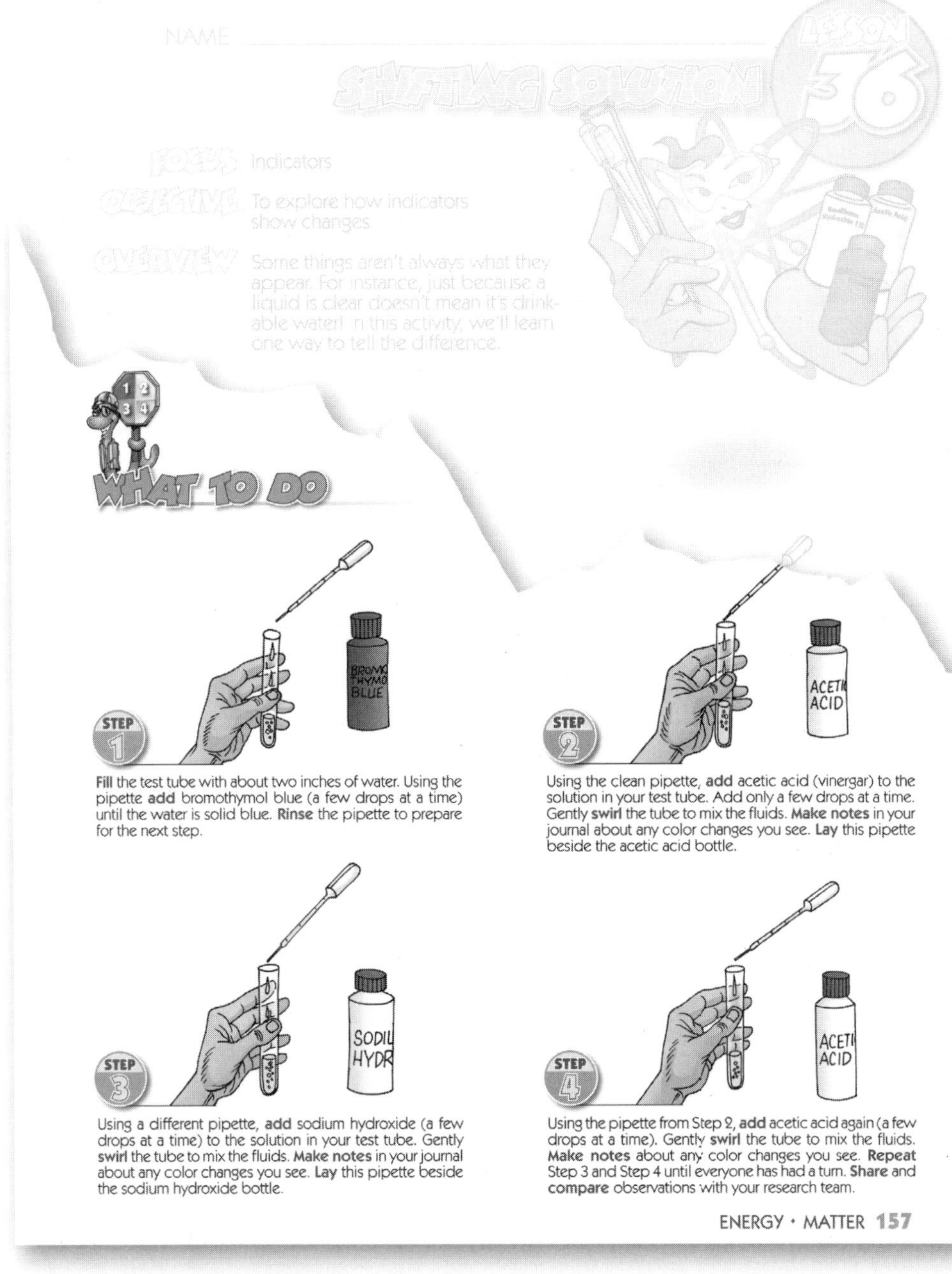

NAME

LESSON 36

SHIFTING SOLUTION

FOCUS Indicators

OBJECTIVE To explore how indicators show changes

OVERVIEW Some things aren't always what they appear. For instance, just because a liquid is clear doesn't mean it's drinkable water! In this activity, we'll learn one way to tell the difference.

WHAT TO DO

Fill the test tube with about two inches of water. Using the pipette **add** bromothymol blue (a few drops at a time) until the water is solid blue. **Rinse** the pipette to prepare for the next step.

Using the clean pipette, **add** acetic acid (vinergar) to the solution in your test tube. Add only a few drops at a time. Gently **swirl** the tube to mix the fluids. **Make notes** in your journal about any color changes you see. **Lay** this pipette beside the acetic acid bottle.

Using a different pipette, **add** sodium hydroxide (a few drops at a time) to the solution in your test tube. Gently **swirl** the tube to mix the fluids. **Make notes** in your journal about any color changes you see. **Lay** this pipette beside the sodium hydroxide bottle.

Using the pipette from Step 2, **add** acetic acid again (a few drops at a time). Gently **swirl** the tube to mix the fluids. **Make notes** about any color changes you see. **Repeat** Step 3 and Step 4 until everyone has had a turn. **Share** and **compare** observations with your research team.

ENERGY • MATTER 157

Teacher to Teacher

Scientists determine the strength of an unknown acid with universal indicator paper, or a process called titration. Indicator paper provides a quick, easy way to do simple testing (like soil or swimming pools). More accurate testing requires titration, similar to the process in this activity, but based on an exact strength solution (acid or base) as the standard.

WHAT HAPPENED?

You first mixed an **indicator** (bromothymol blue) with water to make a **solution**. Indicators change color when **acid** or **base** levels change. Since an indicator was present, adding an acid (vinegar) to the solution caused a color change. Next you added a base (sodium hydroxide), and the color change reversed. This is because the base **neutralized** the acid — bringing the solution back to where it was in Step 1.

Acids and bases are measured on a number scale (1 to 14) called a **pH scale**. Readings from 1 through 6 indicate an acid. Readings from 8 through 14 indicate a base. And anything that reads exactly 7 is **neutral** (neither acid nor base).

Scientists and others use the pH scale in many ways: environmental monitoring, water testing, medical assessments — even checking the soil balance for the best crops.

WHAT WE LEARNED

1 **What does an indicator do? What are two substances that would affect an indicator?**

a) changes color to indicate the presence of an acid or a base

b) acids, bases

2 **How are acids and bases measured? Why are these kinds of measurements useful?**

a) on a pH scale

b) pH levels are important in soil testing, medical testing, water testing, etc.

3 **Would a substance with a pH of 3 be a base, an acid, or neutral? What would it be with a pH of 7?**

a) pH of 3 = acid b) pH of 7 = neutral (neither acid nor base)

4 **Describe the color changes that took place in each step. Explain what each color change meant.**

turned blue in Step 1 due to indicator; turned green then yellow in Step 2 when acid added; turned blue again in Step 3 because acid neutralized; turned green then yellow in Step 4 because acid added again

5 **Name three situations where an indicator might be useful. Explain why the indicator might help.**

a) testing soil, water, environment, medical, etc.

b) answers will vary, but should be logical

What Happened

Review the section with students. Emphasize bold-face words that identify key concepts and introduce new vocabulary.

*You first mixed an **indicator** (bromothymol blue) with water to make a **solution**. Indicators change color when **acid** or **base** levels change. Since an indicator was present, adding an acid (vinegar) to the solution caused a color change. Next, you added a base (sodium hydroxide), and the color change reversed. This is because the base **neutralized** the acid – bringing the solution back to where it was in Step 1.*

*Acids and bases are measured on a number scale (1 to 14) called a **pH scale**. Readings from 1 through 6 indicate an acid. Readings from 8 through 14 indicate a base. And anything that reads exactly 7 is **neutral** (neither acid nor base).*

Scientists and others use the pH scale in many ways: environmental monitoring, water testing, medical assessments – even checking the soil balance for the best crops.

What We Learned

Answers will vary. Suggested responses are shown at left.

Conclusion

Read this section aloud to the class to summarize the concepts learned in this activity.

Food for Thought

Read the Scripture aloud to the class. Talk about the "fruits of the spirit." Discuss how we can learn to produce the right kind of fruit.

Journal

If time permits, have a general class discussion about notes and drawings various students added to their journal pages. Discuss correct and incorrect predictions, and remind students that this "trial and error" process is part of the scientific process.

Indicators help determine the pH of a substance by changing colors. A reading of 1 through 6 indicates an acid; 7 indicates neutral; and 8 through 14 indicates a base.

Matthew 7:15-20 Indicators are a great tool for determining what something really is. A clear liquid might be cool, refreshing water — or it might be a burning acid! An indicator can keep us from harm by helping us tell them apart.

This Scripture describes an indicator you can use for people. Jesus said a person is known by their "fruit" — the way they treat others. Thorn bushes don't produce grapes, and thistles don't bear figs! Delicious fruit comes only from the right fruit tree, just as kind deeds only come from the right kind of heart. When our hearts belong to God, we will produce the right kind of spiritual fruit.

JOURNAL **My Science Notes**

160 ENERGY • MATTER

Extended Teaching

1. Bring a soil testing kit to class (available from agricultural agencies and garden stores). Have teams test various locations around the school to determine the soil pH.

2. Invite a professional gardener to visit your classroom. Discuss differing pH requirements of various plants and how incorrect pH affects them. Have students write a paragraph about one thing they learn.

3. Take a field trip to a pool and spa store. Have a technician demonstrate how to test the water for proper pH. Discuss the importance of such testing. Have students write a paragraph about one thing they learn.

4. Using the Internet, have teams research acid rain. Challenge each team to create a poster showing a particular part of the country where this is a problem and explaining why. Discuss some possible solutions.

5. Take a field trip to a municipal water treatment plant. Find out what is required to keep drinking water safe. Have students write a paragraph about one thing they learn.

ASSESSMENT

NAME____ DATE______________

LESSON 1

FERMENTED FUNGI

True/False (Circle T for true, F for false.)

T F **1.** All fungi are harmful to people and the environment.

T F **2.** Fungi (like yeast) need some form of energy to live.

T F **3.** All fungi can perform photosynthesis, just like plants.

T F **4.** Fungi can cause decomposition, allowing nutrients to be recycled.

T F **5.** The air bubble (Tube A) was produced by the life cycle of yeast.

Multiple Choice (Fill in the circle beside the best answer.)

6. Fermentation . . .

○ **a.** is caused by photosynthesis.
○ **b.** is caused by fungi-like yeast.
○ **c.** is always a harmful process.
○ **d.** is never a harmful process.

7. In science, a life cycle is . . .

○ **a.** a process related to non-living things.
○ **b.** the birth of a living thing.
○ **c.** a process common to all living things.
○ **d.** a kind of exercise machine.

8. The life cycle of yeast . . .

○ **a.** is about the same as that of a human being.
○ **b.** is much shorter than that of a human being.
○ **c.** is much longer than that of a human being.
○ **d.** doesn't exist since yeast is only a fungi.

9. Based on your observations, yeast needs all of the following to live except . . .

○ **a.** air
○ **b.** energy
○ **c.** water
○ **d.** warmth

10. How does yeast affect the making of bread?

○ **a.** It produces heat to help the dough bake faster.
○ **b.** It causes the finished bread to decompose more rapidly.
○ **c.** Since it is a fungi, it is rarely used in the making of bread.
○ **d.** It produces carbon dioxide gas, which makes the dough rise.

NAME________________________________ DATE______________

LESSON 2

INDOOR ONION

True/False (Circle T for true, F for false.)

T F **1.** Unlike humans, plants do not have a life cycle.

T F **2.** Gravity causes roots to grow up and stems to grow down.

T F **3.** A clear bottle can serve as a kind of greenhouse.

T F **4.** The bottle must be clear to let light reach the plant.

T F **5.** A greenhouse is "green" due to the action of chlorophyll.

Multiple Choice (Fill in the circle beside the best answer.)

6. Which of the following was not important in this activity?

○ **a.** light
○ **b.** air
○ **c.** a plant
○ **d.** a fungi

7. Scientists call chemicals needed by living things . . .

○ **a.** energy
○ **b.** light
○ **c.** nutrients
○ **d.** photosynthesis

8. What purpose did the toothpicks serve in this activity?

○ **a.** They poked holes in the onion to let water in.
○ **b.** They poked holes in the onion to let air in.
○ **c.** They held the onion off the bottom of the bottle.
○ **d.** They helped photosynthesis occur more rapidly.

9. What energy source do plants use for photosynthesis?

○ **a.** light
○ **b.** nutrients
○ **c.** oxygen
○ **d.** sugar

10. Why is photosynthesis important to humans?

○ **a.** Photosynthesis in plants and animals creates the primary food source for humans.
○ **b.** Photosynthesis keeps plants green, creating more beautiful landscapes.
○ **c.** Photosynthesis in plants creates the primary food source for humans and animals.
○ **d.** Photosynthesis is not an important process, except to plants.

NAME________________________________ DATE______________

LESSON 3

INDOOR ONION 2

True/False (Circle T for true, F for false.)

T F **1.** Gravity is a type of stimulus.

T F **2.** Gravity has no effect on plants.

T F **3.** All living things respond in some way to their environment.

T F **4.** Plants respond to gravity, but animals do not.

T F **5.** Regardless of a seed's position, roots always grow up and stems down.

Multiple Choice (Fill in the circle beside the best answer.)

6. Based on what you've learned, onions . . .

- ◯ **a.** respond to their environment.
- ◯ **b.** do not respond to their environment.
- ◯ **c.** are sensitive to light, but not to gravity.
- ◯ **d.** are sensitive to gravity, but not to light.

7. Based on what you've observed . . .

- ◯ **a.** gravity causes stems to grow down regardless of a seed's position.
- ◯ **b.** light causes roots to grow up regardless of a seed's position.
- ◯ **c.** roots grow down toward gravity and stems grow up toward light.
- ◯ **d.** gravity and light are both affected by a seed's position.

8. The way a living thing reacts when affected by something is called a . . .

- ◯ **a.** stimulus
- ◯ **b.** response
- ◯ **c.** life cycle
- ◯ **d.** gravity

9. Which of the following was the variable in this activity?

- ◯ **a.** the amount of light
- ◯ **b.** the amount of water
- ◯ **c.** the number of toothpicks
- ◯ **d.** the position of the onion

10. What might happen if a living thing could not respond to its environment?

- ◯ **a.** It would not be able to see or hear.
- ◯ **b.** It would have an easier life.
- ◯ **c.** It would probably die.
- ◯ **d.** It would not be affected in any way.

NAME______________________________ DATE______________

LESSON 4

PROTECTED PLANT

True/False (Circle T for true, F for false.)

T F **1.** Water is able to move through plants.

T F **2.** Plants are not able to perform photosynthesis when sealed in a clear bag.

T F **3.** Plants do not need water to survive.

T F **4.** Plants absorb water through their roots.

T F **5.** Sunlight is an important energy source for plants.

Multiple Choice (Fill in the circle beside the best answer.)

6. Cells that open and close to control the amount of water in a plant are called . . .

○ **a.** water cells
○ **b.** gate cells
○ **c.** photo cells
○ **d.** guard cells

7. The openings in a leaf are called . . .

○ **a.** gate cells
○ **b.** stomach cells
○ **c.** stomata
○ **d.** photons

8. What chemical is necessary for photosynthesis to occur?

○ **a.** oxygen
○ **b.** carbon dioxide
○ **c.** carbon silicate
○ **d.** carbon chloride

9. Guard cells are cells that . . .

○ **a.** open and stay open.
○ **b.** close and stay closed.
○ **c.** can both open and close.
○ **d.** none of the above

10. What energy source helps water leave plants?

○ **a.** nutrients
○ **b.** gravity
○ **c.** electricity
○ **d.** sunlight

NAME________________________________ DATE______________

FLOWER POWER

True/False (Circle T for true, F for false.)

T F **1.** Flowers are important to plant reproduction.

T F **2.** All flowers are exactly the same.

T F **3.** All flowers have both male and female parts.

T F **4.** Wind can help pollinate some plants.

T F **5.** Insects can help pollinate some plants.

Multiple Choice (Fill in the circle beside the best answer.)

6. Taking a plant apart to examine its parts is called . . .

- ○ **a.** pollination
- ○ **b.** dissection
- ○ **c.** fertilization
- ○ **d.** integration

7. Which of the following is not part of the pistil?

- ○ **a.** stigma
- ○ **b.** style
- ○ **c.** ovary
- ○ **d.** pollen

8. Which of the following is produced on the stamen?

- ○ **a.** stigma
- ○ **b.** style
- ○ **c.** ovary
- ○ **d.** pollen

9. Pollen and eggs combine in a process called . . .

- ○ **a.** photosynthesis
- ○ **b.** dissection
- ○ **c.** fertilization
- ○ **d.** stigma

10. Pollination can be caused by all of the following except . . .

- ○ **a.** heat
- ○ **b.** insects
- ○ **c.** wind
- ○ **d.** bees

NAME______________________________ DATE ____________

LESSON 6

MEMBRANE MODEL

True/False (Circle T for true, F for false.)

T F **1.** To remain healthy, cells must allow specific materials to enter and leave them.

T F **2.** Materials can enter through a cell's membrane, but can't leave this way.

T F **3.** Diffusion can only occur in water.

T F **4.** Molecules can't pass through "solid" materials (like the wall of a balloon).

T F **5.** Diffusion makes molecules get further and further apart.

Multiple Choice (Fill in the circle beside the best answer.)

6. What process allows a scented candle to fill a room with fragrance?

○ **a.** combustion
○ **b.** photosynthesis
○ **c.** diffusion
○ **d.** none of the above

7. The balloon in this activity modeled a . . .

○ **a.** nucleus
○ **b.** molecule
○ **c.** cell membrane
○ **d.** fat cell

8. Diffusion . . .

○ **a.** always concentrates materials in a smaller area.
○ **b.** can't help materials enter or leave a cell.
○ **c.** only affects liquids, never gasses.
○ **d.** spreads materials out.

9. Smoke looks lighter the farther it gets from a chimney. What causes this?

○ **a.** combustion
○ **b.** photosynthesis
○ **c.** diffusion
○ **d.** none of the above

10. Diffusion makes materials get . . .

○ **a.** lighter
○ **b.** smaller
○ **c.** farther apart
○ **d.** closer together

NAME______________________ DATE______________

LESSON 7

BALLOON EYE

True/False (Circle T for true, F for false.)

T F **1.** The shape of your eye has no effect on vision.

T F **2.** The lens of your eye helps focus light to create an image.

T F **3.** Contact lenses and glasses bend light to improve vision.

T F **4.** Images appear on the retina upside down.

T F **5.** The eye is the only organ that plays a role in vision.

Multiple Choice (Fill in the circle beside the best answer.)

6. How was the image of the flame in the balloon like the image inside our eyes?

○ **a.** The balloon image was upside down; the image in our eyes was right side up.
○ **b.** The balloon image was right side up; the image in our eyes was upside down.
○ **c.** Both images were right side up.
○ **d.** Both images were upside down.

7. A change in the shape of the eye will . . .

○ **a.** change how clearly we see an image.
○ **b.** not affect the shape of the image seen.
○ **c.** increase the size of the image.
○ **d.** decrease the size of the image.

8. Which of the following would not have a lens?

○ **a.** a telescope
○ **b.** a microscope
○ **c.** your eye
○ **d.** a radio

9. Squeezing the balloon provided a model of . . .

○ **a.** the images seen by babies.
○ **b.** various vision problems.
○ **c.** how heat affects our eyes.
○ **d.** the stress in our lives.

10. The back of your eye is called the . . .

○ **a.** diffusion point
○ **b.** retina
○ **c.** lens
○ **d.** image

NAME________________________________ DATE______________

LESSON 8

HOLLOW HAND

True/False (Circle T for true, F for false.)

T F **1.** To produce vision, the brain and eyes work independently of each other.

T F **2.** The lens is the part of the eye where the image appears.

T F **3.** Light is an important component of vision.

T F **4.** An image is formed by focusing light onto the retina of the eye.

T F **5.** Your brain needs information from both eyes to make the most accurate image.

Multiple Choice (Fill in the circle beside the best answer.)

6. The image that we see is processed in the . . .

○ **a.** lens
○ **b.** eye
○ **c.** retina
○ **d.** brain

7. Most humans have one eye that is . . .

○ **a.** unfocused
○ **b.** focused
○ **c.** dominant
○ **d.** crossed

8. When your brain "sees" something that's not there, it's called . . .

○ **a.** a neuron
○ **b.** an illusion
○ **c.** a retinal
○ **d.** a crossed lens

9. The special cells that carry nerve signals through your body are called . . .

○ **a.** neurons
○ **b.** retinals
○ **c.** lenses
○ **d.** signal cells

10. You saw a "hole" in your hand because . . .

○ **a.** your brain was unable to process any information.
○ **b.** the lens in your eye did not function correctly.
○ **c.** your brain tried to process different information from each eye.
○ **d.** the retina in one eye could not form any images.

NAME________________________ DATE____________

LESSON 9

BODY JOINT

True/False (Circle T for true, F for false.)

T F **1.** Joints allow your bones the ability to move.

T F **2.** Your brain directs movement by controlling your muscles.

T F **3.** Your muscles control the nerves in your body.

T F **4.** Your skeleton supports your body like a framework supports a building.

T F **5.** For a joint to move properly, ligaments, muscles, and tendons must work together.

Multiple Choice (Fill in the circle beside the best answer.)

6. Which of the following is not a body joint?

◯ **a.** knee
◯ **b.** ankle
◯ **c.** elbow
◯ **d.** all of these are joints

7. What is the purpose of a ligament?

◯ **a.** to move muscles
◯ **b.** to hold bones together
◯ **c.** to hook muscles to bones
◯ **d.** to make a joint rigid

8. What is the purpose of a tendon?

◯ **a.** to move muscles
◯ **b.** to hold bones together
◯ **c.** to hook muscles to bones
◯ **d.** to make a joint rigid

9. What is one purpose of nerves?

◯ **a.** to move muscles
◯ **b.** to hold bones together
◯ **c.** to hook muscles to bones
◯ **d.** to make a joint rigid

10. Which of the following diseases most directly affects joints?

◯ **a.** influenza
◯ **b.** arthritis
◯ **c.** asthma
◯ **d.** diabetes

NAME________________________ DATE____________

LESSON 10

MOLECULAR MODELS

True/False (Circle T for true, F for false.)

T F **1.** Molecules bond together to create chemical compounds.

T F **2.** An atom is larger than a molecule.

T F **3.** Atoms bond together to create molecules.

T F **4.** There are chemical bonds between atoms.

T F **5.** A compound is the smallest part of an atom.

Multiple Choice (Fill in the circle beside the best answer.)

6. Which of the following best describes how atoms stick together?

○ **a.** Glue holding paper together.
○ **b.** Nails holding boards together.
○ **c.** Magnets attracting and sticking together.
○ **d.** Screws holding boards together.

7. How are the molecules of different compounds similar?

○ **a.** They have the same number of atoms.
○ **b.** They are composed of atoms.
○ **c.** They are composed of different atoms.
○ **d.** They have the same type of atoms.

8. How are the molecules of different compounds different?

○ **a.** They have the same numbers of atoms.
○ **b.** They are composed of atoms.
○ **c.** They are composed of different atoms.
○ **d.** They have the same type of atoms.

9. Chemical compounds . . .

○ **a.** bond in only one way.
○ **b.** bond in many different ways.
○ **c.** are unable to create bonds.
○ **d.** none of the above.

10. The correct order of these particles from smallest to largest is . . .

○ **a.** atoms, molecules, compounds.
○ **b.** molecules, atoms, compounds.
○ **c.** compounds, atoms, molecules.
○ **d.** atoms, compounds, molecules.

NAME________________________________ DATE______________

LESSON 11

WATER BRIDGE

True/False (Circle T for true, F for false.)

T F **1.** Gravity is a force that pulls things down.

T F **2.** Surface tension is not affected by gravity.

T F **3.** Gravity does not affect small things like water molecules.

T F **4.** Surface tension causes water molecules to stick together.

T F **5.** Falling water forms round drops because of surface tension.

Multiple Choice (Fill in the circle beside the best answer.)

6. The attraction between water molecules is called . . .

○ **a.** chemical bonding.
○ **b.** tensile strength.
○ **c.** surface tension.
○ **d.** gravity.

7. Gravity normally causes objects to . . .

○ **a.** push away from each other.
○ **b.** be attracted to each other.
○ **c.** bounce off surface tension.
○ **d.** fall straight down.

8. Water can travel down an angled wet string because . . .

○ **a.** surface tension can be stronger than gravity.
○ **b.** gravity can be stronger than surface tension.
○ **c.** surface tension and gravity are equal.
○ **d.** none of the above

9. Water drops stick better to wet string than dry string because . . .

○ **a.** dry string has a higher moisture content.
○ **b.** wet string contains water molecules to stick to.
○ **c.** wet string decreases gravitational pull.
○ **d.** all of the above

10. Surface tension causes water molecules to . . .

○ **a.** create a chemical bond.
○ **b.** decrease gravitational pull.
○ **c.** stick together.
○ **d.** pull apart.

NAME________________________________ DATE______________

True/False (Circle T for true, F for false.)

T F **1.** Density refers to how tightly an object's atoms are packed together.

T F **2.** In a way, objects are only "solid" in relationship to your body.

T F **3.** Even though objects look solid, the major ingredient in matter is space.

T F **4.** A rock seems solid because it is less dense than your body.

T F **5.** You can walk through fog because it is less dense than your body.

Multiple Choice (Fill in the circle beside the best answer.)

6. What does cutting do to the molecules in a sheet of paper?

○ **a.** It destroys them completely.
○ **b.** It separates some of them from others.
○ **c.** It chemically changes some molecules.
○ **d.** It has no effect at all.

7. Scientists call the substances we see and touch each day . . .

○ **a.** matter
○ **b.** space
○ **c.** density
○ **d.** chemicals

8. At the molecular level, most matter is primarily . . .

○ **a.** solid
○ **b.** liquid
○ **c.** gas
○ **d.** space

9. Which of the following is less dense than your body?

○ **a.** air
○ **b.** water
○ **c.** rocks
○ **d.** trees

10. Which of the following is more dense than your body?

○ **a.** air
○ **b.** rocks
○ **c.** clouds
○ **d.** fog

NAME_______________________________ DATE______________

LESSON 13
SPINNING STEEL

True/False (Circle T for true, F for false.)

T F **1.** Gravity can temporarily be defeated by other forces.

T F **2.** Velocity is another word for speed.

T F **3.** Linear velocity involves movement along a curved path.

T F **4.** Angular velocity involves movement in a straight line.

T F **5.** Adding energy at just the right time is called resonance.

Multiple Choice (Fill in the circle beside the best answer.)

6. All of the following demonstrate linear velocity except . . .

◯ **a.** an arrow shot from a bow.
◯ **b.** a bullet fired from a gun.
◯ **c.** a wheel turning.
◯ **d.** a dropped weight.

7. All of the following demonstrate angular velocity except . . .

◯ **a.** a merry-go-round.
◯ **b.** a turning wheel.
◯ **c.** a dropped weight.
◯ **d.** Earth's rotation.

8. Resonance . . .

◯ **a.** can make an object go faster.
◯ **b.** will make an object slow down.
◯ **c.** can make an object quieter.
◯ **d.** has no effect on anything but sound.

9. Angular velocity is . . .

◯ **a.** motion along a straight line.
◯ **b.** motion along a curved path.
◯ **c.** motion that is totally random.
◯ **d.** none of the above

10. Linear velocity is . . .

◯ **a.** motion along a straight line.
◯ **b.** motion along a curved path.
◯ **c.** motion that is totally random.
◯ **d.** none of the above

NAME______________________________ DATE______________

LESSON 14

ECCENTRIC EGGS

True/False (Circle T for true, F for false.)

T F **1.** Newton's first law is the "Law of Inertia."

T F **2.** Inertia only relates to moving objects.

T F **3.** An object that is sitting still remains still until a force acts on it.

T F **4.** An object that is moving remains moving until a force acts on it.

T F **5.** Given the same force, a hard-boiled egg spins slower than a fresh egg.

Multiple Choice (Fill in the circle beside the best answer.)

6. The "Law of Inertia" states that . . .

○ **a.** an object that is sitting still remains still until a force acts on it.
○ **b.** an object that is moving remains moving until a force acts on it.
○ **c.** both of the above
○ **d.** neither of the above

7. A seatbelt helps protect you from injury because . . .

○ **a.** it keeps you separate from the car so you can stop faster.
○ **b.** it keeps you attached to the car so when the car stops, you stop.
○ **c.** it keeps the car attached to you so the car stops more quickly.
○ **d.** it keeps the car attached to you so the car stops more slowly.

8. A practical application of the "Law of Inertia" is . . .

○ **a.** a law against littering.
○ **b.** a rule against running in school hallways.
○ **c.** a sign-up sheet for basketball.
○ **d.** a "no parking" zone.

9. An example of inertia is . . .

○ **a.** a rock sitting in a field.
○ **b.** a boy running down the road.
○ **c.** both of the above
○ **d.** neither of the above

10. Wearing a seatbelt is most like which egg in this activity?

○ **a.** the fresh egg because it kept moving
○ **b.** the hard boiled egg because it stopped
○ **c.** both eggs because they both stopped eventually
○ **d.** both eggs because they kept moving

NAME____________________ DATE__________

LESSON 15

RATTLEBACK

True/False (Circle T for true, F for false.)

T F **1.** Torque is what scientists call a turning or twisting force.

T F **2.** An off-center balance point can create preferential spin bias.

T F **3.** Preferential spin bias means an object turns equally well in either direction.

T F **4.** Friction is one force which can stop an object's movement.

T F **5.** Very smooth objects are not affected by friction.

Multiple Choice (Fill in the circle beside the best answer.)

6. Whenever two surfaces rub against each other . . .

○ **a.** gravity is increased.
○ **b.** preferential spin bias occurs.
○ **c.** there is friction.
○ **d.** it creates a fire.

7. The Rattleback's center of gravity . . .

○ **a.** is at the Rattleback's exact center.
○ **b.** is at the Rattleback's narrowest end.
○ **c.** makes the Rattleback spin smoothly in either direction.
○ **d.** is not at the Rattleback's center.

8. When something spins easier in one direction it has . . .

○ **a.** a balanced center of gravity.
○ **b.** preferential spin bias.
○ **c.** no center of gravity.
○ **d.** no friction.

9. Which of the following can help stop an object's movement?

○ **a.** friction
○ **b.** spinning
○ **c.** preferential spin bias
○ **d.** balance

10. Which of the following might demonstrate preferential spin bias?

○ **a.** a weight dropped straight down
○ **b.** a football thrown in a perfect spiral
○ **c.** a jogger running down the street
○ **d.** a car sitting in a garage

NAME________________________________ DATE______________

LESSON 16

BERNOULLI BALL

True/False (Circle T for true, F for false.)

T F **1.** The Bernoulli effect greatly increases the pull of gravity.

T F **2.** Fast moving air has lower air pressure than slow moving air.

T F **3.** Nothing moves unless there is more force in one direction than the other.

T F **4.** Sometimes forces oppose (work against) each other.

T F **5.** Gravity is always stronger than any other force.

Multiple Choice (Fill in the circle beside the best answer.)

6. A force can be . . .

○ **a.** a push.
○ **b.** a pull.
○ **c.** either a push or pull.
○ **d.** none of the above

7. For something to move . . .

○ **a.** it must have an adequate supply of air.
○ **b.** there must be more force exerted in one direction.
○ **c.** the Bernoulli effect is necessary.
○ **d.** it must be alive.

8. When you held the funnel up and blew hard, the ball stayed inside because . . .

○ **a.** the force holding the ball in was greater than the force pushing it out.
○ **b.** the force holding the ball in was less than the force pushing it out.
○ **c.** there was not enough force available to affect the ball in any way.
○ **d.** gravity was not strong enough to have any affect on the ball.

9. When you pointed the funnel down and blew hard, the ball stayed inside because . . .

○ **a.** the force holding the ball in was greater than the force pushing it out.
○ **b.** the force holding the ball in was less than the force pushing it out.
○ **c.** there was not enough force available to affect the ball in any way.
○ **d.** gravity was not strong enough to have any affect on the ball.

10. The Bernoulli Principle is named after the scientist who discovered . . .

○ **a.** slow moving air has lower air pressure than fast moving air.
○ **b.** low moving air has more air pressure than high moving air.
○ **c.** fast moving air has lower air pressure than slow moving air.
○ **d.** high moving air has less air pressure than low moving air.

NAME________________________ DATE____________

LESSON 17

STACKED STRENGTH

True/False (Circle T for true, F for false.)

T F **1.** Fastening layers of a material together to make them stronger is called lamination.

T F **2.** Any force applied to a laminated object is spread evenly through the layers.

T F **3.** Lamination is only found in man-made materials (like plywood).

T F **4.** The greater the number of layers laminated, the greater the strength.

T F **5.** Single sheets laminated together are never as strong as one thick sheet of the same material.

Multiple Choice (Fill in the circle beside the best answer.)

6. Gluing several layers of a material together is a process called . . .

○ **a.** gravitation
○ **b.** inertia
○ **c.** laminatio
○ **d.** stratification

7. The growth rings (layers) in a tree trunk are an example of . . .

○ **a.** gravitation
○ **b.** inertia
○ **c.** lamination
○ **d.** stratification

8. What role does glue play in the lamination process?

○ **a.** It attaches materials together so their strength is shared.
○ **b.** It reduces the pull of gravity on the glued object.
○ **c.** It reduces the effect of inertia on the glued object.
○ **d.** It weakens lamination by making surfaces too sticky.

9. Which of the following is an example of natural lamination?

○ **a.** a sea shell
○ **b.** a tree trunk
○ **c.** a goat's horn
○ **d.** all of the above

10. Why are laminated materials commonly used in the construction industry?

○ **a.** The multiple layers makes them easier to separate into sections.
○ **b.** The increased weight makes them easier to transport.
○ **c.** They are more expensive, making more money for the manufacturers.
○ **d.** They are lighter and stronger than similar materials of the same thickness.

NAME_______________________________ DATE_____________

LESSON 18

PULLEY POWER

True/False (Circle T for true, F for false.)

T F **1.** Simple machines are of little use in the modern world.

T F **2.** A pulley is one kind of simple machine.

T F **3.** Machines are often used to change the direction of a force.

T F **4.** A simple machine can operate without any kind of applied force.

T F **5.** A pulley contains at least one wheel and one axle.

Multiple Choice (Fill in the circle beside the best answer.)

6. Using a screwdriver to pry open the lid of a paint can . . .

○ **a.** does not require the application of force.
○ **b.** is an example of a simple machine called a lever.
○ **c.** is an example of a simple machine called a pulley.
○ **d.** none of the above

7. Which of the following uses a wheel and axle?

○ **a.** a pulley in a hay barn
○ **b.** a hitch on a car bumper
○ **c.** a handle on a shovel
○ **d.** the buckle on a belt

8. A pulley can . . .

○ **a.** eliminate gravity.
○ **b.** eliminate force.
○ **c.** change the direction of gravity.
○ **d.** change the direction of force.

9. A teeter-totter is similar to what simple machine?

○ **a.** a wheel
○ **b.** an axle
○ **c.** a lever
○ **d.** a pulley

10. For a simple machine to operate, what must be provided?

○ **a.** gravity
○ **b.** electricity
○ **c.** force
○ **d.** inertia

NAME ______________________ DATE ____________

LESSON 19

FORCED FOUNTAIN

True/False (Circle T for true, F for false.)

T F **1.** Air is matter.

T F **2.** Air has pressure.

T F **3.** Air is light because it contains no molecules.

T F **4.** Some kind of force is necessary to make anything move.

T F **5.** Liquids are easier to compress than air.

Multiple Choice (Fill in the circle beside the best answer.)

6. When you squeeze air into a smaller volume, it creates . . .

○ **a.** an increase in pressure.
○ **b.** a decrease in pressure.
○ **c.** a vacuum.
○ **d.** no change in pressure.

7. When you blew air into the bottle, the pressure . . .

○ **a.** stayed the same.
○ **b.** decreased.
○ **c.** increased.
○ **d.** caused the bottle to collapse.

8. What caused the water to shoot out of the straw?

○ **a.** a decrease in gravity inside the bottle
○ **b.** a decrease in air pressure inside the bottle
○ **c.** an increase in gravity inside the bottle
○ **d.** an increase in air pressure inside the bottle

9. Air . . .

○ **a.** maintains a constant pressure.
○ **b.** is easier to compress than water.
○ **c.** is more difficult to compress than water.
○ **d.** is unaffected by pressure.

10. Liquids . . .

○ **a.** react to pressure changes exactly like air.
○ **b.** are easier to compress than air.
○ **c.** can't be compressed.
○ **d.** have no relationship to pressure.

NAME____________________________________ DATE______________

LESSON 20

WANDERING WATER

True/False (Circle T for true, F for false.)

T F **1.** Water is always the same state of matter.

T F **2.** Changing the state of matter requires the addition or removal of energy.

T F **3.** When water changes from liquid to gas, water molecules are destroyed.

T F **4.** Condensation is when a gas turns back into a liquid.

T F **5.** Solar energy helps drive Earth's water cycle.

Multiple Choice (Fill in the circle beside the best answer.)

6. Water can exist as what state(s) of matter?

○ **a.** solid, liquid, gas
○ **b.** liquid only
○ **c.** liquid or gas only
○ **d.** none of the above

7. Adding or removing ______ may cause a change in the state of water.

○ **a.** sound
○ **b.** electricity
○ **c.** heat
○ **d.** gas

8. Water molecules move the slowest in which state?

○ **a.** solid
○ **b.** liquid
○ **c.** gas
○ **d.** matter

9. Water molecules move the fastest in which state?

○ **a.** solid
○ **b.** liquid
○ **c.** gas
○ **d.** matter

10. All of the following demonstrate a change in the state of matter except . . .

○ **a.** breaking glass.
○ **b.** boiling water.
○ **c.** freezing water.
○ **d.** melting ice.

NAME____________________ DATE__________

LESSON 21

MINIATURE GLACIER

True/False (Circle T for true, F for false.)

T F **1.** Glaciers are giant masses of ice formed over time by accumulations of snow.

T F **2.** Glaciers are relatively light and move rapidly.

T F **3.** As a glacier begins to melt, the land that it is sitting on sinks.

T F **4.** Currently, there are no glaciers on Earth. They all melted after the Ice Age.

T F **5.** Since glaciers are so large, they are not significantly affected by gravity.

Multiple Choice (Fill in the circle beside the best answer.)

6. As a glacier melts . . .

○ **a.** water flows uphill, causing the glacier to push the earth's crust downward.
○ **b.** water flows downhill, reducing the glacier's weight, causing the earth's crust to rise.
○ **c.** water runs off, but the earth's crust remains the same.
○ **d.** Glaciers never melt.

7. The outer layer of the Earth is called the. . .

○ **a.** core
○ **b.** mantle
○ **c.** crust
○ **d.** glacier holding layer

8. In this activity, which layer of the Earth did the board represent?

○ **a.** core
○ **b.** mantle
○ **c.** crust
○ **d.** magma

9. In this activity, which layer of the Earth did the water represent?

○ **a.** core
○ **b.** mantle
○ **c.** crust
○ **d.** magma

10. In this activity, what did the block of ice represent?

○ **a.** the Earth's core
○ **b.** the Earth's mantle
○ **c.** the Earth's crust
○ **d.** a glacier

NAME______________________________ DATE______________

LESSON 22

RAIN SHADOWS

True/False (Circle T for true, F for false.)

T F **1.** All areas of the United States get the same amount of rainfall.

T F **2.** Mountains have little effect on the weather.

T F **3.** Large areas which receive little annual rainfall are called deserts.

T F **4.** In the U.S., most weather systems travel from the east to the west.

T F **5.** A rain shadow is a dark area of land caused by very wet ground.

Multiple Choice (Fill in the circle beside the best answer.)

6. The sprayer in this activity represented . . .

○ **a.** a mountain
○ **b.** a rain shadow
○ **c.** moisture-laden winds
○ **d.** clouds

7. As moisture-laden winds approach a mountain range, they . . .

○ **a.** move downwards due to the pull of gravity.
○ **b.** move upwards due the rising ground.
○ **c.** continue level, slamming into the mountain.
○ **d.** are stopped completely by the high peaks.

8. In the U.S., deserts usually occur . . .

○ **a.** on top of mountain ranges.
○ **b.** on the west side of mountain ranges.
○ **c.** on the east side of mountain ranges.
○ **d.** The U.S. does not have any deserts.

9. Deserts usually occur in a mountain's . . .

○ **a.** water range.
○ **b.** wet range.
○ **c.** water shadow.
○ **d.** rain shadow.

10. If you were building a ski resort in the U.S., it should probably be located . . .

○ **a.** in a mountain rain shadow to help keep your customers drier.
○ **b.** high on eastern slopes for coldest temperatures and maximum moisture.
○ **c.** low on western slopes for coldest temperatures and minimum moisture.
○ **d.** high on western slopes for coldest temperatures and maximum moisture.

NAME________________________________ DATE______________

LESSON 23

RAZORBLADE ROCK

True/False (Circle T for true, F for false.)

T F **1.** Ancient peoples often used rocks as tools.

T F **2.** Obsidian is a kind of sedimentary rock.

T F **3.** Igneous rocks are formed by layers of silt subjected to huge pressure over time.

T F **4.** Molten rock stays underground until it hardens and rises to the surface.

T F **5.** Obsidian rock is often found where volcanoes were once active.

Multiple Choice (Fill in the circle beside the best answer.)

6. Scientists call molten rock underground . . .

○ **a.** magnum
○ **b.** lava
○ **c.** magma
○ **d.** obsidian

7. Scientists call molten rock on the surface . . .

○ **a.** magnum
○ **b.** lava
○ **c.** magma
○ **d.** obsidian

8. Molten rock usually comes to the surface through a . . .

○ **a.** magma chute.
○ **b.** volcanic opening.
○ **c.** lava box.
○ **d.** obsidian vent.

9. Obsidian is . . .

○ **a.** an igneous rock.
○ **b.** formed by the action of a volcano.
○ **c.** a material prized by early humans.
○ **d.** all of the above

10. How was obsidian used by ancient peoples?

○ **a.** as a cutting instrument
○ **b.** for jewelry
○ **c.** both of the above
○ **d.** neither of the above

NAME________________________ DATE____________

LESSON 24

MOLDED MINERALS

True/False (Circle T for true, F for false.)

T F **1.** Once rock is formed, it is impossible to change it in any way.

T F **2.** The weight of higher rock layers creates pressure on lower rock layers.

T F **3.** Pressure can change the shape and appearance of rock layers.

T F **4.** Wonderstone is a type of sedimentary rock.

T F **5.** Igneous rock was once molten.

Multiple Choice (Fill in the circle beside the best answer.)

6. Igneous rock was . . .

- ○ **a.** formed by wind and water.
- ○ **b.** once molten and underground.
- ○ **c.** never molten and never underground.
- ○ **d.** formed in layers by pressure and time.

7. Obsidian and Wonderstone are both examples of . . .

- ○ **a.** rocks formed by glaciers.
- ○ **b.** sedimentary rocks.
- ○ **c.** igneous rocks.
- ○ **d.** eroded rocks.

8. All of the following are types of rock except . . .

- ○ **a.** glacier
- ○ **b.** igneous
- ○ **c.** metamorphic
- ○ **d.** sedimentary

9. Rhyolite was a type of . . .

- ○ **a.** sedimentary rock
- ○ **b.** super hot lava
- ○ **c.** frozen magma
- ○ **d.** glacier

10. Igneous rocks are usually associated with . . .

- ○ **a.** glaciers
- ○ **b.** rivers and streams
- ○ **c.** extremely cold temperatures
- ○ **d.** volcanoes

NAME______________________________ DATE______________

LESSON 25

GULLIBLE GOLD

True/False (Circle T for true, F for false.)

T F **1.** Testing a mineral helps us identify it.

T F **2.** The color of a mineral always tells us what the material is.

T F **3.** The color of a mineral is always the same, whether powdered or in large chunks.

T F **4.** Minerals are not pure substances. They are always combined with another material.

T F **5.** Materials mined from the Earth are very important to our economy.

Multiple Choice (Fill in the circle beside the best answer.)

6. The test you did in this activity is called a . . .

- ◯ **a.** steak test
- ◯ **b.** powder test
- ◯ **c.** streak test
- ◯ **d.** coloration test

7. The color resulting from this test was . . .

- ◯ **a.** very light, almost gold.
- ◯ **b.** very dark, almost black.
- ◯ **c.** light green.
- ◯ **d.** dark red.

8. Why are rocks and minerals mined from the Earth important?

- ◯ **a.** They provide minerals (like salt) that living things need.
- ◯ **b.** They provide raw materials to make various metals.
- ◯ **c.** They provide useful materials for building construction.
- ◯ **d.** all of the above

9. A "rock" is usually defined as . . .

- ◯ **a.** a pure Earth material.
- ◯ **b.** a mixture of Earth materials.
- ◯ **c.** a form of compressed plant matter.
- ◯ **d.** a type of meteorite.

10. A "mineral" is . . .

- ◯ **a.** a pure Earth material.
- ◯ **b.** a mixture of Earth materials.
- ◯ **c.** a form of compressed plant matter.
- ◯ **d.** a type of meteorite.

NAME______________________________ DATE____________

LESSON 26

TEAPOT TEMPEST

True/False (Circle T for true, F for false.)

T F **1.** Heat is a form of energy.

T F **2.** Heat can be transferred from one place to another.

T F **3.** Heat has no effect on water circulation.

T F **4.** Cold water contains more energy than hot water.

T F **5.** Dissolving tea in water creates a solution.

Multiple Choice (Fill in the circle beside the best answer.)

6. Steam coming off the surface of hot water is . . .

○ **a.** water in a gaseous state changing back to a liquid.
○ **b.** water in a solid state changing into a gas.
○ **c.** water in a liquid state changing into a solid.
○ **d.** water in a liquid state changing into a gas.

7. Cold water is . . .

○ **a.** more dense than hot water.
○ **b.** less dense than hot water.
○ **c.** more a gas than a liquid.
○ **d.** contains more energy than hot water.

8. When liquids swirl and mix due to heating and cooling, it is called . . .

○ **a.** convention
○ **b.** density
○ **c.** convection
○ **d.** solution

9. As Earth's atmosphere heats and cools, it demonstrates . . .

○ **a.** convention
○ **b.** density
○ **c.** convection
○ **d.** solution

10. Liquids and gasses are two forms of . . .

○ **a.** masonry
○ **b.** convection
○ **c.** solids
○ **d.** matter

NAME______________________________ DATE____________

LESSON 27

Wobbling World

True/False (Circle T for true, F for false.)

T F **1.** The Earth rotates in an even and steady way.

T F **2.** One full rotation of Earth is called a day.

T F **3.** One full revolution of Earth around the sun is called a year.

T F **4.** The Earth only moves in two ways: revolution and rotation.

T F **5.** The movement of Earth is related to how we measure time.

Multiple Choice (Fill in the circle beside the best answer.)

6. The Earth rotates at a speed of about . . .

○ **a.** one mile per hour.
○ **b.** one hundred miles per hour.
○ **c.** one thousand miles per hour.
○ **d.** Earth's rotation is impossible to measure.

7. Earth's movement around the sun is called a . . .

○ **a.** rotation
○ **b.** wobble
○ **c.** revolution
○ **d.** wiggle

8. Earth's spinning movement is called a . . .

○ **a.** rotation
○ **b.** wobble
○ **c.** revolution
○ **d.** wiggle

9. A variation in Earth's spinning movement is called a . . .

○ **a.** rotation
○ **b.** wobble
○ **c.** revolution
○ **d.** wiggle

10. Which of the following best describes Earth's three primary movements?

○ **a.** A girl standing in the center of basketball court, spinning in a circle, wobbling slightly.
○ **b.** A boy walking in a circle around the court, weaving slightly from side to side.
○ **c.** A girl spinning in a circle, wobbling slightly, moving in a slow circle around the court.
○ **d.** A boy spinning in a circle, wobbling slightly, moving from goal to goal.

NAME_______________________________ DATE______________

LESSON 28

WAVE TABLE

True/False (Circle T for true, F for false.)

T F **1.** There are many kinds of waves that transfer energy.

T F **2.** Light is one type of wave.

T F **3.** The high point of a wave is called a trough.

T F **4.** Television, radio, and cell phones require waves to operate.

T F **5.** An important aspect of waves is their ability to stop energy.

Multiple Choice (Fill in the circle beside the best answer.)

6. All of the following are types of waves except . . .

○ **a.** light
○ **b.** gravity
○ **c.** sound
○ **d.** radio

7. When a rock hits the smooth surface of a pond . . .

○ **a.** energy moves inward in waves from the point of impact.
○ **b.** energy moves outward in waves from the point of impact.
○ **c.** energy is absorbed by the rock's surface.
○ **d.** energy is destroyed by the rock's impact.

8. How are a wave crest and a wave trough similar?

○ **a.** Neither one can transfer energy.
○ **b.** They are identical parts of a wave.
○ **c.** They are not found in most waves.
○ **d.** They are both parts of a wave.

9. How are a wave crest and a wave trough different?

○ **a.** Neither one can transfer energy.
○ **b.** They are the opposite points on a wave.
○ **c.** They are not found in most waves.
○ **d.** They are both parts of a wave.

10. What affect does a wave crest have on light?

○ **a.** The crest concentrates the light making it brighter.
○ **b.** The crest concentrates the light making it dimmer.
○ **c.** The crest diffuses the light making it brighter.
○ **d.** The crest diffuses the light making it dimmer.

NAME__________________________________ DATE______________

LESSON 29

LIGHT DETECTOR

True/False (Circle T for true, F for false.)

T F **1.** Light is a form of energy that travels in waves.

T F **2.** Light cannot be reflected from a surface.

T F **3.** A material that allows light to pass through is called opaque.

T F **4.** A material that allows little light to pass through is called translucent.

T F **5.** Our eyes do not need reflected light to see an image.

Multiple Choice (Fill in the circle beside the best answer.)

6. Light is a form of . . .

- ◯ **a.** electricity that travels as a particle.
- ◯ **b.** energy that travels as a wave.
- ◯ **c.** particle that travels as electricity.
- ◯ **d.** gravity that travels as a wave.

7. A material that allows light to pass through easily is called . . .

- ◯ **a.** transparent
- ◯ **b.** translucent
- ◯ **c.** opaque
- ◯ **d.** none of the above

8. A material that allows no light to pass through is called . . .

- ◯ **a.** transparent
- ◯ **b.** translucent
- ◯ **c.** opaque
- ◯ **d.** none of the above

9. A material that allows little light to pass through is called . . .

- ◯ **a.** transparent
- ◯ **b.** translucent
- ◯ **c.** opaque
- ◯ **d.** none of the above

10. Which of the following is an opaque material?

- ◯ **a.** clear glass
- ◯ **b.** colored glass
- ◯ **c.** plywood
- ◯ **d.** plastic wrap

NAME________________________________ DATE________________

SOUND SCOPE

True/False (Circle T for true, F for false.)

T F **1.** Sound is a form of energy that travels in waves.

T F **2.** It takes energy to create a sound.

T F **3.** Sound waves are created by the vibration of molecules.

T F **4.** Sound can't travel through a solid or a gas.

T F **5.** Sound travels by destroying energy molecules.

Multiple Choice (Fill in the circle beside the best answer.)

6. Sound is caused by . . .

○ **a.** energy molecules being destroyed.
○ **b.** waves absorbing energy.
○ **c.** the vibration of molecules.
○ **d.** molecules collapsing.

7. Which of the following is necessary for sound to occur?

○ **a.** wires
○ **b.** energy
○ **c.** gravity
○ **d.** inertia

8. Sound can pass through . . .

○ **a.** string
○ **b.** metal
○ **c.** air
○ **d.** all of the above

9. Sound would travel the fastest through . . .

○ **a.** air
○ **b.** fog
○ **c.** steel
○ **d.** clouds

10. For your ear to hear a sound . . .

○ **a.** some air molecules must vibrate.
○ **b.** some air molecules must be destroyed.
○ **c.** some form of wire is required.
○ **d.** some form of inertia is required.

NAME________________________________ DATE______________

LESSON 31

CORK COMPASS

True/False (Circle T for true, F for false.)

T F **1.** Magnetism is a special property found only in a few materials.

T F **2.** Some kinds of metal can be turned into a temporary magnet.

T F **3.** A compass can align itself with the Earth's magnetic field.

T F **4.** A sailor can use a compass to find out the correct time of day.

T F **5.** A simple compass can be made with water, a cork, and a toothpick.

Multiple Choice (Fill in the circle beside the best answer.)

6. The accuracy of a compass might be affected if you were in . . .

- ○ **a.** a rainstorm at night.
- ○ **b.** the middle of a metal building.
- ○ **c.** a major snowstorm.
- ○ **d.** a small camping tent.

7. Which of the following would not be affected by magnetism?

- ○ **a.** a large nail
- ○ **b.** a soft drink bottle
- ○ **c.** iron filings
- ○ **d.** the door of a car

8. Which of the following could be picked up by a magnet?

- ○ **a.** a pencil
- ○ **b.** an eraser
- ○ **c.** a staple
- ○ **d.** a piece of tape

9. A magnetic field is the area where a magnet can . . .

- ○ **a.** pull
- ○ **b.** push
- ○ **c.** either push or pull
- ○ **d.** none of the above

10. Rubbing a small piece of steel with a magnet can . . .

- ○ **a.** create a fire.
- ○ **b.** destroy its magnetic molecules.
- ○ **c.** make it immediately point north.
- ○ **d.** make it a temporary magnet.

NAME________________________________ DATE______________

LESSON 32

ELUSIVE ELECTRONS

True/False (Circle T for true, F for false.)

T F **1.** Atoms are made of protons, neutrons, and electrons.

T F **2.** An electronoscope is a device to detect the presence of neutrons.

T F **3.** Electricity is created when protons move from atom to atom.

T F **4.** Electrons have a negative charge; protons are have a positive charge.

T F **5.** Rubbing a comb with a piece of wool can create static electricity.

Multiple Choice (Fill in the circle beside the best answer.)

6. Electrons are always . . .

○ **a.** positively charged
○ **b.** negatively charged
○ **c.** neutral
○ **d.** static

7. Charges that are alike . . .

○ **a.** attract each other
○ **b.** repel each other
○ **c.** explode
○ **d.** none of the above

8. When electrons are made to move it can create . . .

○ **a.** gravity
○ **b.** inertia
○ **c.** electricity
○ **d.** atoms

9. Static electricity is . . .

○ **a.** identical to household current.
○ **b.** different from household current.
○ **c.** a good power source for appliances.
○ **d.** identical to battery power.

10. Regarding the charges of protons and neutrons . . .

○ **a.** protons are negative; neutrons are positive.
○ **b.** protons are positive; neutrons are negative.
○ **c.** protons are negative; neutrons are neutral.
○ **d.** protons are positive; neutrons are neutral.

NAME ________________________ DATE ____________

LESSON 33

CRYSTAL CORD

True/False (Circle T for true, F for false.)

T F **1.** Primary forces, like gravity, cannot be opposed.

T F **2.** A crystal is a solid whose particles are arranged in a specific pattern.

T F **3.** Salt crystals can bond with each other.

T F **4.** Salt is a mineral that is easy to burn.

T F **5.** A mixture of salt and water is called an infusion.

Multiple Choice (Fill in the circle beside the best answer.)

6. To overcome the force of gravity requires . . .

- ○ **a.** an equal force in the same direction.
- ○ **b.** a greater force in the same direction.
- ○ **c.** a greater force in the opposite direction.
- ○ **d.** Gravity can't be overcome.

7. In the Crystal Cord activity, what solution did you use?

- ○ **a.** saltwater and string
- ○ **b.** saltwater and crystals
- ○ **c.** salt and water
- ○ **d.** string and water

8. When saltwater completely evaporates, it can leave behind . . .

- ○ **a.** salt crystals
- ○ **b.** salt solutions
- ○ **c.** saltines
- ○ **d.** none of the above

9. When salt crystals stick to each other it is called a . . .

- ○ **a.** mixture
- ○ **b.** solution
- ○ **c.** bond
- ○ **d.** force

10. In the Crystal Cord activity, the paperclip was held up because . . .

- ○ **a.** gravity was temporarily suspended.
- ○ **b.** the string fibers wouldn't burn.
- ○ **c.** the salt was completely destroyed.
- ○ **d.** the salt crystals bonded together.

NAME________________________________ DATE______________

RAGING ROCKET

True/False (Circle T for true, F for false.)

T F **1.** A chemical change results in a new substance.

T F **2.** A physical change results in a different form of the same material.

T F **3.** Energy is required for a physical or chemical change to take place.

T F **4.** Changes are constantly happening all around us.

T F **5.** Mixing vinegar with an antacid does not produce chemical change.

Multiple Choice (Fill in the circle beside the best answer.)

6. Which of the following is not a physical change?

○ **a.** breaking glass
○ **b.** burning wood
○ **c.** boiling water
○ **d.** melting ice

7. Which of the following is not a chemical change?

○ **a.** breaking glass
○ **b.** burning wood
○ **c.** mixing vinegar and an antacid
○ **d.** baking a cake

8. A chemical reaction can produce . . .

○ **a.** pressure
○ **b.** heat
○ **c.** gas
○ **d.** all of the above

9. Pressure inside the Raging Rocket . . .

○ **a.** decreased greatly, causing the rocket to take off.
○ **b.** decreased greatly, causing the tube to collapse.
○ **c.** increased greatly, causing the rocket to take off.
○ **d.** increased greatly, causing the tube to collapse.

10. Chemical and physical changes require . . .

○ **a.** gravity
○ **b.** inertia
○ **c.** energy
○ **d.** pressure

NAME________________________________ DATE____________

LESSON 35

RATTLEBACK LENS

True/False (Circle T for true, F for false.)

T F **1.** A lens works by bending light.

T F **2.** Scientists call the bending of light "refraction."

T F **3.** All lenses must be shaped identically to function.

T F **4.** A lens that is bowed out is called concave.

T F **5.** A concave lens makes the image look smaller.

Multiple Choice (Fill in the circle beside the best answer.)

6. What effect does a lens have on light passing through it?

○ **a.** It increases the light's speed.
○ **b.** It decreases the light's speed.
○ **c.** It bends the light.
○ **d.** It straightens the light.

7. The process of bending light is called . . .

○ **a.** retraction
○ **b.** translucence
○ **c.** reflection
○ **d.** refraction

8. A convex lens is . . .

○ **a.** perfectly flat
○ **b.** bowed out
○ **c.** dished in
○ **d.** all of the above

9. A concave lens is . . .

○ **a.** perfectly flat
○ **b.** bowed out
○ **c.** dished in
○ **d.** all of the above

10. Which of the following does not use a lens?

○ **a.** contacts
○ **b.** glasses
○ **c.** a mirror
○ **d.** a camera

NAME________________________________ DATE______________

LESSON 36

SHIFTING SOLUTION

True/False (Circle T for true, F for false.)

T F **1.** Mixing an indicator with water creates a solution.

T F **2.** An indicator changes color to show the presence of an acid or base.

T F **3.** An indicator can't change back to its original color.

T F **4.** Vinegar is an example of a base.

T F **5.** A pH scale must be used only by trained scientists.

Multiple Choice (Fill in the circle beside the best answer.)

6. Adding a base to an acid can _____ a solution.

- ○ **a.** explode
- ○ **b.** neutralize
- ○ **c.** freeze
- ○ **d.** melt

7. On the pH scale, a reading of exactly 7 is . . .

- ○ **a.** an acid
- ○ **b.** a base
- ○ **c.** a neutral
- ○ **d.** a solution

8. On the pH scale, any reading below 7 is . . .

- ○ **a.** an acid
- ○ **b.** a base
- ○ **c.** a neutral
- ○ **d.** a solution

9. On the pH scale, any reading above 7 is . . .

- ○ **a.** an acid
- ○ **b.** a base
- ○ **c.** a neutral
- ○ **d.** a solution

10. Which of the following would be a good place to use an indicator?

- ○ **a.** a municipal swimming pool
- ○ **b.** a field used to grow soybeans
- ○ **c.** a laboratory doing medical tests
- ○ **d.** all of the above

Lesson 1
Fermented Fungi

1. F
2. T
3. F
4. T
5. T
6. b
7. c
8. b
9. a
10. d

Lesson 2
Indoor Onion

1. F
2. F
3. T
4. T
5. F
6. d
7. c
8. c
9. a
10. c

Lesson 3
Indoor Onion 2

1. T
2. F
3. T
4. F
5. F
6. a
7. c
8. b
9. d
10. c

Lesson 4
Protected Plant

1. T
2. F
3. F
4. T
5. T
6. d
7. c
8. b
9. c
10. d

Lesson 5
Flower Power

1. T
2. F
3. F
4. T
5. T
6. b
7. d
8. d
9. c
10. a

Lesson 6
Membrane Model

1. T
2. F
3. F
4. F
5. T
6. c
7. c
8. d
9. c
10. c

Lesson 7
Balloon Eye

1. F
2. T
3. T
4. T
5. F
6. d
7. a
8. d
9. b
10. b

Lesson 8
Hollow Hand

1. F
2. F
3. T
4. T
5. T
6. d
7. c
8. b
9. a
10. c

Lesson 9
Body Joint

1. T
2. T
3. F
4. T
5. T
6. d
7. b
8. c
9. a
10. b

Lesson 10
Molecular Models

1. T
2. F
3. T
4. T
5. F
6. c
7. b
8. c
9. a
10. c

Lesson 11
Water Bridge

1. T
2. F
3. F
4. T
5. T
6. c
7. d
8. a
9. b
10. c

Lesson 12
Paper Portal

1. T
2. T
3. T
4. F
5. T
6. b
7. a
8. d
9. a
10. b

Lesson 13
Spinning Steel

1. T
2. T
3. F
4. F
5. T
6. c
7. c
8. a
9. b
10. a

Lesson 14
Eccentric Eggs

1. T
2. F
3. T
4. T
5. F
6. c
7. b
8. b
9. c
10. b

Lesson 15
Rattleback

1. T
2. T
3. F
4. T
5. F
6. c
7. d
8. b
9. a
10. b

Lesson 16
Bernoulli Ball

1. F
2. T
3. T
4. T
5. F
6. c
7. b
8. a
9. a
10. c

Lesson 17
Stacked Strength

1. T
2. T
3. F
4. T
5. F
6. c
7. c
8. a
9. d
10. d

Lesson 18
Pulley Power

1. F
2. T
3. T
4. F
5. T
6. b
7. a
8. d
9. c
10. c

Lesson 19
Forced Fountain

1. T
2. T
3. F
4. T
5. F
6. a
7. c
8. d
9. b
10. c

Lesson 20
Wandering Water

1. F
2. T
3. F
4. T
5. T
6. a
7. c
8. a
9. c
10. a

Lesson 21
Miniature Glacier

1. T
2. F
3. F
4. F
5. F
6. b
7. c
8. c
9. b
10. d

Lesson 22
Rain Shadows

1. F
2. F
3. T
4. F
5. F
6. c
7. b
8. c
9. d
10. d

Lesson 23
Razorblade Rock

1. T
2. F
3. F
4. F
5. T
6. c
7. b
8. b
9. d
10. c

Lesson 24
Molded Mineral

1. F
2. T
3. T
4. F
5. T
6. b
7. c
8. a
9. b
10. d

Lesson 25
Gullible Gold

1. T
2. F
3. F
4. F
5. T
6. c
7. b
8. d
9. b
10. a

Lesson 26
Teapot Tempest

1. T
2. T
3. F
4. F
5. T
6. d
7. a
8. c
9. c
10. d

Lesson 27
Wobbling World

1. F
2. T
3. T
4. F
5. T
6. c
7. c
8. a
9. b
10. c

Lesson 28
Wave Table

1. T
2. T
3. F
4. T
5. F
6. b
7. b
8. d
9. b
10. a

Lesson 29
Light Detector

1. T
2. F
3. F
4. T
5. F
6. b
7. a
8. c
9. b
10. c

Lesson 30
Sound Scope

1. T
2. T
3. T
4. F
5. F
6. c
7. b
8. d
9. c
10. a

Lesson 31
Cork Compass

1. T
2. T
3. T
4. F
5. F
6. b
7. b
8. c
9. c
10. d

Lesson 32
Elusive Electrons

1. T
2. F
3. F
4. T
5. T
6. b
7. b
8. c
9. b
10. d

Lesson 33
Crystal Cord

1. F
2. T
3. T
4. F
5. F
6. c
7. c
8. a
9. c
10. d

Lesson 34
Raging Rocket

1. T
2. T
3. T
4. T
5. F
6. b
7. a
8. d
9. c
10. c

Lesson 35
Rattleback Lens

1. T
2. T
3. F
4. F
5. T
6. c
7. d
8. b
9. c
10. c

Lesson 36
Shifting Solution

1. T
2. T
3. F
4. F
5. F
6. b
7. c
8. a
9. b
10. d

This **"Shopping List"** is provided for your convenience. It contains all the items that are not common classroom supplies (paper, pencil, scissors, etc.) or components found in your Materials Kit.

Please note: There are a few items (like tissue paper rolls) that require advance planning for effective collection.

Lesson 1
Baby food jars (2)
Spoon

Lesson 2
Small onion
Soft drink bottle (2 liter)
Aluminum foil
Knife

Lesson 3
Small onion
Aluminum foil

Lesson 4
Potted plant
Clear plastic bag
String

Lesson 5
Flower

Lesson 6
Vanilla extract

Lesson 7
Match

Lesson 9
Toilet tissue rolls (2)

Lesson 10
Colored marshmallows

Lesson 11
Paper towels

Lesson 14
Fresh egg
Hard boiled egg

Lesson 16
Antiseptic wipes

Lesson 19
Soft drink bottle (2 liter)

Lesson 21
Bucket

Lesson 22
Plastic sheet
Spray bottle

Lesson 23
Gloves
Apple

Lesson 26
Tea bag

Lesson 28
Plastic wrap
Flashlight

Lesson 2
Plastic wrap
Milk jug (transparent)
Cardboard

Lesson 30
Coat hanger

Lesson 31
Bowl (non-metallic)
Compass

Lesson 32
Aluminum foil

Lesson 33
Paper towel
Match

Lesson 34
Paper towel

Lesson 35
Newspaper